teach yourself...

HARVARD GRAPHICS

ROB KRUMM

'E.P.L. - MNA

MIS: PRESS

A Subsidiary of
Henry Holt and Co., Inc.

Second Edition — 1991

ISBN 1-55828-133-9

Printed in the United States of America
10   9   8   7   6   5   4   3   2   1

MIS:Press books are available at special discounts
for bulk purchases for sales promotions, premiums,
fund-raising, or educational use. Special editions
or book excerpts can also be created to specification.

For details contact:

Special Sales Director
MIS:Press
a subsidiary of Henry Holt and Company, Inc.
115 West 18th Street
New York, New York 10011

TRADEMARKS

Contents

Preface

Since you are taking the time to read this preface, you are probably standing in a bookstore, surrounded by shelves of computer books, trying to decide which one to buy. The function of this preface is to explain the concept of this book to help you make that decision.

There are three ideas that sum up the approach used in *teach yourself...Harvard Graphics*, which I believe make it different from most books about software applications.

Education. The purpose of this book is to help you learn to use Harvard Graphics. All learning takes place through a *structured* experience that guides you through a working session with the program where you will discover for yourself the concepts behind the command structure of the program.

In-Context Examples. The examples given in the book are complete keystroke-for-keystroke lessons. This means the features and techniques are explained within the context of an actual project. This is very important when you are trying to learn to use a program well, because it reveals not just how the features work, but how they work with each other.

Visual Reinforcement. This book contains more than 150 illustrations. The illustrations are an important part of learning. They show how charts and drawings are constructed, step-by-step, and serve as a point of reference for comparing your results to those in the book.

From my experience of writing 28 computer books since 1983, I have found that the detailed, step-by-step method used in this book is the best way to learn and understand a new software application. This method not only allows you to get started with the program, but also encourages you to continue learning after you have finished the material in the book.

ROB KRUMM

Introduction

This introduction will show you how to load Harvard Graphics, how to select commands, and how to move around the menu. It also shows the keyboard conventions and the setup of the examples used in this book.

KEYBOARD CONVENTIONS

The following conventions are used in this book to represent keystrokes or mouse operations.

Symbol	Key
↵	Return or Enter
⇐	Left Arrow
⇑	Up Arrow
⇒	Right Arrow
⇓	Down Arrow
[Home]	Home
[Esc]	Escape
[Tab]	Tab
[End]	End
[Pg Up]	Page Up
[Pg Dn]	Page Down
[Ins]	Insert
[Del]	Delete
[Backspace]	Backspace
[Spacebar]	Spacebar
[Fn]	Function key n (where n is the function key number)

ENTERING KEYSTROKES

Keystrokes, key sequences, and text entries that you should enter as you work through these examples will appear in **Helvetica Bold** typeface. For example:

Press:

   [F10] [↵]

Key Combinations

Key combinations appear in the following format:

   [Ctrl-F10]

This example indicates that you are to press the first key, [Ctrl], then—while holding down the first key—press the second key, [F10].

Key Repetition

Instructions to press a key several times in succession appear as follows:

   [Tab] *(5 times)*

Key Sequences With Text

Key sequences contained within text may appear in the following format:

   [Shift-F10] 2 7

A sequence such as this contains spaces to separate individual keystrokes from other keystrokes and key combinations. The above example is an instruction that tells you to enter the [Shift-F10] key combination, release, press the [2] key, release, then press the [7] key.

KEYBOARD AND MOUSE PROCEDURES

Although *Harvard Graphics* provides support for a mouse, many users do not have mice installed in their computers. To accommodate both keyboard and mouse users, some sections of the book contain procedures that appear twice—once for keyboard entry and another for mouse entry. For example, in chapter 2 you will encounter the headings "Moving the Cursor with the Mouse" and "Moving the Cursor with the Keyboard" consecutively in the text. These sections explain two ways to perform the identical action: one uses the mouse and the other uses the keyboard as the respective entry devices. In these instances, you should enter only the commands for method you choose. Topics that do not specify keyboard or mouse should be entered by all readers.

LOADING THE PROGRAM

The *Harvard Graphics* program can be loaded from the operating system by accessing the hard-disk directory in which the program is stored and entering **HG.** In most cases, it will be installed in a directory called **\HG.** Thus, the typical command sequence for starting the program is as follows:

cd\hg [↵]

hg [↵]

When you start the program, the *Harvard Graphics* logo, shown in figure i.1, will appear and remain on screen for a few seconds.

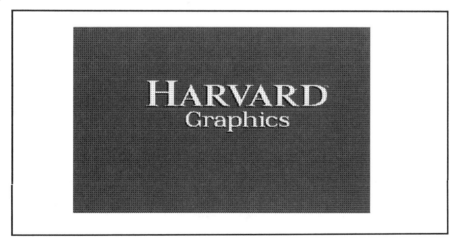

Figure i.1. Harvard Graphics Logo

After the logo disappears, the program will display the main program menu.

HARVARD GRAPHICS MENUS

The vast majority of software applications running on MS-DOS machines today are *menu-driven* applications. This means that all program operations are selected from lists of commands, in contrast to older, command driven applications. A command-driven application simply displays a prompt that tells you the program is active. You must then type in a command sentence to make the program perform a certain task. The most common example of a command-driven program is the MS-DOS operating system. Harvard Graphics, on the other hand, is menu driven, making is much easier to for most people to use.

The menus in Harvard Graphics are *tree structured.* This just means that you always begin with the Main Menu, shown in figure i.2. The Main Menu consists of a list of items that leads to other submenus that display more detailed commands and command options. Each item off of the Main Menu is assigned a single-digit number from 1 through 9. The only exception is the **Exit** command, which is assigned the letter **E.** The **Exit** command terminates the Harvard Graphics program and returns you to the operating system.

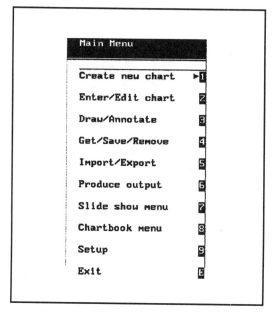

Figure i.2. Harvard Graphics Main Menu

MAKING MENU SELECTIONS

When a menu is displayed, you can make selections using the following methods:

Arrow-Key By default, the first item on any menu will appear in a contrasting set of colors (on a multicolor screen) or underlined (on some single-color screens). This is called the *highlight*. The highlight can be moved to any of the items on the menu with the [⇓] or [⇑] keys. If you want to select the highlighted menu item, you can press either [↵] or [F10].

When you first load the Harvard Graphics program, the highlight is positioned on the first menu item on the menu, **Create new chart.** In addition, the program displays a triangular arrowhead next to the **1** on the menu. This is called the *selection marker*. It indicates the item that is currently selected on the menus and data-entry screens.

Number A more direct method is to enter the number that corresponds to the command you want to select. When you press the number (1 through 9), its item is immediately selected, eliminating the need to press [↵] or [F10].

Mouse You can also use a mouse to select menu items, if your computer is equipped with one. Moving the mouse up or down will move the highlight in the same direction on the menu. The actual distance the mouse travels to move the menu highlight will vary with the mouse you are using. Note that Harvard Graphics does not display a unique mouse cursor in the way that applications such as Microsoft Word do. This means that you must experiment with your mouse to get a feel for degree of movement necessary to change the highlight's position.

To select the highlighted item, press the *left* mouse button, which performs the sam function as pressing [↵]. The *right* mouse button which performs the same function as [Esc]. If you have a three-button mouse, Harvard Graphics ignores the center button.

To select the **Setup** option from the Main Menu use any one of the following three methods:

1. Arrow-Key   [⇓] *(8 times)*
                            [↵]

2. Number   **9**

3. Mouse   **move down to Setup**
                            [Click left]

When you select a menu item, the program responds by displaying a submenu; in this case, it is the **Setup** submenu. For this example, select the **Defaults** option using one of the following methods:

1. Arrow-Key   [↵]

2. Number   **1**

3. Mouse   **[Click left]**

DATA-ENTRY SCREENS

You have worked your way through a menu tree and arrived at a more detailed screen display. These displays are called *data-entry* or *options* screens, depending on the activity you have selected. In general, similar displays are found at the lowest level of each menu tree. In this example, the Default Settings screen, shown in figure i.3, is currently displayed.

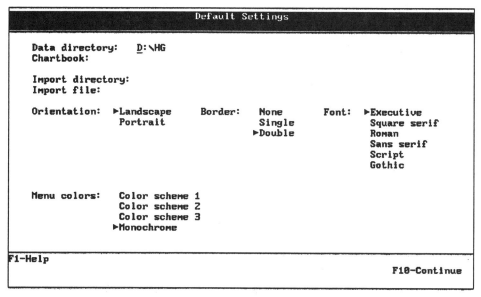

Figure i.3. Default Settings entry screen

There are two types of items on these screens.

Entry An *entry* item is one that requires a typed entry. For example, the **Data directory** option is filled in by typing the name of the directory in which you want to store your charts. By default this will usually be set to the **\HG** directory.

Selection A *selection* item is one that has a fixed list of options from which you can choose. For example, the item labeled **Orientation** has two options listed, **Landscape** and **Portrait**. The currently selected option is indicated by the triangular selection marker. There will be only one selection marker for each item. The current selection for **Orientation** is **Landscape**.

Changing Screen Items

The data-entry/options screens are provided for two purposes. First, they summarize the current selections. Second, they give you the means to change those selections. The Harvard Graphics program indicates which item on the menu is selected by displaying it in white (on multicolor screens) or bold white (on single-color screens).

7

The best way to get from one option to another is to use [Tab] and [Shift-Tab]. You can also use a mouse to move the bold highlighting.

For example, to change the **Orientation** to **Portrait**. Move the cursor to **Orientation** item by pressing:

   [Tab] *(4 times)*

There are three ways to change a selection:

Arrow/[↵]   Use the arrow key to change the highlighted option. Pressing [return] moves the selection marker to the new option. If you have a mouse, you can use it to move the highlight and then [Click left] to move the selection to the new option.

Letter   Select an option by typing in the first letter of the item. For example, *L* for **Landscape** or *O* for **Orientation**. If more than one item begins with the same letter, the selection marker moves to the next item with the letter to the right of the currently selected item.

[Spacebar]   Rotate the selection mark through all of the options using the [Spacebar]. Each time [Spacebar] is pressed, the selection mark moves to the next item. When it reaches the end of the list it cycles back to the first item.

Note that the **Arrow/[↵]** method will automatically advance you to the next item on the screen, and the other methods do not.

Change the orientation with one of the following methods:

1. Arrow-Key   **[⇓][↵]**

2. Letter   **I**

3. Spacebar   **[Spacebar]**

Change the setting back to the original using one of the following methods:

1. Arrow-Key   **[Shift-Tab][⇑][↵]**

2. Letter   **P**

3. Spacebar   **[Spacebar]**

Exiting the Screen

When you have completed a screen, you can exit it by entering:

[F10]

The program then returns to the previous menu level. To exit a menu and return to the previous menu level, either press the [Esc] key or [Click right] on the mouse. Exit the **Settings** menu for the current example, using either of the following methods:

1. Keyboard   **[Esc]**

2. Mouse   **[Click right]**

FUNCTION KEY COMMANDS

In addition to the menu commands, Harvard Graphics lists special operations at the bottom of the screen, which can be performed with the functions keys [F1] through [F10]. Note that not all of the function keys will be listed at any one time. Only those keys that have a function for the current activity will appear. For example, when the Main Menu is displayed, four function-key commands are listed at the bottom of the screen:

[F1]	Help
[F2]	Draw Chart
[F4]	Spell Check
[F8]	Options

You can activate the function-key commands in two ways:

Keyboard   Simply press the function key.

Mouse   First, display a special function-key menu by clicking *both* mouse buttons at the same time. This displays a menu at the bottom of the screen that reacts to mouse movements. While this menu is active, use the mouse to move a highlight to the function-key command you want to execute. Clicking the left mouse button will activate that function-key command.

One very handy function-key command that will appear on all Harvard Graphics menus is **Help.** The **Help** command is *context-sensitive*. This means that it displays screens that give you information about the current menu and options. Display the help for the Main Menu by one of the following methods:

1. Keyboard   **[F1]**

2. Mouse   **[Click both]**
                  Move to *F1-Help*
                  [Click left]

The program displays a screen or, if you are in the drawing mode, a panel that explains the menu (or screen) you are currently working with.

To return to the previous screen and resume operations, use either of the following methods:

1. Keyboard   **[Esc]**

2. Mouse   **[Click right]**

COMMANDS IN THIS BOOK

This introduction has revealed that there are several ways to perform the same task. To make the clearest possible presentations of examples in this book, you are asked to enter instructions primarily from the keyboard, using the simplest keystrokes available. Many people will find that, when they use the *highlight/[↵]* method to make menu selections, they are actually entering more keystrokes than they would if they typed the menu numbers.

In this book, you will find menu-selection instructions written using the *number* method, because it is the clearest way to write down instructions. This does not imply that the alternative methods are wrong or inferior. Once you are comfortable with the program's organization, feel free to use whichever method you like best to accomplish the results.

Return the highlight to the first item on the menu by entering:

    C

You are ready to begin working with Harvard Graphics.

Chapter 1

Text Charts

One of the simplest types of charts that you can produce with Harvard Graphics is a *text* chart. The charts are simple because they are composed of standard alphanumeric characters arranged into a specific layout. Creating text charts is similar to word processing; in both processes you directly enter the information that will appear on the chart. Text charts are useful for organizing lists of information or tables of data, and they commonly are used as text displays for title pages, lecture notes, and seminar notes.

PRESTRUCTURED CHARTS

If you have used a word-processing program such as WordPerfect or Microsoft Word, you are probably aware that you can create lists and tables with those applications. However, there are several important advantages to using Harvard Graphics, rather than a word-processing program, to create these items. Word processing programs can cover a wide range of text applications. In Harvard Graphics you can enter text in a predefined text-chart format, which simplifies the creation of standard text charts useful for presentations or seminar outlines.

The primary difference between Harvard Graphics and a word processor for creating a page of text is the *orientation* of each application. A word-processing program is oriented toward pages of paragraph text. It automatically assumes that you want to enter a continuing stream of text from left to right across the page, beginning at the top of the page and flowing to the bottom. If you fill up a page, the word processor creates new pages, so you are not limited in the amount of data you can enter. Unless you specify otherwise, the word-processing program assumes that you want all of the text in all of the paragraphs to look the same.

Text entry in Harvard Graphics is oriented toward the *display frame of reference,* which is the rectangular area of the chart. The program assures that all of the text you want to enter must fit into this frame, in contrast to word processors that create new pages as you enter more text. In addition, Harvard Graphics does not assume that all of the text should look the same. Each type of text chart is *prestructured* for certain types of text. When you select a particular type of text chart, Harvard Graphics automatically divides the *display frame* into a number of areas. Because of its location on the chart, each area will automatically display text in a different way. For example, figure 1.1 shows information entered into a two-column style of text chart. Notice that the chart title, subtitle, column headings, column items and footnote are all displayed differently.

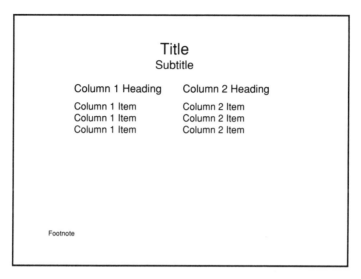

Figure 1.1. Text displayed in two column chart

In Harvard Graphics it is not necessary to specify the size and position of the items in a chart, because the areas of a two-column chart are automatically assigned formatting by the program. Figure 1.2 shows what looks like a single-chart display, but it is really composed of a variety of distinct sections, each carrying its own special formatting.

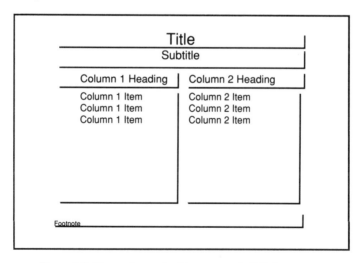

Figure 1.2. Two-column chart is composed of distinct areas

The predefined formatting areas make it possible to create text charts easier and faster, because the structure—that is, the character size, position, and column layout—is already there. You simply fill in the text. You also have the option of changing the details of the chart to suit your own needs or desires.

Harvard Graphics offers six types of predefined text charts.

Title Chart   This chart is used to display a title page. The text is placed into one of three areas: top, middle, or bottom. An example is shown in figure 1.3.

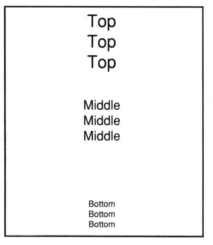

Figure 1.3. Title Chart

Simple List   A simple list chart has a heading that is followed by a column of items. An example is shown in figure 1.4.

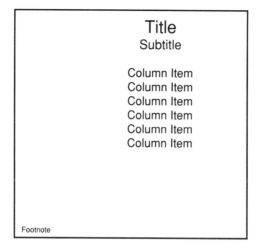

Figure 1.4. Simple list chart

Bullet List

The bullet chart is similar to the list chart, except that it has two levels of items in the column. A bullet character is placed to the left of major items in the list. An example is shown in figure 1.5.

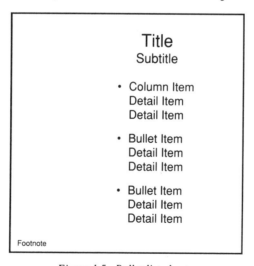

Figure 1.5. Bullet list chart

Two Columns

This chart style divides items into two columns. An example is shown in figure 1.6.

Three Columns   This chart style divides items into three columns as shown in figure 1.6.

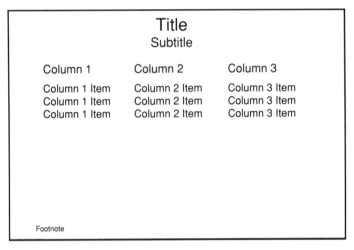

Figure 1.6. Three column text chart

Free Form   In addition to the five preset charts, you can create a *free form* chart. This chart has special areas for title, subtitle, and footnote. The rest of the chart can be filled with any type of text.

Generally, the predefined charts operate the same. In this chapter, you will work with two examples, a bullet chart and a two-column chart. These two examples will cover most of the details you will need to understand and operate the other three text charts.

Load the Harvard Graphics program in the usual manner. To begin the next section you should be at the Main Menu display.

Bullet List Charts

The Bullet List text chart is one of the most useful predefined text charts in Harvard Graphics. It is organized in two major sections. In the first section, space is automatically allocated for a chart title, subtitle, and footnote. The footnote is used typically to identify the source of data in the chart. Almost all of the charts created in Harvard Graphics have these three elements.

The second section of the chart is the list of items. This section allows you to have two levels, a bulleted heading and a subheading under the bullet.

The term *bullet* refers to the character placed at the left of the text to draw attention to the text item. Bullets are common in advertising and sales brochures, where they typically are used for lists of benefits and features.

Create a Bullet List chart by selecting the **Create new chart** option from the Main Menu. Press:

1

A second menu title, **Create New Chart,** appears to the right of the Main Menu. Select the **Text** option from this chart by pressing:

1

A third menu, shown in figure 1.7, now appears on the screen and lists the six text-chart styles you can create.

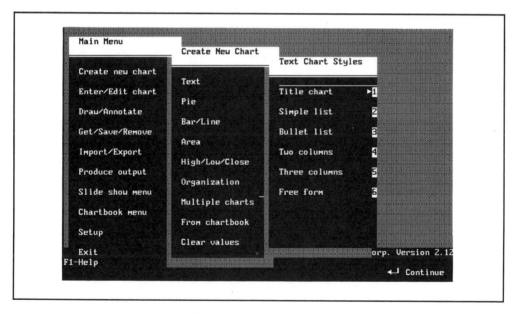

Figure 1.7. Text-chart styles

Select a **Bullet List** chart by pressing:

3

Text Entry Screens

The program changes the screen and displays one entitled Bullet List. This screen is the *text entry* screen for the Bullet List chart. In Harvard Graphics, the raw material (that is, the data or text) that is to be used as the basis for the chart is entered into a screen similar to the one currently displayed. It is important to understand that the organization of this screen does not necessarily indicate how the information will appear when the chart is displayed or printed. This screen is not a *what-you-see-is-what-you-get* (WYSSIWYG) type of display.

Rather, the data-entry screen is organized to help you enter the raw data (text, in the case of text charts) from which the final chart will be composed. The Harvard Graphics data-entry screen is divided into three sections: *Frame Text, Data Area,* and *Command Menu Area.*

Frame Text

The frame text usually consists of a title, subtitle and footnote, as shown in figure 1.8. The term *Frame Text* refers to the idea that this information appears in the same position on all charts. However, keep in mind that even though all three items are entered in one section of the data-entry screen, they will not necessarily appear that way on the final chart. For example, the footnote text, which is the third item in the section, will print in the bottom-left corner of chart, not directly below the subtitle.

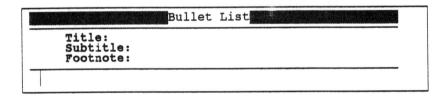

Figure 1.8. Frame text section

Data Area

The area in the center of the screen is used entering information that will make up the body of the chart. In the Bullet List chart, this area is blank. In other charts, the area may be organized in columns.

Command Menu Area At the bottom of the data-entry screen, Harvard Graphics reserves room for a list of commands, typically function keys, that can be issued from the current screen. The following function keys are always used for the same general purposes.

Key	Function
[F1]	Display Help
[F2]	Draw Chart
[F4]	Redraw Chart
[F5]	Text Attributes
[F6]	List Colors or Patterns
[F7]	Size and Placement
[F8]	Options
[F10]	Exit to next screen

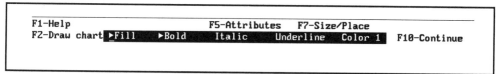

Figure 1.9. Command menu area

Note that not all function-key commands appear on all screens.

Text and Spacing

The text chart that you will create will be a list of the most popular plays written by Shakespeare. You will begin by entering the text for the title, subtitle, and footnote. You can enter up to 50 characters on each of these lines. However, it is important to keep in mind that the actual number of characters that will fit onto the final chart is affected by two factors: character size and spacing.

Size Harvard Graphics will display the text using different-size letters, depending upon what role they play in the chart. For example, the characters entered for the title will be printed with letters that are larger than any of the other text on the chart. Conversely, the footnote is printed with the smallest characters on the chart. In Harvard Graphics, the size of the characters is specified by a number from 0.5 to 100. Harvard Graphics automatically sets text sizes for each section of the chart.

The best way to understand the effect of different text sizes is to experiment with them. As a general guide, you will find that text set at 5.5 will allow you to fit about 40 characters across the chart.

If you are familiar with the measurement of characters in points (1 point = 1/72 of an inch) keep in mind that the text size values entered in Harvard Graphics are not point size measurements.

Spacing
When text is typed into the data-entry screen, all of the characters are the same size and width. This is called *monospaced* text. However, when Harvard Graphics displays text in the final chart, the letters are *proportionally* spaced. Proportional spacing refers to a process in which the amount of horizontal space taken up by a character changes, depending on which character is printed. For example, the letter *M* will take up more space than the letter *i*. Figure 1.10 shows that each character in monospaced type, illustrated by lines {1} and {2}, takes up the same amount of space, regardless of whether it is upper- or lowercase. But in proportionally spaced type, illustrated by lines {3} and {4}, a character's case changes the width of the lines.

Monospaced text:

{1}   `To be or not to be.`
{2}   `TO BE OR NOT TO BE.`

Proportional Spaced Text:

{3}   To be or not to be.
{4}   TO BE OR NOT TO BE.

Figure 1.10. Monospaced and proportionally spaced text

This means that when you enter text such as an all-uppercase title, the characters will take up more space than mixing upper- and lowercase characters.

Enter the title for the chart:

Popular Plays [↵]
By William Shakespeare [↵]
Dates shown are the generally accepted dates

The [F2] command allows you to display the chart at any point. For example, you might want to see what the frame text looks like when displayed as a chart. Press:

[F2]

When you press [F2], Harvard Graphics changes its display mode from the normal text display to a high-resolution graphics mode that paints the screen to look like the final form of a chart. An example is shown in figure 1.11.

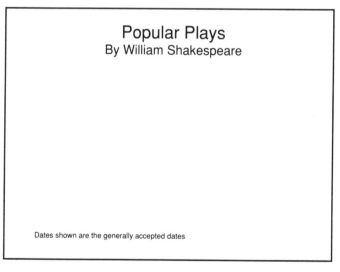

Figure 1.11. Chart displayed by [F2] key

You can return to the text-entry screen by pressing any key. Press:

[Esc]

When the keystroke is pressed, Harvard Graphics returns to the text-entry screen. Note that the cursor is still positioned in the same location as it was when you displayed the chart.

Entering a Bullet List

Following the frame-text items, you can enter a bulleted list. In this list type of there are two categories of items: bullet ed and sub-item.

Bulleted These are the main items on the list. Each is preceded by a bullet character (a solid black dot).

Note that a bullet character can be inserted at any location in the text by pressing the key combination [Ctrl-b].

Sub-item You can add items that fill in details under a bulleted (main) item. These items will not have bullets in front of them.

To begin entering bulleted text, move the cursor into the middle section of the entry screen, using one of the following keys: the [⇓], the [↵] or the [Tab] keys. Press:

[Tab]

When the cursor moves to the middle section of the entry screen, the program adds a bullet character, on the left side of cursor position. Enter the text for this line:

Comedies [↵]

The cursor moves to the next line, but no bullet appears to the left of the cursor; Harvard Graphics assumes that the line directly following a bulleted item is a subordinate detail line that should not have a bullet. If you were to leave this line blank and move to the next line, Harvard Graphics would display a bullet.

In this case, you want to enter details under the bulleted heading. Press

The Merchant of Venice (1595) [↵]
The Taming of the Shrew (1596) [↵]

While *The Merchant of Venice* is not a particularly funny play it is technically classified as a comedy because the heroes achieve their ends. You are ready to start a new classification. To create a bulleted line leave the current line blank by pressing:

[↵]

The program displays a bullet at the beginning of this line. The bullet was triggered by the blank line following the title, *The Taming of the Shrew*. Continue the chart with Shakespeare's historical plays. Type in:

Histories [↵]
King Richard III (1593) [↵]
King Henry V (1599) [↵]
[↵]

Add the tragic plays:

Tragedies [↵]
Romeo and Juliet (1593) [↵]
Hamlet (1602) [↵]
MacBeth (1606)

The data-entry screen should now look like figure 1.12.

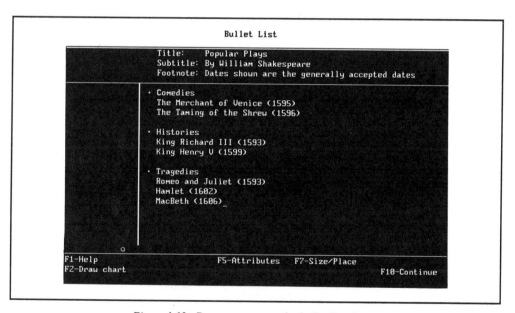

Figure 1.12. Data-entry screen for bullet-list chart

Display the chart based on this data by pressing:

[F2]

The chart that is displayed will look like figure 1.13. Note that, although the text in the data-entry screen is similar to the final chart, the two are not exactly the same. The final chart used a variety of character sizes for its text. The result is that the text fills the entire chart frame, even though it filled only part of the data-entry screen. Data entry screens generally can hold more text than can be displayed in a single chart. From this example you can see that by using the default text values, a bullet chart is limited to about 12 lines, including blanks, of text.

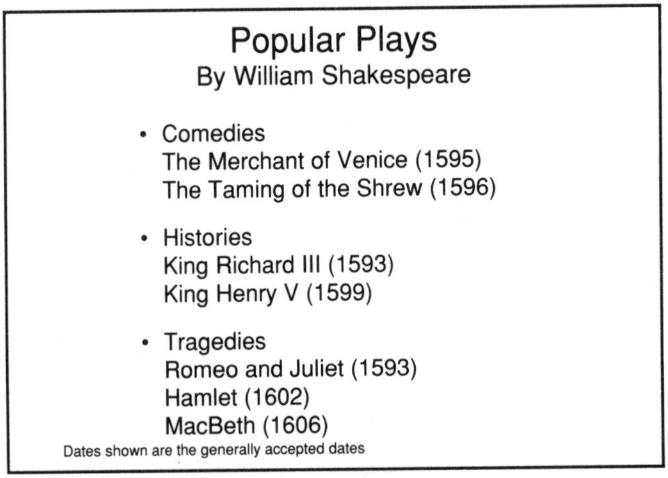

Popular Plays
By William Shakespeare

- Comedies
  The Merchant of Venice (1595)
  The Taming of the Shrew (1596)

- Histories
  King Richard III (1593)
  King Henry V (1599)

- Tragedies
  Romeo and Juliet (1593)
  Hamlet (1602)
  MacBeth (1606)

Dates shown are the generally accepted dates

Figure 1.13. Chart based on entered data

Return to the data-entry screen by pressing:

[Esc]

CONTROLLING THE APPEARANCE OF TEXT

As the name implies, text charts consist entirely of standard characters arranged on a page. To simplify the creation of text charts, the program makes a number of assumptions about the way that text should appear on the final chart.

Size   The sizes of the characters that appear on the final chart are set automatically. You can use the [F7] command to make changes in text size. Harvard Graphics automatically sets the following text sizes for a bullet-list chart:

Item	Size
Title	8
Subtitle	6
Footnote	3.5
All others	5.5

Place   In Harvard Graphics the term *place* refers to the alignment of text on a line. Text can be aligned on the left side of the frame, centered in the frame, or aligned on the right side of the frame. By default, the text in a bullet chart is aligned as follows:

Item	Size
Title	center
Subtitle	center
Footnote	left
All others	center

Attribute   A text attribute is an enhancement added to the basic shape of a character. Harvard Graphics supports the three most common text attributes: boldface, italics, and underscore. In addition, you can select either *outlined* or *filled* characters; you can also choose the color of the text. By default, all text on the chart is filled, boldface,, and white.

Font   The term *font* refers to the basic style of lettering used to display characters in the text. In Harvard Graphics displays all text on a chart in the same font. By default, text is displayed in the **Executive** font. Other fonts you can use include *Roman* and *Gothic*. However, you can change the font used for text.

In many cases, you will be satisfied with the chart as displayed with the default values. However, commands available in Harvard Graphics make it possible for you to change any or all of the settings to produce a chart that fits your personal preferences.

The default size value for text in the body of a bulleted list is 5.5. Subtitles are displayed at size 6, very close to what is used for the bulleted text. You might improve the appearance of the chart by changing the size of some items to produce a greater contrast between chart titles and the text in the list section.

The [F7] key accesses to a special menu that lists text sizes you have used in a chart. Press:

[F7]

You should see a menu that shows the size and place settings for each section of the chart. Figure 1.14 shows the size and place menu.

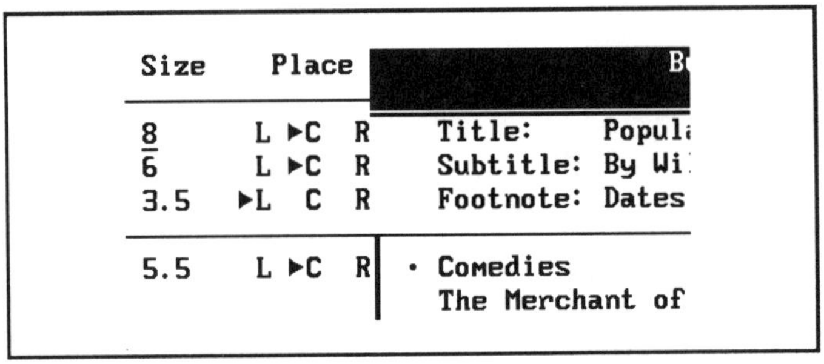

```
    Size      Place                          B
    ___
     8        L ►C   R      Title:     Popul
     6        L ►C   R      Subtitle:  By Wi
    3.5       ►L  C  R      Footnote:  Dates

    5.5       L ►C   R    · Comedies
                           The Merchant of
```

Figure 1.14. Size and place menu displayed

In this example, you will change the size of the list text from 5.5 to 3.8. You will also change the size of the footnote text to 2.2. The change will increase the quantity of text size on the chart. Press:

[⇓] *(2 times)*
2
[⇓] **[Ctrl-Del]**
3.8

You can display the chart directly from the Size/Place menu by pressing:

[F2]

The text of the list section of the chart is significantly smaller than it was in the previous version, shown in figure 1.15. Because the character size has been reduced, the amount of vertical space used by the 12 lines is reduced leaving a blank area between the last line and the bottom of the chart. You can see that one way to get more text on a chart is to reduce the size of the characters. Also note that the reduced size of the footnote makes it less prominent in the display.

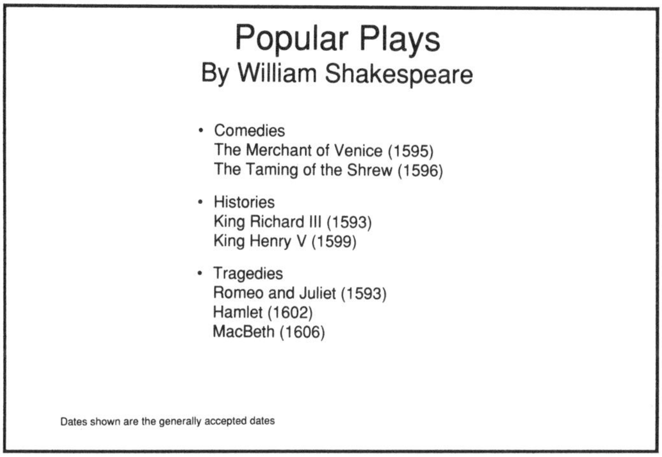

Figure 1.15. Chart with text size altered

Return to the text entry screen by pressing:

[Esc]

Note that when you returned to the text-entry screen, the [F7] Size/Place menu was automatically deactivated.

CHANGING PLACEMENT

The alignment (left, center, or right) of the lines in a chart is set automatically by Harvard Graphics. You can use the [F7] Size/Place menu to change the alignment. In a bulleted list chart, all text in the main section is centered. Suppose you wanted the chart text to be aligned on the left side of screen. Begin by displaying the Size/Place menu. Press:

[F7]

The second column in the menu is labeled *Place*. The alignment characteristics are shown as letters: L = left, C = center, and R = right. The position of the right-pointing triangle indicates the currently active option.

You can see from the display that the center section of the chart has **Center** alignment chosen. Move the cursor to the **Place** option for the middle section of the chart. Press:

[⇓] *(3 times)*
[Tab]

You can change the alignment by pressing either the letter of the option (L, C, or R) or the [Spacebar]. The [Spacebar] will select the next option each time it is pressed. Change to left alignment by pressing:

[Spacebar]

The selection marker moves to the **R.** Press:

[Spacebar]

The marker moves again, this time back to the first option, **L.** You have now selected Left alignment for the list.

Left alignment of text will usually place the text too close to the edge of the frame. Unlike word processing programs, Harvard Graphics does not automatically create a margin at the edge of the chart frame. The last option in the Size/Place menu is **Indent.** It allows you to establish a left margin for left-aligned text. The default value is zero. Change the value to 10 by pressing:

[End]
10

Display the revised chart by pressing:

[F2]

The chart now aligns the bullet-list section on the left side of the screen, shown in figure 1.16. Note that the 10 used for the indenting prevents placement of text too close to the left side of the chart frame.

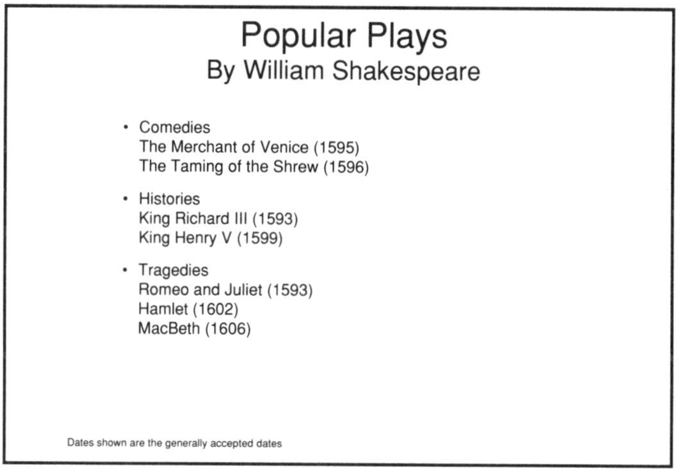

```
                  Popular Plays
              By William Shakespeare


        •  Comedies
           The Merchant of Venice (1595)
           The Taming of the Shrew (1596)

        •  Histories
           King Richard III (1593)
           King Henry V (1599)

        •  Tragedies
           Romeo and Juliet (1593)
           Hamlet (1602)
           MacBeth (1606)



     Dates shown are the generally accepted dates
```

Figure 1.16. Text alignment changed

Return to the text entry screen by pressing:

[Esc]

BULLET SHAPE

By default, the bullet symbol is a solid, black dot. You can use the [F7] Size/Place menu to change the bullet to a different character, such as a check mark, a dash, or a small square. You also have the option of changing the bullet to a sequential number, which means that a bullet would appear as the number *1.* for the first bullet, *2.* for the second, and so on.

The most interesting of these options is the numbering option. Display the [F7] **Size/Place** menu by pressing:

[F7]

The center section of this menu, shown in figure 1.17, shows the alternative bullet characters. The # option creates the consecutive numbering effect.

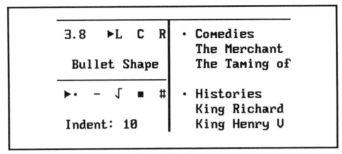

Figure 1.17. Bullet Shape menu

Select the # style of bullet by pressing:

[⇓] *(4 times)*
#
[F10]

Note that all the bullets change to the # character. Harvard Graphics does not display the numbers for bullet lines in the data-entry screen. They will appear only when the actual chart is displayed or printed. Press:

[F2]

When the chart is displayed, the # characters are replaced with the actual numbers, as shown in figure 1.18.

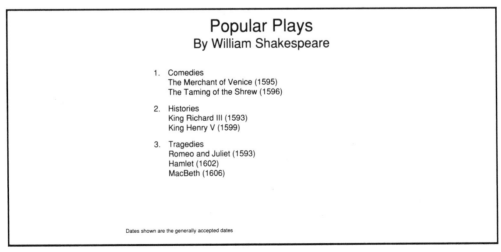

Figure 1.18. Bullets automatically numbered

Return to the data-entry screen by pressing:

[Esc]

TEXT ATTRIBUTES

By default, all text on a bullet-list chart is displayed as **bold** text. The [F5] and [Shift-F5] commands can be used to change the attributes of text on the chart. Recall that Harvard Graphics provides five text attributes: fill, bold, italic, underscore, and color.

Looking at the information on this chart in figure 1.18, you might realize that the name of the plays should be displayed in italic text to indicate that they are taken from the actual plays. In addition, you might want to add variety to the display by removing the boldface attribute from all text, except in the title and subtitles.

Begin by moving the cursor to the top of the data-entry screen. Press:

[Home]

Move the cursor to the footnote line:

[⇓] *(2 times)*

Starting at this location, you want to remove the bold attribute from text items drawn to the bottom of the display. Two commands affect text attributes: [F5] and [Shift-F5].

[F5]   The [F5] command lets you change the attribute of one or more characters starting at the current cursor location. When you press [F5], Harvard Graphics highlights the current character and displays the attribute menu at the bottom of the screen. If you want to include more characters in the attribute change, use either the [⇒] or [⇓] key to extend the highlight to the next character or the next line, respectively. By moving the highlight, you can include as much text as in the attribute change as necessary.

[Shift-F5]   The [Shift-F5] command works the same way as [F5], with the exception highlighting. With [Shift-F5], highlighting is on a line-by-line basis. When [Shift-F5] is entered, the entire line of text on which the cursor is positioned is highlighted and the attribute menu is displayed at the bottom of the screen. The [⇓] key extends the highlight one line at a time down the screen.

In this case you will use the [Shift-F5] key and work on a line-by-line basis. Press:

[Shift-F5]

The entire footnote line is highlighted, and the attribute menu, shown in figure 1.19, appears at the bottom of the screen. Selection markers on the menu indicate that the text is currently set as filled, bold text.

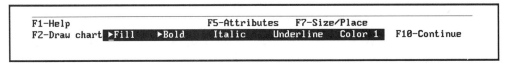

Figure 1.19. Text attribute menu

Extend the highlight to cover the remainder of the text on that page by pressing:

[⇓] *(12 times)*

To remove the bold attribute from the text, move the cursor on the attribute menu to **Bold** by pressing:

[Tab]

Remove the selection marker from **Bold** by pressing:

[Spacebar]

Save the change by pressing:

[↵]

In addition to removing the bold attribute from most of the chart, you want to add italics to the names of the plays. Press:

[⇓] *(2 times)*
[Shift-F5]
[⇓]

The two comedies are highlighted. The cursor is positioned on the **Bold** attribute, because that was the selection when you last used the **Text Attribute** menu. Add italics by pressing:

[Tab] *(2 times)*
[Spacebar] [⏎]

Repeat the process for the next two groups of plays:

[⇓] *(4 times)*
[Shift-F5] [⇓]
[Spacebar] [⏎]

[⇓] *(4 times)*
[Shift-F5]
[⇓] *(2 times)*
[Spacebar] [⏎]

When you have completed the task, display the chart by pressing:

[F2]

The chart now displays a variety of type styles, as shown in figure 1.20. The removal of the bold allows the title and subtitle to stand out more. The italics properly indicate the names of the plays. The use of text attributes is always a tricky matter. Too many attributes used inconsistently can detract from the appearance of your chart. Once you establish a pattern of attributes to use, you should try to maintain that pattern through all of the charts in any given presentation.

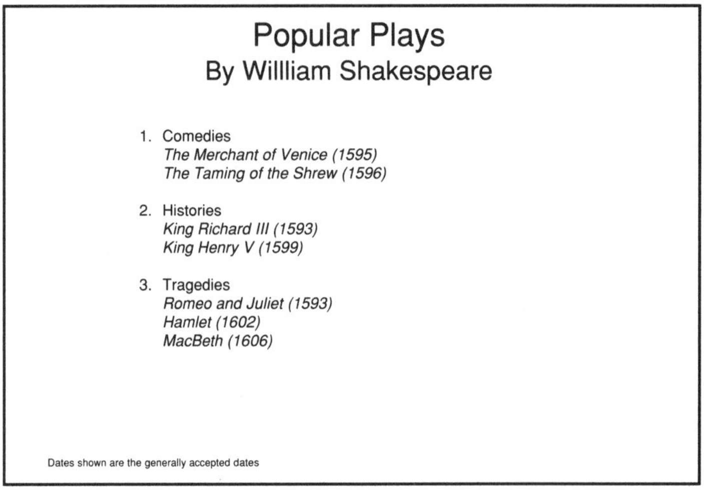

```
┌────────────────────────────────────────────────────┐
│                                                      │
│                   Popular Plays                      │
│                By Willliam Shakespeare               │
│                                                      │
│                                                      │
│          1. Comedies                                 │
│             The Merchant of Venice (1595)            │
│             The Taming of the Shrew (1596)           │
│                                                      │
│          2. Histories                                │
│             King Richard III (1593)                  │
│             King Henry V (1599)                      │
│                                                      │
│          3. Tragedies                                │
│             Romeo and Juliet (1593)                  │
│             Hamlet (1602)                            │
│             MacBeth (1606)                           │
│                                                      │
│                                                      │
│                                                      │
│     Dates shown are the generally accepted dates     │
└────────────────────────────────────────────────────┘
```

Figure 1.20. Chart shows changes in text attributes

Return to the data entry screen by pressing:

[Esc]

Changing Fonts

A *font* is a unique set of printing characters. Some fonts, such as Courier, the typewriter font, form letters of uniform thickness; letters in other fonts, such as Times (which you're reading now), vary in thickness. The default font used by Harvard Graphics is the **Executive** font. This font is similar to Helvetica.

Harvard Graphics allows you to change the font used for the text in a given chart. Note that a font change effects *all* of the text in the chart. You cannot change the font in a part of the chart.

To change the font of the chart return to the main menu by pressing:

[F10]

At the bottom of the screen you will see the [F8] **Options** command listed in the command menu. Press:

[F8]

The program displays the **Current Chart Options** menu which lists three types of options that effect the overall appearance of the chart, as shown in figure 1.21.

Orientation   Controls the orientation of the chart. **Landscape** places the *wide* side of the frame or printed page on the horizontal. The **Portrait** orientation places the *narrow* side of the frame or paper on the horizontal. The default is **Landscape.**

Border   Controls the border that will print around the chart. The default is a double-line border.

Font   Selects the font used for all of the text in the current chart. The default is the **Executive** font.

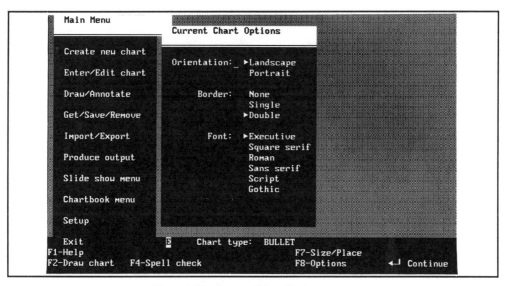

Figure 1.21. Current Chart Options menu

Change the font from *Executive* to *Roman* by pressing

[Tab] *(2 times)*
[⇩] *(2 times)*
[Spacebar] [↵]

Display the revised chart by pressing the following command at the Main Menu:

[F2]

The chart remains the same in all respects except that the characters have been changed to a Roman font. Note that a Roman font uses lines that vary in thickness.

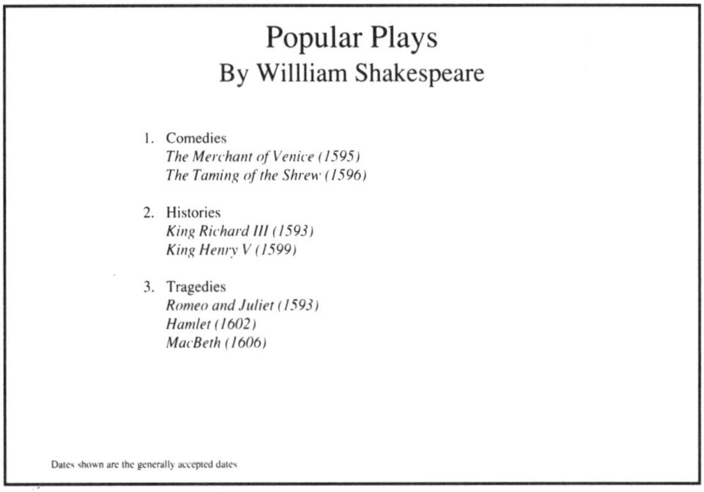

Figure 1.22. Chart that uses Roman font for text characters

Return to the data-entry screen by pressing:

[Esc]
2

Changing Colors

You can also use the attribute menu to change the color of the text. In general, text charts look best when they are in black and white. This affords the reader the greatest degree of contrast making the text easier to read. Also keep in mind that most printers print only in black and white. However, occasional use of color can brighten up the text charts when using a color display or a color printer.

To display a title and subtitle of the example text chart in yellow, first highlight the title and subtitle of the chart by pressing:

[Shift-F5]
[⇓]

To change the color move the cursor to the option on the attribute menu that reads **Color 1** by pressing:

[Tab] *(2 times)*

Colors in Harvard Graphics are entered as numbers ranging from 1–16. If you do not know the number of the color you want to select, you can display a menu of available colors by pressing:

[F6]

The program displays a menu that list the colors and the corresponding numbers. Yellow is color 7. Select that color by pressing:

y
[↵] *(2 times)*

Display the chart by pressing:

[F2]

The first two lines of the chart will appear in yellow. Return to the data-entry screen by pressing:

[Esc]

SAVING THE CHART

When you have created the chart you desire you should save a copy of the chart in a disk file. The disk file can be reloaded into Harvard Graphics for output or further modification. Saving is performed from the **Get/Save/Remove** menu. Press:

[F10] 4

Select the **Save Chart** option by pressing:

2

Harvard Graphics automatically enters the title of the chart as the description. Enter a valid DOS file name for the chart. In this example, call the chart BULLET. Press:

bullet [↵]
[↵]

The current chart is stored on the disk as a file with a CHT extension. Return to the main menu by pressing:

[Esc]

PRINTING A CHART

Once a chart has been created it can be sent to an output device such as a printer, plotter, or film-recording device. The most common output devices are printers.

In general, there are two kinds of printers that will print the charts you create with Harvard Graphics.

Dot Matrix   Dot matrix printers create an image as a series of dots. They vary greatly in speed and quality depending on how many *dots per inch* they are capable of printing. The fewer dots per inch, the lesser the quality, but the faster the image is printed. The time it takes some printers to print a high-quality chart with many dots per inch is quite substantial. For example, an older dot matrix printer such as an Epson MX-80 might take 30 to 45 minutes to print a high quality chart.

Many later model dot-matrix printers can print in color. This is achieved by using a multicolor ribbon and a special program supplied in the form of a Read Only Memory (ROM) chip set.

Laser   Laser printers combine high rates of speed, high print quality with easy of use and quiet operation. Most of them print at a resolution of 300 dots per inch.

Another form of printing charts is to use a *pen plotter.* Pen plotters are generally more expensive and slower than comparable dot matrix printers, but their color rendition, due to the use of individual pens for each color, is superior. When combined with specially coated plotter paper, the ink drawings produced by a plotter can be of a very high quality.

Black and White Reversal

When text is printed on a black and white printer (either laser or dot-matrix), the roles of black and white as they appear on the screen are reversed. On the screen the charts are composed of white letters on a black background; when printed on white paper, the chart will be black on a white background.

Checking The Printer Selection

Before you attempt to print a chart you must set up the program to work with the particular printer you are using. This is usually done when the Harvard Graphics program is installed on the computer. Once a printer or printers have been selected the choices will be recorded on the disk and be retained until you decide to change them; you are not required to select printers every time you use Harvard Graphics. In this example, check the program's setup to make sure that the correct printer has been installed. Display the **Setup** menu.

[Esc] 9

The **Setup** menu lists two printers, **Printer 1** and **Printer 2.** This enables you to install two different printers if you are working in an environment where there is more than one type of printer available. Select the **Printer 1** menu by pressing

2

The **Printer 1 Setup** menu (figure 2.23) lists the printers supported by Harvard Graphics. When you select a printer, keep in mind that many printers that do not appear on this list emulate popular printers. If your printer does not appear on the list, select the printer that your printer emulates. For example, Citizen printers can emulate IBM or Epson models and the Qume CrystalPrint Publisher emulates the Apple Laserwriter.

You can change the selected printer by using the [⇓] or [⇑] keys to move the bold highlight to the desired printer.

```
                          Printer 1 Setup

IBM   Graphics Printer     EPSON   FX,LX,RX        TOSHIBA  P1340,P1350,P1351
      Proprinter,XL,II              EX,JX                   P321,P341,P351
      ProprinterX24,XL24            MX                      P351C
      QuietwriterII,III             LQ 800,1000             PageLaser12
      Color Printer                 LQ 1500
      Color Jetprinter              LQ 2500         QUME     LaserTEN,+
      Personal PagePrinter          GQ 3500
                                                   AST      TurboLaser
HP    LaserJet,+,500+,II   OKIDATA  ML 84,92,93
      ThinkJet                      ML 182,183      APPLE    LaserWriter
      QuietJet,+                    ML 192,193
      PaintJet                      ML 292,293      CALCOMP  ColorMaster
      DeskJet                       ML 294
                                    LaserLine 6     MATRIX   TT200
NEC   P5,P6,P7
      P5XL,P9XL,CP6,CP7   XEROX     4020            TEKTRONIX 4696
      LC-860 (LaserJet)             4045
      LC-890 (PostScript)                           UDI      Printer

      Printer: LaserWriter                          TEKTRONIX Phaser CP

F1-Help
                                                           F10-Continue
```

Figure 1.23. Printer 1 Setup menu

Save your selection by pressing

[F10]

Harvard Graphics displays a menu (figure 1.24) that lets you to specify the *printer interface*, the port in your computer to which the printer is attached. The default printer port is LPT1, the parallel printer port.

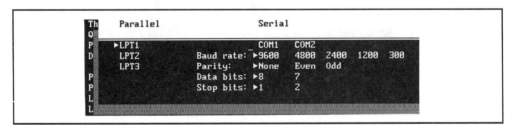

Figure 1.24. Printer Port menu

Exit the setup menus by pressing:

[F10] [Esc]

Printing the Chart

When you have selected the correct printer you can print a chart form the **Produce Output** menu by pressing

6

The first option on this menu is for the **Printer.** Press:

1

The program displays the **Printer Chart Options** menu, shown in figure 1.25.

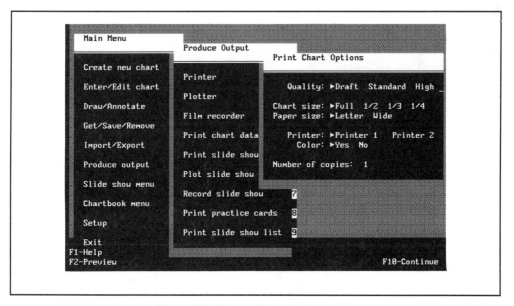

Figure 1.25. Printer Chart Options menu

Quality   You can select **draft, standard,** or **high.** The default is **draft,** which provide the lowest quality, but the highest speed printout. Keep in mind that the effect of the quality selection will vary with the type of printer you are using. On some printers the standard and high options will not effect the printed image.

Chart Size   This option specifies the chart size relative to the page, assumed by default to be an 8.5-by-11-inch page. The chart size default is **full,**

meaning that the chart will fill the entire page. You can reduce the size of the chart to **1/2, 1/3,** or **1/4** page size.

Paper size   The paper options allow you to choose between **Letter** (8.5-by-11-inch) or **Wide** (14-by-11-inch) paper. The default is **Letter** size paper.

Printer   You can select **Printer 1** or **Printer 2.** The default is **Printer 1.**

Color   Select whether or not you want to print in color. If you select **no,** the printout will be in black and white. This option has no effect on black and white printers.

Copies   Sets the number of copies of the chart to be printed. The default is a single copy.

Print the chart by pressing:

[F10]

When the printing is complete the program returns to the Main Menu.

TWO-COLUMN CHARTS

Two- and three-column text charts are useful for presenting data tables. The data in the tables is often the basis of the graphic you will create in the later chapters. Two- and three-column tables are frequently used to display the raw data as part of a presentation.

Create a new two column chart by pressing:

1 1 4

Harvard Graphics asks you if you want to keep the current data. This option allows you to copy the text entered in the current chart into the new chart. This is useful when you want to change the chart type without having to enter the data again. In this case, select not to copy the data from the current chart by entering:

n [↵]

The data-entry screen for a two-column chart is similar to the screen used for the Bullet List chart with the exception that the middle section of the chart is divided into columns. On this display there are only two columns because the area on the left, which appears to be a narrow column, is reserved for the Size/Place menu.

Begin the entry with the title section of the chart:

Passenger Car Production [↵]
1988 [↵]
Motor Vehicle Manufacturers Assc. [↵]

The boxes at the top of the columns are the locations where you can enter the column headings. The cursor should be in the box at the top of the first column. By default the column headings will be displayed at the text size 5.5. The text will be filled, bold, underlined text. The items in the columns will be slightly smaller, size 5, and be filled and bolded, but not underscored. Type the headings for both columns:

Company [Tab]
Vehicles [Tab]

Entering Data in Columns

You can enter information in the two-column layout in two ways:

[Tab]   Pressing the [Tab] key after an entry moves you to the next entry position. If you are located in the first column the cursor moves to the entry area on the same line in column 2. From column 2 the cursor jumps to the next line down in column 1. Using [Tab] lets you enter data column-by-column.

[↵]   The [↵] key advances you to the next line in the same column. Using [↵] at the end of each item allows you to work down a column.

For this example, work down each column by entering:

Chrysler [↵]
Ford [↵]
General [↵]
Motors [↵]
Volkswagen [↵]
Honda [↵]
Mazda [↵]

Nissan [↵]
Toyota

Return the cursor to the top of the next column and enter the corresponding values:

[⇑]
[Tab]

Enter the following values in the second column:

1,072,845 [↵]
1,805,741 [↵]
3,501,124 [↵]
35,998 [↵]
366,354 [↵]
163,289 [↵]
109,879 [↵]
55,480

Changing Attributes by Column

In a two- or three-column chart, Harvard Graphics enables you to change text attributes on a column-by-column basis. When you use [F5] or [Shift-F5] to highlight text, the cursor will move up and down only in the current column.

For example, by default all text displayed in text charts is displayed in bold. In this example, change the attributes of the values in the **Vehicles** column to normal text.

Move the cursor to the top of the column by pressing:

[⇑] *(7 times)*

Display the attribute menu and begin the highlighting by pressing:

[Shift-F5]

Note that the highlight covers only the section of the line in the right-hand column. Extend the highlight down the column by pressing:

[⇓] *(7 times)*

Remove the bold attribute from this text by pressing:

[Tab] [Spacebar] [↵]

Display the two-column chart by pressing:

[F2]

The program displays the two column chart (figure 1.26). Note that the numeric data in the right-hand column has been aligned on the right side of the column so that the numbers are aligned correctly, according to place value. Harvard Graphics will automatically implement this type of alignment if *all* of the items in the column are numeric. If you mix numbers and text in the same column, the text and numbers in the column will be left aligned.

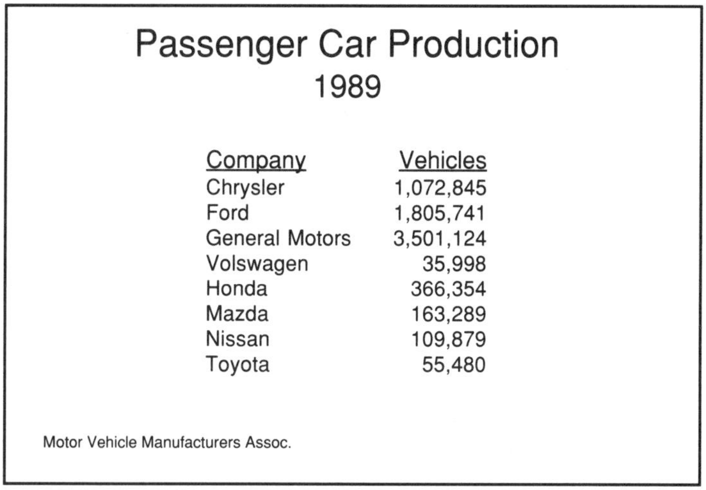

Passenger Car Production
1989

Company	Vehicles
Chrysler	1,072,845
Ford	1,805,741
General Motors	3,501,124
Volswagen	35,998
Honda	366,354
Mazda	163,289
Nissan	109,879
Toyota	55,480

Motor Vehicle Manufacturers Assoc.

Figure 1.26. Two-column chart

Return to the data entry screen by pressing:

[Esc]

Column Spacing

The two- and three-column text charts have the same Size/Place menu options as do the other text charts with one addition, the **Column Spacing** option. To see this new option, first display the Size/Place menu by pressing:

[F7]

The last item on this menu is **Column Spacing** which shows four options: **S**=small, **M**= medium, **L**= large and **X**= extra large. The default value is **M** for medium spacing between the column. Change the spacing to extra large by pressing:

[⇓] *(5 times)*
X

Display the chart by pressing:

[F2]

The chart now displays the column with additional space between the two columns, as shown in figure 2.27.

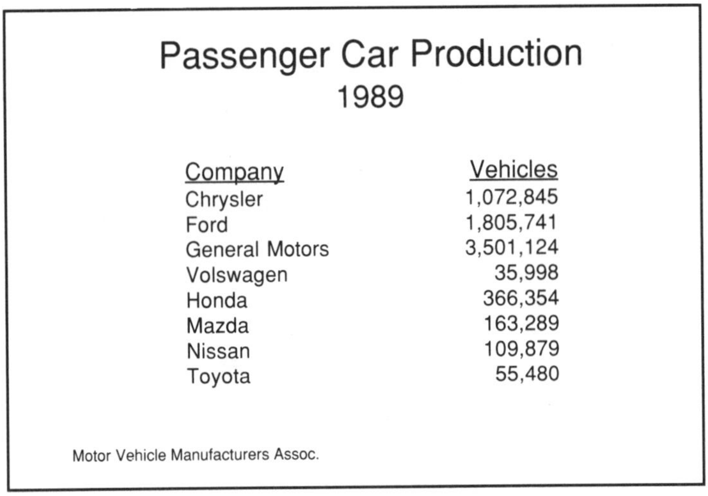

```
Passenger Car Production
           1989

       Company              Vehicles
       Chrysler             1,072,845
       Ford                 1,805,741
       General Motors       3,501,124
       Volswagen               35,998
       Honda                  366,354
       Mazda                  163,289
       Nissan                 109,879
       Toyota                  55,480

Motor Vehicle Manufacturers Assoc.
```

Figure 1.27. Space between columns widened

Save this chart by pressing:

[Esc] [F10] 4 2
twocols [↵]
[↵]

Return to the Main Menu by pressing:

[Esc]

SUMMARY

The charts discussed in this chapter were text charts. These charts do not use graphic images or pictures but are composed simply of text. The advantage of text charts is that they are prestructured for the creation of title pages, summary listings, or tables of data. These predefined structures can speed up the creation of text displays.

Chart Structure. The text charts in Harvard Graphics are divided into discrete sections. All charts have a frame text section that includes items such as the chart title. Each section of the chart is assigned a distinct set of size, place and text attributes. You can create a chart using the default values or you can modify them to suit your own needs.

Bullets. A bullet is a character used to draw attention to a line of text. Bullets are automatically inserted in bullet-list charts. You can manually insert a bullet character in any location in the chart using the key combination [Ctrl-b]. The # symbol will be replaced with consecutive numeric values when the chart is displayed or printed.

Text Attributes. The text characters have five different attributes: **fill, bold, italic, underline and color.** The defaults are **fill, bold,** and **color 1** (white). The [F5] and [Shift-F5] keys allow you to change the attributes of one or more characters or of lines of text. You can use the [⇒] and [⇓] keys to extend the highlight to cover the desired area of text.

Size. The [F7] command displays a special menu that lists the text size for each of the sections of the chart. The size of the text is set by default, but you can change the size of the text by entering any value from .5 to 100. Obviously, the larger the size, the fewer characters can be displayed on the chart. Conversely, reduction in the size of the text will permit more text on the chart.

Place. The [F7] menu also lists the placement characteristics for the lines in the sections of the chart. You can align text left, center, or right in the chart frame. You can also enter an indent factor. On bulleted lists you can select the bullet character. On two- and three-column charts you can adjust the spacing between the columns.

Font. Fonts allow you to change the basic style of text used in the chart. In Harvard Graphics all of the text in a given chart will have the same font. You can select that font by using the [F8] command from the Main Menu of the program.

Saving. Charts can be saved using the **Get/Save/Remove** menu. Charts are stored in files with CHT extensions.

Printing. Once you have selected a printer from the setup menu you can use the **Produce Output** menu to print the chart.

Chapter 2

Pie Charts

The purpose of a pie chart is to illustrate, in as dramatic a fashion as possible, the size or magnitude of each item in a series of related items. Pie charts are very good at highlighting how each of the parts compares to the whole or other individual parts.

A typical example of a series of values that can be expressed in a pie chart is the budget of a business or government. In a budget, the whole value (the whole pie) can be expressed as the total amount of income. Each source of income (each slice of the pie) combines to make up a value series that shows the significance of each income source relative to the whole.

As an example, take the projected budget of the Federal government of the United States for 1990. Figure 2.1 shows the sources of income of the Federal government in billions of dollars.

Projected Federal Budget
Fiscal 1990

Income Source	Amount(in billions)
Individual Income Tax	466.7
Corporate Income Tax	117.4
Social Security	391.5
Estate Taxes	8.1
Excise Taxes	35.5
Misc	40.4

Source: President's Office of Management and Budget

Figure 2.1. Table of income sources

The table could be represented by a pie chart because each item in the table is a part of the overall whole: the total income of the federal government. The goal of creating a pie chart from these figures would be to illustrate the relative importance of each income source to the total amount of federal revenue. Figure 2.2 shows a pie chart created using the data shown in the previous table.

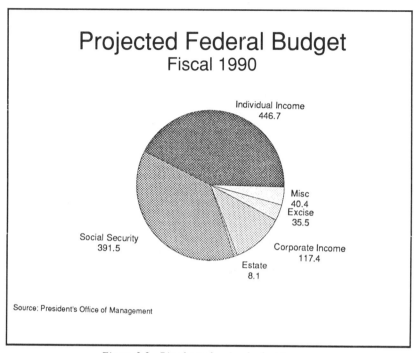

Figure 2.2. Pie chart showing budget income

Your first task in this chapter is to create a pie chart of the data shown in the table. In addition you will learn how to use special pie-chart features to augment the basic pie chart with special graphic features. Begin by loading the Harvard Graphics program in the usual manner. When loaded you will see the Main Menu displayed.

CREATING A PIE CHART

The first step in the process of creating a pie chart is to select the **Pie Chart** option from the **Create new chart** menu. Press:

1

The programs displays a second menu parallel to the Main Menu (figure 2.3) that lists the major categories of charts that can be created in Harvard Graphics.

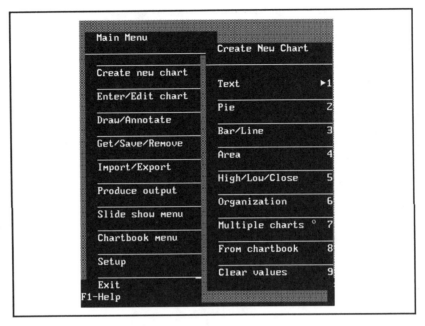

Figure 2.3. Create New Chart menu

For this example, create a Pie chart by pressing:

2

When you select option 2 the menus are removed from the screen and the Pie Chart data-entry screen (figure 2.4) is displayed. The display is divided into two parts. The large area in the center of the screen is the data-entry area. It is divided into rows and columns, each of which represents some detail about each slice in the pie chart. The first three columns are labeled *slice, label,* and *value.*

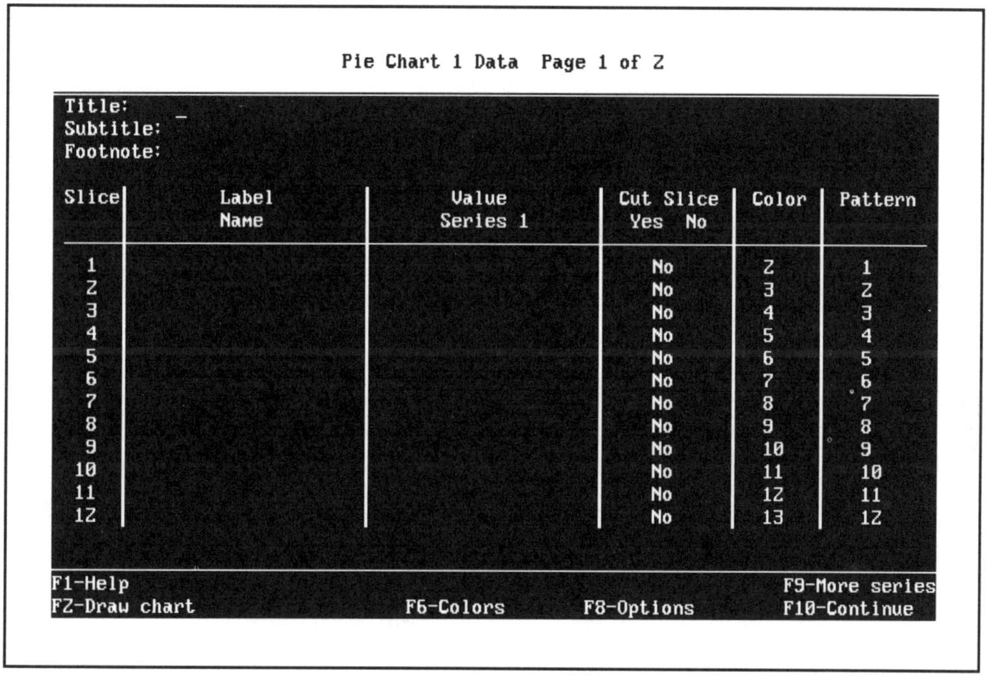

```
                    Pie Chart 1 Data   Page 1 of 2

 Title:         _
 Subtitle:
 Footnote:

 Slice|  Label              |      Value        | Cut Slice | Color | Pattern
      |  Name               |      Series 1     | Yes   No  |       |

   1  |                     |                   |    No     |   2   |   1
   2  |                     |                   |    No     |   3   |   2
   3  |                     |                   |    No     |   4   |   3
   4  |                     |                   |    No     |   5   |   4
   5  |                     |                   |    No     |   6   |   5
   6  |                     |                   |    No     |   7   |   6
   7  |                     |                   |    No     |   8   |   7
   8  |                     |                   |    No     |   9   |   8
   9  |                     |                   |    No     |  10   |   9
  10  |                     |                   |    No     |  11   |  10
  11  |                     |                   |    No     |  12   |  11
  12  |                     |                   |    No     |  13   |  12

 F1-Help                                                    F9-More series
 F2-Draw chart              F6-Colors      F8-Options        F10-Continue
```

Figure 2.4. Pie chart data entry screen, page 1

At the very bottom of the screen are a list of function-key commands available in the current mode. For example, the [F2] key activates the **Draw Chart** command. This command appears on most menus and lets you to see the chart based on the current settings at any time.

If you look at the very top of the screen you will see the title *Pie Chart 1 Data Page 1 of 2*. When a Harvard Graphics screen title refers to a *page* it signifies that all of the options available for a particular chart cannot fit onto a single screen. The [Pg Dn] key will move you to the next page of the display; the [Pg Up] key will move you to the previous page of the display. To display the second page of example data display, press:

[Pg Dn]

In this example, you need to look carefully at the display to see what has changed since page 2 is very much like page 1. Notice that at the top of the screen the title has changed to *Pie Chart 2 Data Page 2 of 2*. The current screen is used to define a second pie for the same chart. When you use this second pie screen your chart will contain two pies instead of just one. Multiple pie charts are useful when you want to contrast the proportions of slices of two different pies. Later in this chapter you will create charts with two pies. For now, return to the first pie screen by pressing:

[Pg Up]

DIRECT DATA ENTRY

Once you have selected the type of chart you want to create (a pie chart in this example), you must enter the data that will define this particular chart. Data entry is a task which is common to all of the charts and the basic techniques are the same throughout the applications.

Table 2.1 summarizes the keys which can be used to change the position of the cursor.

Table 2.1. Cursor Movement Keys

Key	Cursor Movement
[⇐]	one character to the left
[⇒]	one character to the right
[⇑]	one line up
[⇓]	one line down
[Tab]	next entry item
[Shift-Tab]	previous entry item
[Home]	first item on screen
[End]	last item on screen
[Ctrl-⇐]	one word left
[Ctrl-⇒]	one word right

In Harvard Graphics (as in all applications from Software Publishing), the [Tab] and [Shift-Tab] keys are the preferred method of moving from one item to another because they always position the cursor at the beginning of an entry area. The keys listed in table 2.2 show the edit keys, used to make corrections and deletions.

Table 2.2. Editing Keys

Key	Function
[Backspace]	delete character to the left
[Del]	delete character at cursor position
[Ctrl-Del]	deletes all text in current item
[Ins]	switch between typeover and insert modes

Note that by default, Harvard Graphics operates in a *typeover* mode. This means that if you position the cursor on an existing character and type a new character, the existing character is replaced with the one that you type. If you want to add the character without overwriting any of the existing characters, you must activate the *insert* mode by pressing the [Ins] key. Once activated, the insert mode stays on until you press [Ins] again, at which time the typeover mode is reactivated. Harvard Graphics uses the shape of the cursor to indicate the current mode. In the *typeover* mode the cursor is a flashing *line*. When the *insert* mode is active the cursor shape changes to a flashing *block*.

Entering Titles

The first items on any chart menu are usually the titles for the chart. In the case of a pie chart, you have room to enter a *title, subtitle,* and a *footnote*. The title and subtitle of the chart will appear centered at the top of the chart. Enter the title and subtitle of this chart:

Federal Revenues [↵]
Fiscal 1990 [↵]

To add the word *Projected* to the title of the chart, move the cursor back to the title entry area by pressing:

[Shift-Tab] *(2 times)*

Recall that by default Harvard Graphics operates in the overtype mode. In this case you need to insert the word in front of the current title. Activate the insert mode by pressing:

[Ins]

Note that the cursor changes shape from a flashing line to a flashing block. Any characters that you type will be inserted into the entry at the current cursor position. Press:

Projected [Spacebar]

The title is now revised, as shown in figure 2.5. Note that the insert mode will continue to stay active until you press [Ins] again. For now, leave the insert mode on.

```
    Title:    Projected Federal Revenues
    Subtitle: Fiscal 1990
    Footnote:
```

Figure 2.5. Text inserted in entry area

Move the cursor to the Footnote entry area by pressing:

[Tab] *(2 times)*

The footnote will appear in the lower-left corner of the chart in smaller print than the the text. The footnote is typically used to indicate the source of the data. In this example, that is the *Office of Management and Budget*. Press:

Source: Office of Management and Budget [↵]

Note that the title, subtitle, and footnote entries are limited to 40 characters.

Entering Slice Information

The next section of the pie-chart screen is the entry of the details for each slice in the pie. There are five items that define each slice in the pie. A pie can have up to 12 different slices.

Label   The label is the text that identifies the meaning of each of the pie slice. You can enter up to 20 characters for each pie slice.

Value   The value is a numeric value that represents the magnitude of the slice.

Cut Slice   A **cut** slice is one that is broken out from the pie itself. This effect is often used to emphasize a particular slice. It is possible, however, to have all of the slices exploded. The default setting for this option is **no.**

Color   Harvard Graphics supports sixteen colors. The colors are entered using the numbers 1-16, as shown in table 2.3. By default, Harvard Graphics assigns the colors to the slices consecutively beginning with color 2, cyan, for the first slice.

Table 2.3. The numbers assigned to the pie-slice colors

Number	Color
1	White
2	Cyan
3	Magenta
4	Green
5	Blue
6	Red
7	Yellow
8	Orange
9	Royal Blue
10	Gold
11	Violet
12	Pink
13	Grey
14	Crimson
15	Dark Green
16	Black

Pattern   In Harvard Graphics a *pattern* is a method of drawing lines to fill in an area instead of using solid colors. If you have a black-and-white printer, all colors are automatically converted to patterns of black and white when they print. Harvard Graphics automatically assigns a different pattern to each slice of the pie. Note that by default, the patterns are ignored when the chart is displayed on screen unless you specifically select to use patterns.

Enter the first slice of the pie:

Individual Income [Tab]
466.7 [Tab] *(4 times)*

When you press [Tab] in the **Cut Slice, Color**, and **Pattern** columns the default values will be used. Enter the next slice:

Corporate Income [Tab]
117.4 [Tab] *(4 times)*

The Sequences of Slices

When you are entering slice information in a pie chart, it is common to enter the slices in a logical order, such as alphabetically or by size. However, when using Harvard Graphics it is important to keep in mind how the final pie chart will appear before deciding upon a slice order. For example, if you decide to group the slices in order of decreasing size so that three small slices are grouped together (such as slices 4, 5, and 6 in the current example), you might find that when you displayed the pie chart, the labels of the small slices would be crowded together and difficult to read, as shown in figure 2.6.

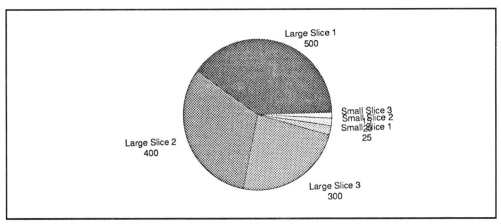

Figure 2.6. Small slice labels crowded together

You can avoid this problem by changing the order in which the slices are written into the chart data screen. The chart in figure 2.7 shows how the readability of labels is improved when you alternate between large and small slices.

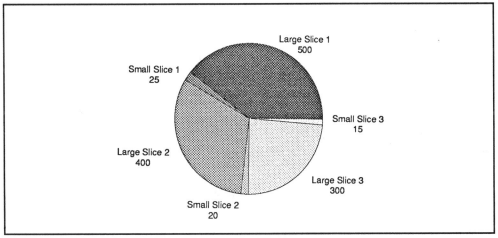

Figure 2.7. Slice rearranged to improve label display

In the current chart, mix in the small slices with the larger ones in order to avoid places to many small slices in one section of the chart. Enter the next three slices of the pie chart:

Estate [Tab]
8.1 *(4 times)*
Social Security [Tab]
391.5 *(4 times)*
Excise [Tab]
35.5 *(4 times)*

Enter the final slice exactly as it appears in the text. The error in spelling is made intentionally so that you can experiment with the built-in spell check. Press:

Miscellanous [Tab]
40.4

Displaying the Chart

You can display the chart, at any time while you are working on the Pie Chart screen by pressing:

[F2]

The screen changes from the data entry screen to a graphic image of the chart, as shown in figure 2.8. Note that in this book the colors are represented by patterns. If you are using a color monitor you will see each slice represented by a different solid color.

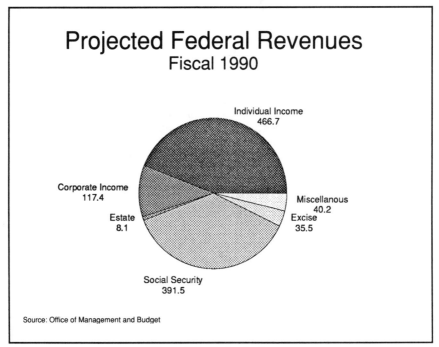

Figure 2.8. Basic pie chart

Return to the previous screen by pressing any key. For example, press:

[Esc]

Exploding a Slice

You can draw attention to one particular slice of the budget pie by using the **Cut Slice** option to create a *cut* or *exploded* slice. For example, to draw attention to the Social Security slice, change the **Cut Slice** setting to *Yes*. To do this, move the cursor to the line for slice 4 which is Social Security. Press:

[⇑] *(2 times)*

Move the cursor to the **Cut Slice** column by pressing:

[Tab]

You can change the setting in this column in two ways: by typing the letter of the option you want (*Y* for Yes or *N* for No) or by pressing the [Spacebar] to toggle the entry between Yes and No. Press:

[Spacebar]

The column changed to *Yes* for that slice. Display the revised graph by pressing:

[F2]

The display now shows the Social Security slice cut away from the pie (figure 2.9), creating a contrast between that slice and the other slices of the pie.

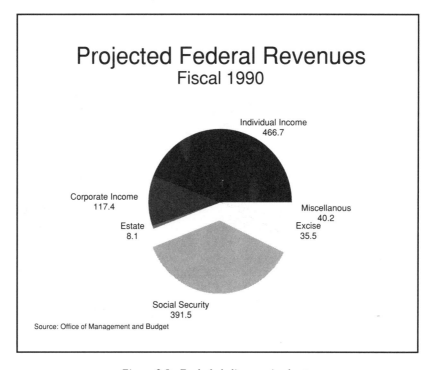

Figure 2.9. Exploded slice on pie chart

Return to the data entry screen by pressing:

[Esc]

Slice Labels

Once you have created a basic pie chart you can alter small details of its appearance by using the **Options** command, **[F8]**. Pie-chart options cover a wide range of features that can make small or major changes in the appearance of the chart.

First, use the options that alter the appearance of the slice labels. By default, Harvard Graphics labels each slice with the name entered into the **Labels** column and the number entered into the **Value** column. Since pie charts show *part-to-whole* relationships, it is often useful to label each slice with a percentage that shows what portion of the whole each slice actually represents.

Begin by displaying the options screen by pressing:

[F8]

When the **Options** command is issued, the screen changes to show a new set of items (figure 2.10). Note that the chart titles, entered on the data screen, appear on the options screen as well.

```
        Pie Chart Titles & Options   Page 1 of 2              ▼

         Title:      Projected Federal Revenues
         Subtitle:   Fiscal 1990

         Footnote:   Source: Office of Management and Budget


         Pie 1 title:

         Pie 2 title:



         3D effect          Yes    ►No
         Link pies          Yes    ►No
         Proportional pies  Yes    ►No
         Fill style        ►Color     Pattern      Both


F1-Help                    F5-Attributes   F7-Size/Place
F2-Draw chart                              F8-Data          F10-Continue
```

Figure 2.10. Pie Chart Titles & Options screen

This screen is labelled 1 of 2 in the top-right corner. The options that control the display of slice labels are located on page two of the screen. Press:

[Pg Dn]

This screen is divided into two columns labeled *Pie 1* and *Pie 2*. In the case of a simple pie chart, you will be concerned only with the settings in the *Pie 1* column. The options are divided into four basic groups. The first group of four options effect the entire pie. The second group affects the name labels, the third affects, the value labels, and the fourth affects the display of percentages.

The structure of the menus allows you to turn on and off the name, value, and percentage labels independently using the **Show labels, Show values,** and **Show percent** options. This means you can create different combinations of name, value, and percent labels. By default, **Show labels** and **Show values** are *Yes,* while **Show percent** is *No.* Note that the current setting is indicated by the position of the triangle.

To add percent labels to the current chart, move the cursor down to the **Show percent** option and press:

[⇓] *(10 times)*

You can change the setting by pressing:

[Spacebar]

The triangle moves from *No* to *Yes,* indicating that percent labels will be added to the chart. In addition to the display of the percents, you can select the position on the chart where the percents will be placed relative to each slice. You have three choices under the **Place percent** option: **Below, Adjacent,** and **Inside.**

Below   The percent labels will be placed below the name and value labels.

Adjacent   The labels will be placed next to the name labels.

Inside   The percents will appear inside the slices of the chart.

Inside positioning makes it very clear exactly how large each slice is compared to the other slices of the pie, but one drawback of the inside position is that the percentages do not stand out clearly against some colors or patterns. On the screen display, text is usually displayed in white, which does not contrast well with lightly colored slices such as yellow or cyan. When printed, the letters are black and will sometimes be hard to read against dark patterns. To see the drawbacks and advantages of inside placement, press:

[⇒]
i

Display the revised chart by pressing:

[F2]

The percentages for each slice appear inside of each slice on the pie (figure 2.11). With the exception of the yellow slice, percents can be read fairly easily.

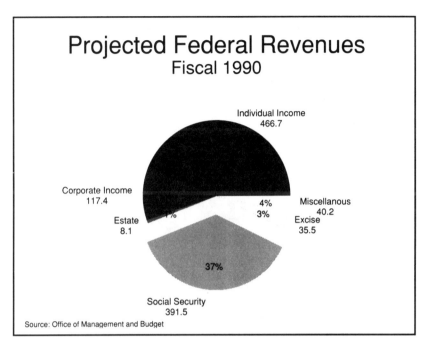

Figure 2.11. Percent labels placed inside pie slices

In order to improve the appearance of the chart, you might want to change the yellow slice (number 6) to a different color. Return to the options screen by pressing:

[Esc]

Switch back to the data-entry screen by using the **Options** command:

[F8]

Move to the **Color** column for slice 6 by pressing:

[⇓] *(5 times)*
[Tab] *(3 times)*

The current color is 7, which you know from viewing the chart is yellow. If you do not recall the number for the color you want to choose you can display a list of colors by pressing:

[F6]

Harvard Graphics pops up a special menu from which you can pick the color you want. In this case, select a dark color. Choose a number greater than 7 so that you do not select the same color used for one of the other slices. Color 8 is orange. On most screens that color is a rust color that looks reddish brown instead of a bright orange. Select orange for this slice by pressing:

[⇓] [↵]

Display the revised chart by pressing:

[F2]

The orange color provides a much better background against which the percent is displayed. Return to the chart-entry screen by pressing:

[Esc]

Colors and Patterns

Keep in mind that if you use a back-and-white printer to output a chart, the patterns selected may not produce good contrast with the percents. For example, on a Postscript laser printer the color cyan is printed as a dark gray pattern against which the black letters are hard to read. Figure 2.12 shows the patterns used for printing the colors as output on a Postscript type laser printer; keep them mind when when you select colors for a chart to be printed.

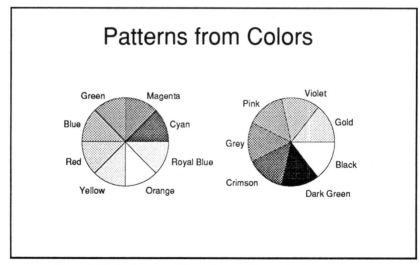

Figure 2.12. Patterns used for color on a Postscript laser printer

Formatting Values

The value labels are displayed with the exact values entered into the **Value** column. Harvard Graphics allows you to clarify the significance of these numbers by *formatting* their display. The term *format* refers to the way that the values are displayed. For example, the values shown on the chart are actually in billions of dollars. You might want the entries to be followed by the word *billion*. You can create value formats by placing instructions into the **Value format** option on page 2 of the Pie chart options display. The instructions are entered in the form of special codes.

,

The comma tells Harvard Graphics to insert comma separators every three decimal places (for example, 1000 = 1,000).

0-9

Entering the numbers 0–9 tells Harvard Graphics to show all values with the specified number of decimal places. For example, if you entered 2, all of the values would appear with two decimal places. Zeros are added to values that did not have significant figures for those digits. Conversely, if you used a value lower than the actual number of decimal places, the display of decimals would be suppressed.

xxxx | xxxx

The **xxxx** stands for text, such as the word *billion* which you want to print before and/or after the value. The bar symbol (|) is used to indicate the position of the value relative to the text. If you entered *billion* | the values would look like *billion 466.7*. The symbol | *billion* would display *466.7 billion*. Note that | is the vertical line character that is on the same keys as the \.

!

The ! causes Harvard Graphics to use scientific notation to display the values.

In addition to these format options, Harvard Graphics allows you to add a dollar sign ($) by selecting *Yes* at the **Currency** options.

Display the second page of the options screen by pressing:

[F8] [Pg Dn]

Move the cursor to the **Value format** option by pressing:

[⇓] *(8 times)*

To create the effect you desire you will have to enter several symbols in the same format. Type:

|0 billions

Move the cursor to the **Currency** option and change it to **Yes.** Press:

[⇓] y

Display the modified chart by pressing:

[F2]

Figure 2.13 shows the chart with the values with $ sign, zero decimal places, and the word *billion* added.

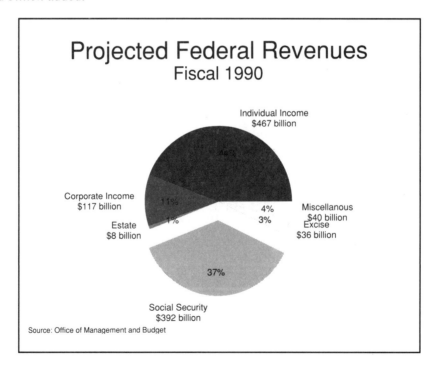

Figure 2.13. Values formatted on chart display

Return to the options screen by pressing:

[Esc]

Note that the percent group of commands also has an option for **Percent format.** You can use the same symbols as the **Value format** to control the appearance of the percent display. Keep in mind that a percentage always has a % following the value.

Checking Spelling

To spell check a chart you must return to the main menu of the program. The [F10] key, labeled **Continue,** will exit you from the current mode. Press:

[F10]

To execute the spell-check press:

[F4]

Harvard Graphics scans the text used in the chart and looks for any words that are not stored in its dictionary file. Harvard Graphics has a limited number of words in its dictionary; it will not recognize proper nouns or technical terms. In this case, it finds the misspelled word *Miscellanous* (figure 2.14). The menu has two sections. The top section lists three actions that you can take.

Word OK, continue	Select this option when the word is corrected spelled.
Add to dictionary	This option is used when you want to add a word to the dictionary.
Type correction	Select this option if you want to manually type in a correction.

If Harvard Graphics can locate any words in its dictionary that closely resemble the misspelled word, the bottom section will list them.

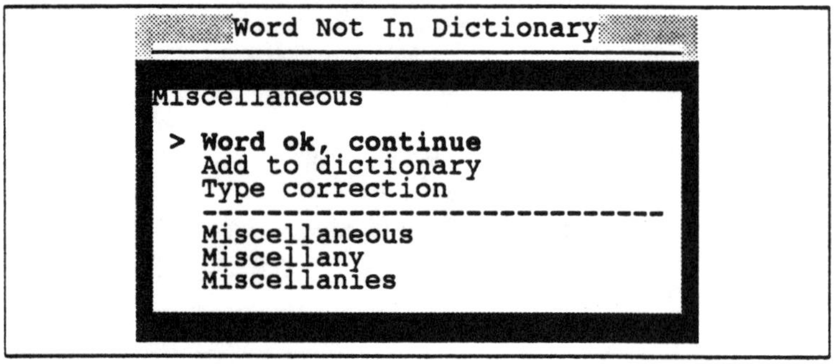

Figure 2.14. Spell-check correction menu

In this case, you can select an alternate spelling to replace the misspelled word. Press:

[⇓] *(3 times)*

[↵]

The correction is entered into the chart data. Harvard Graphics proceeds to look for other spelling errors. When the entire chart has been checked, the message *Spell check complete* appears at the bottom of the screen.

The Save Chart Menu

You should save a copy of the current chart because it will be the basis of several additional pie charts you will make in this chapter.

Select the **Get/Save/Remove** option from the Main Menu by pressing

4

The highlight automatically falls on **Save chart** because you currently have an unsaved chart in the computer's memory. To save this chart press:

[↵]

The **Save Chart** menu, shown in figure 2.15, displays the default disk and directory, in this example C:\HG. The title of the chart is automatically inserted as the file description.

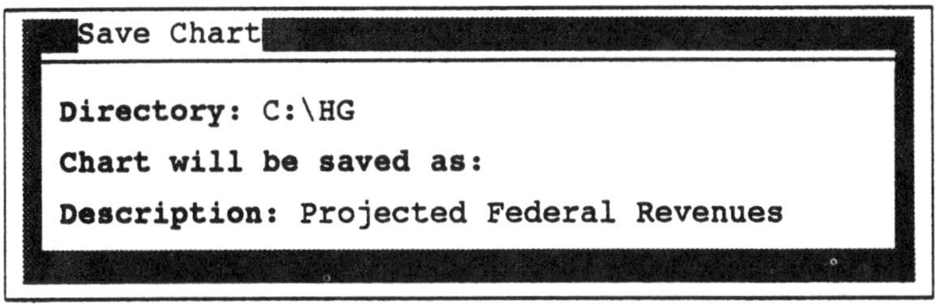

```
Save Chart

Directory: C:\HG
Chart will be saved as:
Description: Projected Federal Revenues
```

Figure 2.15. Save chart menu

You need to enter the name for this chart file. In this case, call the file PIE-01. Press:

pie-01 [⏎]
[⏎]

The name of the chart file, PIE-01.cht appears in the lower right corner of the screen. Exit the **Get/Save/Remove** menu by pressing:

[Esc]

Harvard Graphics stores charts in files with CHT file extension. As with all MSDOS applications, you are limited to using an 8 characters file name.

The program returns to the Main Menu. Note that at the bottom center of the screen the words *Chart type: PIE* appear. This indicates that, even though it cannot be seen on the screen, there is currently a pie chart defined. In Harvard Graphics you can only work on the design of one chart at a time.

3-D Charts

Harvard Graphics includes an option that will give a pie chart a three-dimensional appearance. To do this, select the **Enter/Edit chart** option from the Main Menu and press:

2

By default, the first page of the data screen appears. Move to the Options screen by pressing:

[F8]

In the bottom section of the screen the option **3D effect** is listed. By default this option is set on **No.** Change the option to 3-D and display the resulting chart by pressing:

[Tab] *(5 times)*
y [F2]

The pie chart now appears in 3-D, as shown in figure 2.16. Note that the **Cut Slice** option is ignored when 3-D is in effect. Also note that labels for adjacent small slices may run together.

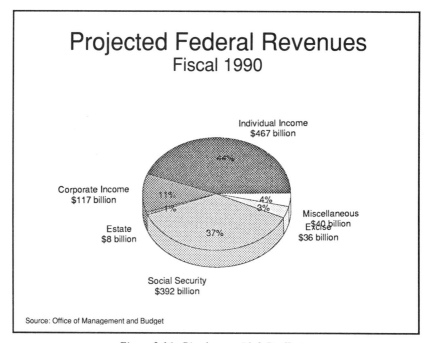

Figure 2.16. Pie shown with 3-D effect

Return to the **Options** screen by pressing:

[Esc]

Pie Size

The actual size of the pie in the pie chart can be altered by using the **Pie Size** option on page 2 of the Options screen. Press:

[Pg Dn]

The current **Pie Size** setting is set to the default value of 50. Pie size can be set to a value from 0 to 100. When you enlarge a pie you may find that some of the labels are no longer fully displayed.

Change the size of the pie to 75 by pressing:

[⇓] *(3 times)*
75
[F2]

The pie has expanded to fill a larger area of the chart frame (figure 2.17). The increased size has also resulted in a conflict between the labels for the *Social Security* slice and the footnote at the bottom of the frame and the loss of the letter C in the *Corporate Income* label.

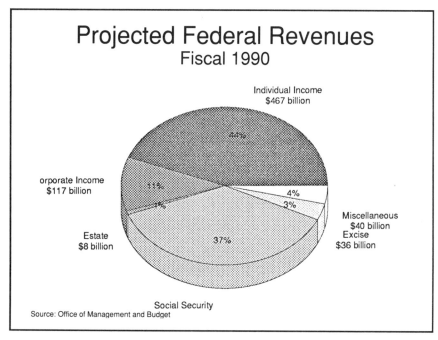

Figure 2.17. Pie expanded to size 75

Return to the options menu by pressing:

[Esc]

Rotating the Slices

To clear up the conflict between the *Social Security* slice and the footnote and to display the *Corporate Income* slice in full, *rotate* the pie using the **Starting angle** option. By default, Harvard Graphics places the edge of the first slice (in this example, *Individual Income*) at the 3:00 position. The slices are then drawn in a counterclockwise direction starting from that point. The **Starting angle** option allows you to move the staring position of the first slice a specified number of degrees in a counterclockwise direction. For example, to make the first slice to start at the 12:00 position. You would enter a **Starting angle** value of 90 to rotate the pie a full 1/4 turn to the left. Because there are 360 degrees in a full circle, every 30 degrees will rotate the pie to a different hour position (for example, 30 = 2:00 and 60 = 1:00).

One useful effect of this is that the adjacent labels will also move along with the pie slices. In this example, you can rotate the pie so that no slice labels falls at the bottom of the chart where there is insufficient room to display them. Rotate the starting slice to 2:00 by entering 30 for the **Starting angle** option:

[⇑]
30
[F2]

The slices are now rotated so that all of the slice labels are displayed clearly (figure 2.18). Note that the 30 degree entry was simply a guess as to the required rotation. You may need to make several tries to get the exact angle needed to allow all of the labels to appear.

In some cases it may be necessary to change some other aspect of the chart—such as label position or pie size—to accommodate the text when the rotation solution cannot resolve the problem.

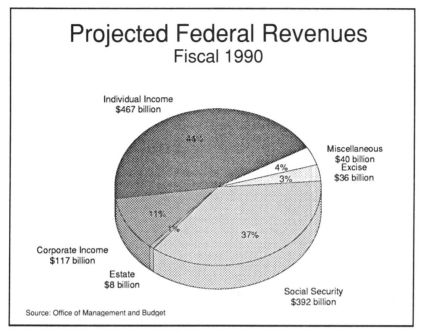

Figure 2.18. Pie slices rotated

Save this revised chart as PIE-02 by pressing:

[Esc]
[F10] 4 2
PIE-02 [⏎]

Note that the description of the chart is still the same; to save the updated chart you must change the chart description. Erase the current description and then enter a new description by pressing:

[Ctrl-Del]
3-D Pie Chart [⏎]

Loading An Existing Chart

The next section of this chapter will begin with the original exploded slice pie chart stored as PIE-01. You can load that chart using the **Get chart** command. Press:

1

When you enter this command, Harvard Graphics changes the screen to the Select Chart display (figure 2.19). On this display, the program lists all of the charts stored in the default directory. In addition, the display shows the date on which the charts were saved, the type of chart, and the description of the chart entered when the chart was saved. Entering a meaningful description will help you locate the chart you are looking for when you display this listing.

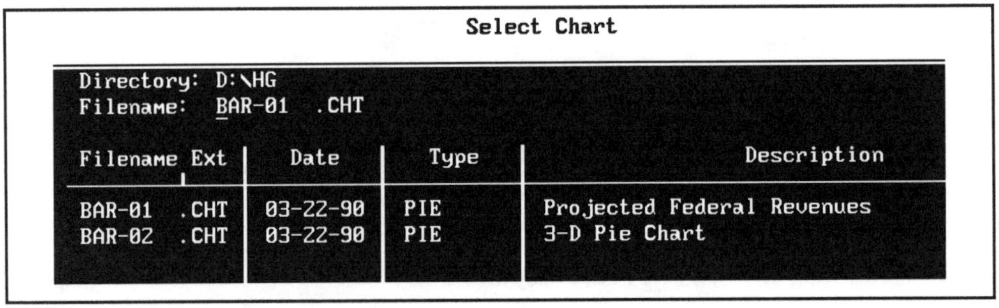

```
                         Select Chart

   Directory:  D:\HG
   Filename:   BAR-01   .CHT

   Filename Ext  |   Date    |  Type   |          Description

   BAR-01   .CHT | 03-22-90  | PIE     | Projected Federal Revenues
   BAR-02   .CHT | 03-22-90  | PIE     | 3-D Pie Chart
```

Figure 2.19. Select chart to load menu

You can select a chart by moving the highlight, currently positioned on the first chart on the list, to the name of the chart you want to load with the [⇓] or [⇑] keys. In this example, the highlight is correctly positioned on PIE-01.CHT. To load the highlighted chart simply enter [↵]. Note that the list of charts that appears on your screen will vary depending upon what files, if any, have already been stored on the disk. For that reason the instructions in this book will ask you to type in the name of the chart you want to load.

pie-01 [↵]

When you load a chart, Harvard Graphics immediately displays the chart on the screen so that you can confirm whether or not you have loaded the chart you want to work with. Press:

[Esc]

After loading and viewing a chart, Harvard Graphics displays the Enter/Edit Chart screen that matches the type of chart you have loaded.

MULTIPLE PIE CHARTS

You can create pie charts that contain two pies. There are two reasons for creating this type of display:

Show Details   In a given pie chart you may encounter a situation where it would be useful to be able to show a detailed breakdown of the parts which make up one of the pie slices. For example, the *Social Security* slice is actually composed of three different types of revenue. You might want to add a second pie to the chart that shows the parts that go into the *Social Security* slice. Harvard Graphics has a special feature that shows a link between the specified slice and the second pie.

Compare Pies   A second pie can be used as a comparison to the first pie. For example, you might want to add a pie to the current chart that shows the expenditure side of the federal budget. Harvard Graphics has a special feature that will scale the sizes of the two pies proportionally creating an easy way to see which pie represents the greater total value.

Adding a Detail Pie

Recall that the pie chart data screen consists of two pages. *Page 1* defines the information for the first pie. *Page 2* can be used to create a second pie. At this point Page 1 of the Pie entry screen is visible. Change to the second page by pressing:

[Pg Dn]

The second pie in this chart will contain three slices which show the details of the *Social Security* section of the federal budget. When you entered the data for pie 1 you used the [Tab] key to work across each slice row. Another way to enter data is to work in a column by column fashion. For example, you might want to enter all three labels and then move to the next column and enter all three values. If you want to work down a particular column you would end each entry with [↵]. This would move you to the next row in the same column. Enter the labels for this chart as follows. Note that the labels are abbreviations; because there is less room on a dual pie chart for labels you should try and limit the labels to 10 characters.

Type in the labels:

Emp. Tax [↵]
UP Ins. [↵]
Retirement

Move the cursor to the top of the next column by pressing:

[⇑] *(2 times)*
[Tab]

Enter the values for these slices:

364.4 [↵]
22.4 [↵]
4.7

Because computer users get in the habit of using the [↵] key after entering an item, the column entry method may feel more natural than moving horizontally with the [Tab] key.

Before you display the chart, return to the pie 1 data screen and shorten the labels for that chart

[Pg Up]
[Ctrl- ⇒]
[Del] *(6 times)*
[↵]
[Ctrl- ⇒]
[Del] *(6 times)*
[↵] *(2 times)*
Soc. Sec.
[Del] *(5 times)*
[↵] *(2 times)*
[⇒] *(4 times)*
[Del] *(8 times)*

The labels should now look like figure 2.20.

Slice	Label Name	Value Series 1	
1	Individual	466.7	
2	Corporate	117.4	
3	Estate	8.1	
4	Soc. Sec.	391.5	
5	Excise	35.5	
6	Misc.	40.2	

Figure 2.20. Abbreviated slice labels

Before you display the chart, return to the second page of the options screen. Recall that this screen has settings for pie 1 and pie 2. You should change the options so that only the slice names appear on the chart. Press:

[F8] [Pg Dn]

Turn off the Value and Percent labels for pie 1 and pie 2. Press:

[⇓] *(6 times)*
n [Tab]
n [Tab]
[⇓] *(3 times)*
n

Display the dual pie chart by pressing:

[F2]

The program displays a chart with two pies, as shown in figure 2.21.

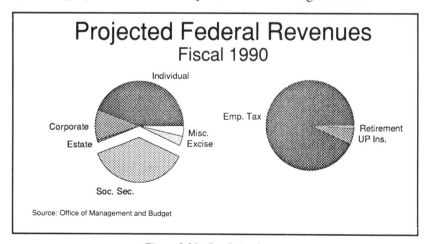

Figure 2.21. Dual pie chart

Return to the **Pie Options** screen by pressing:

[Esc]

Linking Pies

Harvard Graphics has a special option called **Link pies** that is designed to show a relationship between the second pie and a slice from first pie. In this example, the purpose of having two pies on the same chart is to use the second pie as a detail for the Social Security slice of the first pie.

The relationship is defined between the *first* exploded (cut) slice in the first pie and the second pie. To show the relationships between the slices, the program will rotate the linked slice so that it appears on the right side of the first pie, the position closest to the second pie. Harvard Graphics then draws lines between the exploded slice and the second pie.

To create a link you must select *Yes* for the **Link pies** option on the first page of the **Pie Options** screen. Press:

[Pg Up]
[Tab] *(6 times)*
y

Display the chart by pressing:

[F2]

The selection of **Link pies** changes the rotation of the first pie. Dashed lines are drawn between the exploded slice and second pie (figure 2.22):

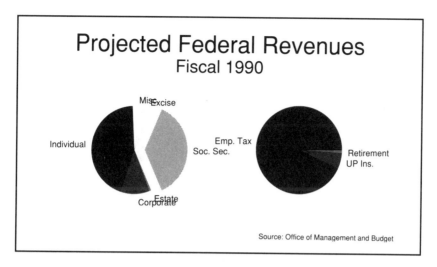

Figure 2.22. Slice linked to second pie

Return to the options screen by pressing:

[Esc]

Using the Column Format

As a variation of the layout of pie charts, Harvard Graphics provides a *column* format under the **Chart style**. When the column format is selected, the data used for the pie is displayed as a stacked column in which each pie slice appears as a layer. This format is often used to detail the information shown in the second pie. The advantage of using the column format for the second pie is that it more clearly indicates that the second pie is subordinate to the first.

To change the format of the second pie, display the second page of the pie options screen:

[Pg Dn]

Change the format of the second pie by pressing:

[Tab] c

Display the chart by pressing:

[F2]

The modified chart is displayed showing the second pie as a stacked column of values, as shown in figure 2.23.

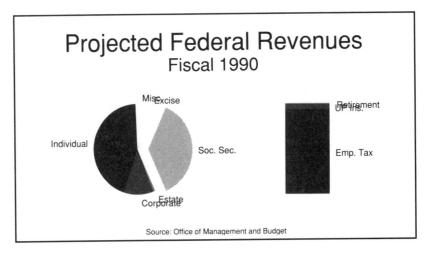

Figure 2.23. Second pie displayed as stacked column

Save this chart as PIE-03 with the description *Dual Pies - Detail* by pressing:

[Esc] [F10]
4 2
pie-03 [↵]
[Ctrl-Del]
Dual Pies - Detail [↵]

COMPARING TWO INDEPENDENT PIE CHARTS

Chart PIE-03 showed how a multiple pie chart could be used to show details of a particular slice. Another use of multiple pies is to compare two independent but related groups of values. For example, you might want to have the first pie show revenue and a second pie show expenditures. Harvard Graphics has an option that will cause the size of the pies to be scaled proportionally to the overall total of all of the slices. This would mean that if the government spent more than it took in, as is usually the case, the expenditure pie would be proportionally larger.

To create this chart, begin by loading the PIE-01 chart from the disk. The **Get/Save/Remove** menu should still be displayed from the previous section. Press:

1

The highlight should fall on PIE-01.CHT. If there are files that are on your disk, unrelated to this book listed in the directory use the [⇓] key to highlight PIE-01.CHT. Load the chart by pressing:

[↵]
[Esc]

The data screen for pie 1 is displayed. Turn off the **Cut Slice** option for *Social Security* by pressing:

[⇓] *(3 times)*
[Tab] *(2 times)*
n

Move to the data entry screen for pie 2:

[Pg Dn]

This screen is empty because you defined only one pie in the original PIE-01 chart. Enter the labels for the slices:

Defense [↵]
Social Security [↵]
Education [↵]
Interest [↵]
Health [↵]
Others

Enter the corresponding values in the Values column:

[⇑] *(5 times)*
[Tab] 320.3 [↵]
246.7 [↵]
39.5 [↵]
170.1 [↵]
52.2 [↵]
323.6

The values for the second pie have now been entered, as shown in figure 2.24.

Slice	Label Name	Value Series 2	
1	Defense	320.3	
2	Social Security	246.7	
3	Education	39.5	
4	Interest	170.1	
5	Health	52.2	
6	Others	**323.6**	
7			

Figure 2.24. Values for Expenditure Pie

Setting Up Proportional Pies

With the data entered you can use the **Options** screens to layout the pie. Press:

[F8]

On the first page of the options screen you can see that there are items called *Pie 1 title* and *Pie 2 title*. These items can be used to add titles to each of the individual pies in addition to the overall chart title. Note that these titles have room for two lines of text, allowing you to add a subtitle for each pie if desired. To add titles for the pies, press:

[Tab] *(3 times)*
Revenues [Tab]
Expenditures

In order to have Harvard Graphics scale the pies proportionally, select *Yes* for the **Proportional pies** option:

[Tab] *(3 times)*
y

Move to the second page of the options screens:

[Pg Dn]

Adjust the format settings for the pie labels so that only the name labels appear on the chart. Press:

[⇓] *(6 times)*
n [Tab] n [Tab]
[⇓] *(3 times)*
n

Display the chart:

[F2]

The chart shows the two pies of roughly equal size (figure 2.25). If you look carefully you can detect that the Expenditure pie is slightly larger than the revenues. In this case, the difference between the totals of the two pies is not great enough to show a dramatic difference between the revenue and expenditure pies.

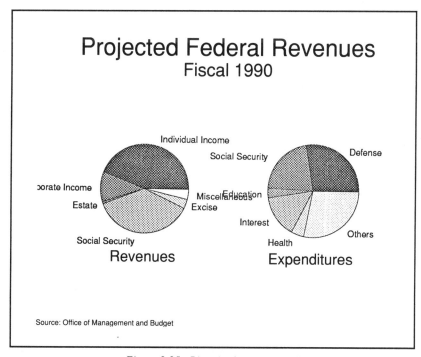

Figure 2.25. Pies sized proportionally

Note that the Coporate Income label has been truncated. You could solve this by rotating the slice. For now, however, save the new chart by pressing:

[Esc] [F10] 4 2
pie-04
[Ctrl-Del]
Proportional Pies [⏎]

Revising the Data

The current charts show the projected federal budget including income and expenditures for Social Security. There is some discussion in Washington that the Social Security funds should not be included in the annual operating budget. You can find out how the current chart would look if you removed the slices for Social Security from both pies by editing the data screens for the current chart. Display the data-entry screens for the current charts by pressing:

[Esc] 2

You can delete an entire slice from a chart with the [Ctrl-Del] command. Move the cursor to the *Social Security* slice by pressing:

[⇩] *(3 times)*

Remove the data for that slice by pressing:

[Ctrl-Del]

All of the information for that slice has been removed and the slices below moved up to fill in the gap. Move to the data screen for pie 2 and repeat the deletion.

[Pg Dn]
[⇩] [Ctrl-Del]

Display the revised chart by pressing:

[F2]

Figure 2.26 shows that the difference between the two pies is significantly greater when the Social Security amounts are removed from both pies. The proportional sizing adjusts to the revised data in order to accurately show the relationship between the two pies.

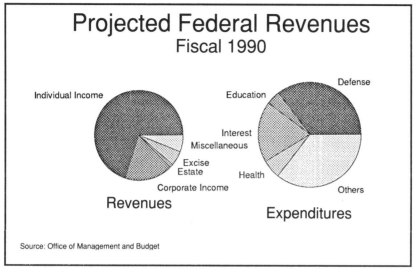

Figure 2.26. Revised chart displayed

Save the current chart as PIE-05 by pressing:

[Esc] [F10] 4 2
pie-05 [⏎]
[Ctrl-Del]
Same as PIE-04, SS removed [⏎]
[Esc]

You are now back at the main Harvard Graphics menu.

SUMMARY

The contents of this chapter serve to illustrate two points. First, the chapter shows how to create and organize pie charts in Harvard Graphics. Second, the chapter introduces the basic structure of Harvard Graphics showing the basic command and menu structure that applies to all of the charts that you can create with this program.

Pie Charts. Pie charts are circular charts that display a series of values as slices of a pie. Pie charts are used to show the relationships between individual parts and the whole which they make up. Pie charts lend themselves to the display of information that might otherwise be expressed as percents. The entire pie always represents 100%.

Data Entry Screens. Information that defines the individual slices of the pie is entered on the pie chart data-entry screens. You can define up to 12 different slices for each pie chart. You can also enter a title, subtitle, and footnote for the chart.

Options Screens. Options are settings that affect the overall appearance of the chart. The [F8] key toggles the screen between data entry and options modes. Options for pie charts include sorting, changing the starting angle, and adjusting the size of pie.

Cut Slices. A cut slice is displayed broken out from the main pie. You can set any or all of the slices to appear as cut. Note that cut slices will not appear if you select the 3-D option.

Labels. Each slice in the pie can potentially have three types of labels: the name of the slice, the value or the slice, and the percent of the slice. You can use special codes to establish a *format* for value or percent labels.

Colors. Colors are automatically assigned to each slice. You can use the [F6] key to list the available colors if you want to change the automatic color selection.

Dual Pies. Harvard Graphics allows you to define two pies as part of the same chart. The data for the second pie is entered on page 2 of the pie chart data-entry screen. You can set separate options for each pie with regard to basic style and labels.

Linked Pies. The linked pie chart is one in which the second pie is a detailed breakdown of a slice from the first pie. The second pie must be related to a *cut* slice of the first pie. When the linked pie option is selected, the first pie is rotated so that the cut slice is on the right side and lines are drawn from that slice to the second pie. You have the option of showing either pie as a stacked column of values.

Proportional Pies. When two pies are displayed, Harvard Graphics can scale the pies so that the size of the pies is proportional to the sum of all the slices in each pie. This option allows for a quick comparison of the overall magnitude of the two pies.

Get and Save. Harvard Graphics allows you to work on one pie at a time. You can save the data and options of the current pie in a disk file using the **Save** command found on the Get/Save/Remove menu. All charts are saved in files with CHT extensions. You can enter a description of the chart when you use the **Get** command load stored charts.

Chapter 3

Bar and Area Charts

In chapter 2 you learned how to use pie charts to demonstrate graphically how each of components of a whole compare to each other and to the total sum of all of the parts.

However, there are many cases where you might want to create a chart that compares a group of values that are not related to a particular whole. For example, you might want to create a chart that shows the tax rates for various cities across the country. A pie chart would not be useful since the value found by adding up all of the items would not represent a meaningful total. A bar chart would provide a better analysis of this data.

Figure 3.1 shows a bar chart that compares the tax rates of three different cities. Using a bar chart to display this data is an appropriate choice for two reasons. First, the items selected for the chart do not represent parts of a whole and therefore would not be applicable to a pie chart. The bars can be arranged in any order without effecting the meaning of the chart. Second, the bars are a clear way of showing the relative magnitude of various items in the chart.

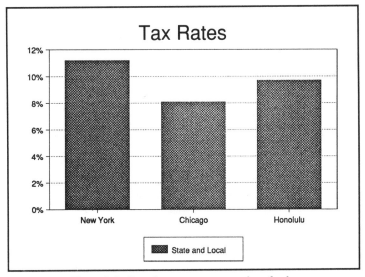

Figure 3.1. Bar chart compares a series of values

In this chapter you will learn how to create bar charts and use the bar-chart options.

Load the Harvard Graphics program in the usual way in order to begin this chapter.

A BASIC BAR CHART

Suppose that you wanted to create a chart that displays information about the number of people employed in certain professions and how that is projected to change by the year 2000.

Begin at the main program menu. Select the command to create a new chart:

1

Select to create a bar chart by pressing:

3

The **Bar/Line** option does not immediately display a data-entry screen for the chart. Instead, you are presented with a menu in the middle of the screen labeled **X Data Type Menu** (figure 3.1). The menu refers to the organization of the horizontal axis of the chart. The **Bar/Line** chart option can be used to create either bar charts, line charts, or charts that combine both types. The horizontal axis of these charts can be organized in two ways: **Free Form Names** and **Chronological/Numeric Sequence**.

Free Form Names

In the chart shown in figure 3.1, the horizontal axis lists the names of the items associated with each bar. The list is called *free form* because there is no standard arrangement of the items. In figure 3.1 the bars were listed from east to west. They might just as well been listed alphabetically, in order of population size, or in no particular order of any kind. You can select to create this type of chart by using the **Name** option in the **X data type** entry area. **Name** is selected by default each time you create a new **Bar/Line** chart.

Chronological/Numeric Sequence

In addition to **Name** there are 10 other options available for **X data type**. All of these options create an X axis that is organized according to a specific chronological or numeric sequence. The items on this type of axis are automatically generated by entering the starting and ending values. For example, if you choose **Month** and entered **Jan** and **Jun**, Harvard Graphics would fill in the months in between. These options are useful when you are creating a *time series* chart, which are discussed in detail in chapter 4.

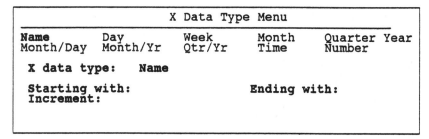

```
                        X Data Type Menu
_____
Name          Day        Week       Month      Quarter  Year
Month/Day     Month/Yr   Qtr/Yr     Time       Number

  X data type:      Name

  Starting with:                    Ending with:
  Increment:

```

Figure 3.2. X Data Type Menu

In this case, choose the free-form axis by accepting the default entry, **Name.** Press:

[F10]

Once you have selected the type of X axis you want to use in this chart, the data entry screen for the bar and line charts appears (figure 3.3). Each bar or line chart can hold up to 60 different data items. The chart is also capable of displaying up to 8 different data series at a time. Multiple data-series charts will be covered later in this chapter.

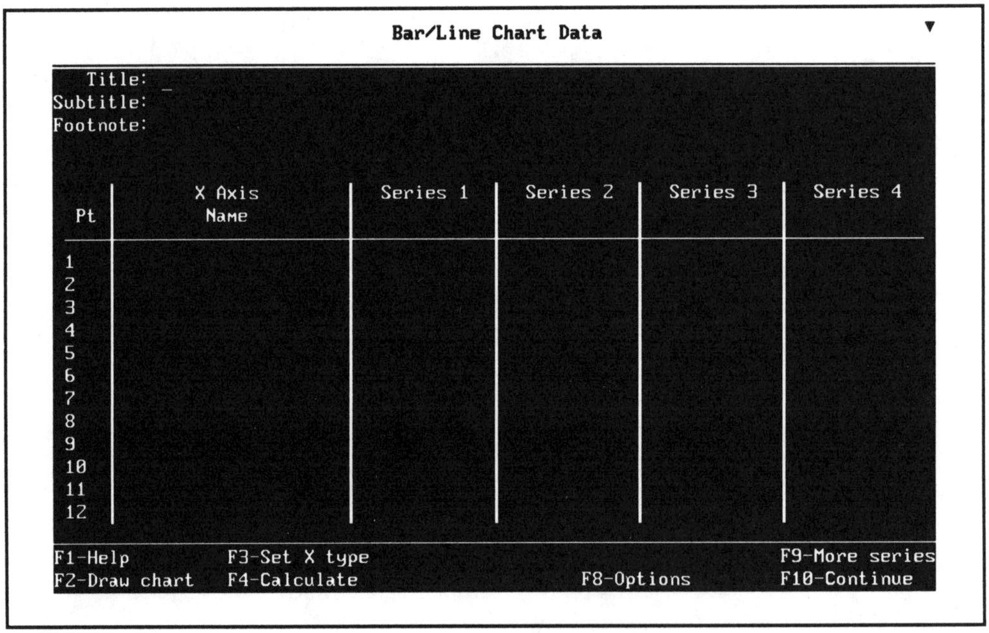

```
                           Bar/Line Chart Data                         ▼
┌──────────────────────────────────────────────────────────────────────┐
│     Title: _                                                           │
│  Subtitle:                                                             │
│  Footnote:                                                             │
│                                                                        │
│          │  X Axis  │ Series 1 │ Series 2 │ Series 3 │ Series 4        │
│      Pt  │  Name    │          │          │          │                 │
│                                                                        │
│      1                                                                 │
│      2                                                                 │
│      3                                                                 │
│      4                                                                 │
│      5                                                                 │
│      6                                                                 │
│      7                                                                 │
│      8                                                                 │
│      9                                                                 │
│     10                                                                 │
│     11                                                                 │
│     12                                                                 │
│                                                                        │
│  F1-Help        F3-Set X type                      F9-More series      │
│  F2-Draw chart  F4-Calculate          F8-Options   F10-Continue        │
└──────────────────────────────────────────────────────────────────────┘
```

Figure 3.3. Bar/Line Chart Data screen

To create a simple bar chart, first enter the title, subtitle, and footnote for the chart by pressing:

Occupational Employment [↵]
Selected Job Categories [↵]
US Department of Labor[↵]

The cursor now moves to the column labeled **X Axis.** On this chart the **X axis** will show the names of various occupations using Department of Labor statistics gathered in 1986. Type:

Comp Prog [↵]
Janitors [↵]
Cashiers [↵]
Lawyers [↵]
Guards [↵]
Secretary

Move the cursor to the top of the next column labeled **Series 1.** This column is used to hold the values which will be represented by the bars. Press:

[⇑] *(5 times)*
[Tab]
479 [↵]
2676 [↵]
2165 [↵]
527 [↵]
794 [↵]
3234

You have now created a basic bar chart. Display the chart by pressing:

[F2]

Harvard Graphics displays a simple bar type chart using the data you have just entered (figure 3.4). The program automatically calculates the scale of the value (Y axis). In this case the axis begins at zero and goes to a value of 3500, slightly larger than the largest value in the series. At the bottom of the screen the color used for the bars is associated with the label **Series 1.** This is called the *legend* of the chart.

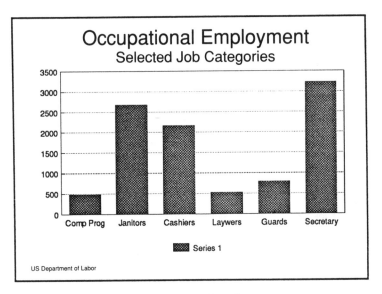

Figure 3.4. Basic Bar chart

Return to the data entry screen by pressing:

[Esc]

Adding More Series

Bar charts can be used to display multiple data series. In the case of this type of bar chart, each additional series represents another value that is related to the names in the X axis column. For example, the values listed under series 1 are the employment figures for 1986. Suppose that you also wanted to show the projected employment figures for the year 2000. You could enter those into the **Series 2** column. Move the cursor to the top of the **Series 2** column and enter the values for the year 2000:

[⇑] *(5 times)*
[Tab]
813 [↵]
3280 [↵]
2740 [↵]
718 [↵]
1177 [↵]
3658

Display the revised chart by pressing:

[F2]

Harvard Graphics now displays two bars of different color (or patterns when printed) at each name on the X axis (figure 3.5). To make room for the additional bar, the program reduces the width of the bars so that they can fit into the same amount of space. Note that the scale of the Y axis is automatically adjusted to the include the increased values. The legend is also expanded to include keys for both series.

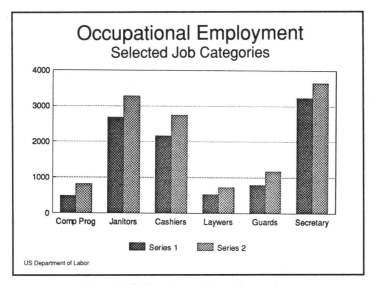

Figure 3.5. Bar chart with two data series

Return to the data entry screen by pressing:

[Esc]

Calculated Series

The two data series you have entered into this chart have been entered manually by typing in each value. But suppose you wanted to show a third series of values that shows the number of additional jobs projected to be created between 1986 and 2000 in each category. You could manually enter these values. However, since the data in this series would be the difference between the values in series 2 subtracted from the values in series 1, you can save yourself some time and improve the accuracy of your chart by having Harvard Graphics automatically calculate the values. The [F4] **Calculate** command allows you to specify an arithmetic formula by which Harvard Graphics can calculate the value of a series. The formulas use the following symbols:

Symbol	Function
+	addition
-	subtraction
*	multiplication
/	division
#*n*	series *n*

The key to writing a formula is the use of a *series reference*. A series reference begins with the # character and is followed by a single-digit number (1–9) corresponding to the series column. For example, to subtract the values in series 2 from series 1 you would enter **#2-#1.** The program would then perform one subtraction for each data item on the chart creating a new data series based on the calculation.

When you create a data series using a formula you should place the cursor in the column for which you want to create a formula. You can place the cursor in any row in that column. Press:

[Tab]

To create or revise a formula for the current series press:

[F4]

The program displays the **Calculate** menu (figure 3.6). The menu shows the number of the series, *3,* the series label, *Series 3,* and a blank area for the formula.

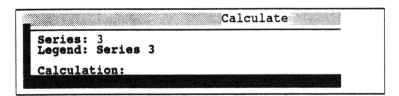

Figure 3.6. Calculate a series menu

In this menu you can change two items, the series name and the calculation formula. You can change the number of the series that will be calculated. In this case, leave the series name as it is (you will find out later how to revise all of the series names) and enter the calculation formula:

[↵]
#2-#1

When you press [↵] from the calculation line, Harvard Graphics will automatically fill in the Series 3 column with the results of the formula. Note that a diamond-shaped symbol appears in the series column heading. This symbol will appear on all series which are calculated. Press:

[↵]

Harvard Graphics uses the formula to fill in values into the Series 3 column as shown in figure 3.7.

X Axis Name	Series 1	◆ Series 2	Series 3	
Comp Prog	479	813	334	
Janitors	2676	3280	604	
Cashiers	2165	2740	575	
Lawyers	527	718	191	
Guards	794	1177	383	
Secretary	3234	3658	424	

Figure 3.7. Values inserted in series 3 by calculation formula

Display the chart which includes the calculated series by pressing:

[F2]

The chart now shows three bars for each item on the X axis (figure 3.8).

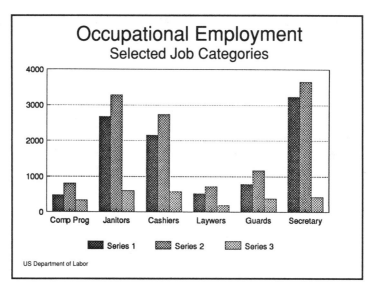

Figure 3.8. Chart with calculated series

Return to the data entry screen by pressing:

[Esc]

Chart and Series Labels

The layout of a bar chart allows you to define labels for the X and Y axis and the individual series names that appear in the legend. By default the X and Y axis names are left blank and the series names are *Series 1, Series 2, etc.* These options can be found on the Options screens for Bar/Line charts which is activated with the [F8] command. Press:

[F8]

The **Bar/Line** options screen is displayed in figure 3.9. Note that this is page 1 of 4 option pages. The top section of the screen is used to enter the title that refers to the overall organization of the chart. The bottom section lists options that affect individual data series.

Legend Title   The title of a series is the name that appears in the chart legend.

Type   The Bar/Line chart menu allows you to display the series data as bars or lines. The **trend, curve,** and **pt** options are special variations on line charts that relate to time series analysis, covered in chapter 4. By default all series are displayed as bars.

Display   This option suppresses the display of data series that are used for calculations, but do not need to be displayed on the chart.

Y Axis   This option allows you to specify **Y axis 1** or **Y axis 2** as the scale by which the series will be proportioned on the chart. There two Y axis options because Harvard Graphics can display a Y axis scale on the left and on the right side of the chart. By default, the program only displays the Y1 axis on the left side of the chart. The Y2 axis is used when the values in one or more data series have vastly different scales. For example, suppose you wanted to display a list of percentages as a series in this chart. Percentages always range from 0 to 100. On the current chart bars with a value of 100 would be so small that you could hardly see them on the chart. You will see how the Y2 axis is used a bit later in this chapter when you calculate the percent change in values from 1986 to 2000. By default all data series are scaled according to the Y1 (left side) axis.

```
  ▲       Bar/Line Chart    Titles & Options    Page 1 of 4       ▼

                  Title:       Occupational Employment
                  Subtitle:    Selected Job Categories

                  Footnote:    US Department of Labor


              X  axis title:
              Y1 axis title:
              Y2 axis title:
   Legend              │ Cum   │ Y Label │ Color │ Marker/ │ Line
   Title:              │ Yes No│ Yes  No │       │ Pattern │ Style

   1   Series 1        │ No    │ No      │  2    │   1     │  1
   2   Series 2        │ No    │ No      │  3    │   2     │  1
   3   Series 3        │ No    │ No      │  4    │   3     │  1
   4   Series 4        │ No    │ No      │  5    │   4     │  1
   5   Series 5        │ No    │ No      │  6    │   5     │  1
   6   Series 6        │ No    │ No      │  7    │   6     │  1
   7   Series 7        │ No    │ No      │  8    │   7     │  1
   8   Series 8        │ No    │ No      │  9    │   8     │  1

  F1-Help                  F5-Attributes   F7-Size/Place
  F2-Draw chart            F6-Colors       F8-Data          F10-Continue
```

Figure 3.9. Bar/Line options, page 1

Add a title for the X axis by pressing:

[Tab] *(3 times)*
Jobs [↵]

The cursor moves to an item labeled **Y1 axis title.** Below that is an item labeled **Y2 axis title**.

The title for the Y axis will typically explain the values on the scale. For example, in this chart the series values are entered in thousands of jobs (for example, the value **479** stands for **479** times **1000 = 479,000**). Type:

In thousands

The bottom section of the screen lists the names of the data series as they will appear in the chart legend. By default, the names are simply entered as *Series 1, Series 2, etc*. You can change the names by moving the cursor into the **Legend Title** column and entering descriptive names for the series. You can also create a title for the legend itself. Press:

[Tab] *(2 times)*
Employment [↵]

The cursor is now positioned on the legend name for series 1. Replace the default name by pressing:

[Ctrl-Del]
Year 1986 [↵]

Repeat the process for the next two series:

[Ctrl-Del]
Year 2000 [↵]
[Ctrl-Del]
Change

Display the modified chart by pressing:

[F2]

The chart now appears with the new axis, legend, and series labels (figure 3.10). Note that the addition of the these labels reduces the amount of room on the chart available for plotting the bars.

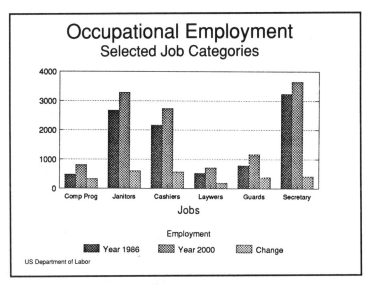

Figure 3.10. Axis and series labels modified

Size and Place Attributes of Labels

Recall that on the options screen you added the Y axis label *In thousands*. If you look at the top of Y axis you will see the label *In thousands* written horizontally across the top of the axis, flush with the left side of the chart. Each of the titles added to the chart are displayed in different sizes of lettering. These aspects of the chart titles are controlled by the **Size/Place** command, [F7]. Return to the options screen by pressing:

[Esc]

Enter the **Size/Place** command by pressing:

[F7]

When you press this command key, a new menu of items appears in the upper-left corner of the screen (figure 3.11). The menu lists values in two columns, **Size** and **Place**. The menu runs parallel to the that appear at the top of the options screen. Each line of the title, subtitle, footnote, and axis titles is assigned a **Size** and **Place** option.

Size   The **Size** option determines the size of the characters used to display the specified text on the chart. The value for text size can range from 1 to 100. By default the main title is assigned size 8, the subtitle size 6, the footnote size 2.5, the X axis title size 4, and the Y1 and Y2 axis titles are size 3.

Place   Place refers to the position of the text on the line on which it prints. Place generally refers to L(eft), C(enter) or R(ight) alignment. However, on the Bar/Line chart options, the Y axis titles have the option of [⇒] (horizontal orientation) or [⇓] (Vertical orientation).

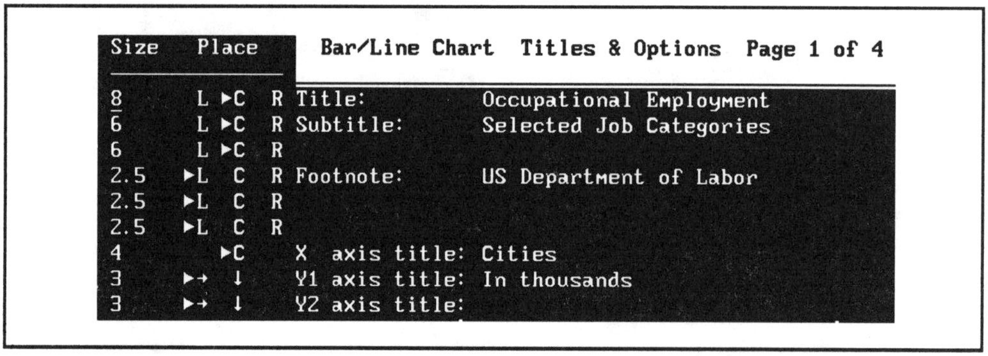

```
 Size     Place     Bar/Line Chart   Titles & Options   Page 1 of 4

 8        L ▶C  R Title:         Occupational Employment
 6        L ▶C  R Subtitle:      Selected Job Categories
 6        L ▶C  R
 2.5      ▶L  C  R Footnote:      US Department of Labor
 2.5      ▶L  C  R
 2.5      ▶L  C  R
 4           ▶C    X  axis title: Cities
 3        ▶→  ↓    Y1 axis title: In thousands
 3        ▶→  ↓    Y2 axis title:
```

Figure 3.11. Displayed Size and Place menus

Change the position of the footnote from the left side of the chart to the right side. Press:

   [⇒] *(3 times)*
   [Tab] r

The appearance of the chart might be improved if the X and Y axis titles were displayed with the same size text. Press:

   [⇓] *(3 times)*
   [Shift-Tab] 3 [↵]

It would also improve the appearance of the chart if the Y axis label would be written vertically, parallel to the Y axis rather than horizontally above the Y axis. Change the alignment of the Y1 axis title to vertical by pressing:

   [Tab] [Spacebar]

Display the revised chart by pressing:

[F2]

The chart (shown in figure 3.12) now shows the text with the type size and position you specified.

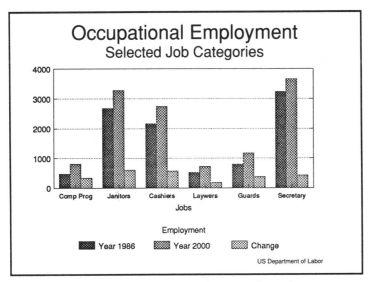

Figure 3.12. Text size and placement changed

Return to the options screen by pressing:

[Esc]

Note that the **Size/Place** menu has been automatically closed following the display of the chart. Save this version of the chart as BAR-01. Press:

[F10] 4 2
bar-01 [↵]
[↵]

Dual-Scale Bar Charts

In the previous section it was mentioned that a bar chart could contain two Y axis scales, one on the left and one on the right side of the chart. The purpose of having dual Y axis scales is to accommodate data series with vastly different ranges of values. One common case where this occurs is when one of the data series contains percentages. Percentages always fall between 0 and 100, but the raw data upon which these percentages are based can vary greatly in magnitude.

For example, suppose you used the calculation command to generate a data series that showed the percentage increase in jobs from 1986 to the year 2000. This could be done by dividing the changed values in series 3 by the initial values in series 1. To change the decimal values to percentages, you would multiply the results of the division by 100.

Return to the data entry area for the bar chart by pressing:

[Esc] 2

Move the cursor to the series 4 column:

[Tab] *(4 times)*

To calculate the percentage of change enter the following formula using the [F4] command. Note that you can also change the series name to a descriptive name at the same time as you enter the calculation formula. Press:

[F4]
% Change [↵]
#3/#1*100 [↵]

The column is filled with percent values in this case ranging from 13 to 69.7 percent. Display the chart by pressing:

[F2]

The addition of this new series does not make a useful addition to the chart because the values, 13 to 70, are too small to generate substantial bars on the chart, as shown in figure 3.13. The series appears in the legend, but the areas in each bar cluster where the value would be charted are simply blank.

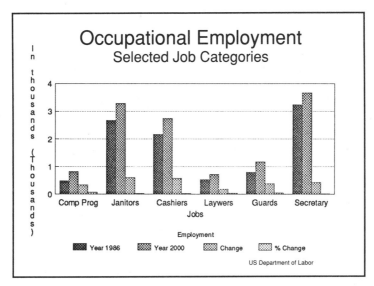

Figure 3.13. Percentages bars are insignificant on chart

Also note that the change in the chart has caused Harvard Graphics to change the values on the scale to single digits in order to accommodate the new series. The program automatically inserts the word *(thousands)* as the Y1 axis label. However, since you had already entered *In thousands* as the Y1 axis label you get *In thousands (thousands)* as the axis label. This is confusing, although accurate. The single digits are thousands in thousands, i.e., millions. You can clear up this confusion on the options screen.

Return to the data entry screen by pressing:

[Esc]

The solution to the disparity in scale between series 4 and series 1, 2, and 3 can be resolved by using the Y2 scale, drawn on the right side of the chart. Display the options screen for Bar/Line charts by pressing:

[F8]

The Y axis column assigns the data series to either the Y1 axis (the default setting) or to the Y2 axis. When all of the series are assigned to the Y1 axis, as is the case at this point, no Y2 axis is drawn. If you change the settings in that column so that at least one series is assigned to the Y2 axis, Harvard Graphics will generate a scale for that axis based on the values in the series assigned to that axis.

Change the scale used for series 4 by pressing:

[Tab] *(7 times)*
[↵] *(3 times)*
[Tab] *(3 times)*
[Space bar]

The item in the column changes from **Y1** to **Y2.** Display the chart by pressing:

[F2]

The bars for the **% change** series now appear on the chart, basing their size on the right-hand scale rather than the left-hand scale (figure 3.14). Note that when you add a new scale to the chart the title for the Y1 axis is deleted by Harvard Graphics. The title you manually entered is also deleted.

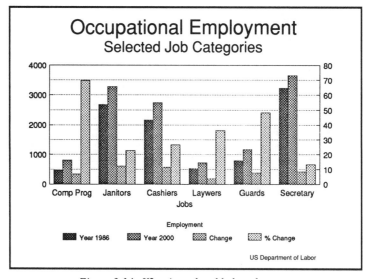

Figure 3.14. Y2 axis scale added to chart

Return to the options screen by pressing:

[Esc]

Suppressing Series Display

The addition of the **% change** series changes the logic of the chart in some ways. If you wanted to emphasize the growth in various job markets, you might want to display just series 3 and 4, the amount and percentage of change. However, the calculation series 3 and 4 *depends* upon the values in series 1 and 2; if you were to delete the values in series 1 and 2, Harvard Graphics would have no way of calculating the values in series 3 and 4. It is for situations such as this that the **Display Series** option is provided. This option allows you to suppress the display of one or more series without having to remove the values from the chart. In this case, suppress the display of series 1 and 2, leaving their values so that series 3 and 4 can be calculated. Press:

[⇑] *(3 times)*
[Shift-Tab]
n [↵]
n

Before you display the chart, enter new titles for the Y1 and Y2 axis:

[Home]
[Tab] *(4 times)*
thousands of jobs [↵]
percent

While you are located on the Y2 axis title line, use the [F7] **Size/Place** command to change the orientation of the Y2 title from horizontal to vertical by pressing:

[F7]
[⇓] *(8 times)*
[Tab] [Spacebar]

Display the chart by pressing:

[F2]

The chart (shown in figure 3.15) now displays only the bars for the number of new jobs and the percent increase. This chart reveals that while the greatest number of new jobs will occur in the janitorial area, the greatest percentage of growth will be in computer programming. The ease with which you can spot these facts exemplifies the advantages of using a bar chart to compare the magnitude of values.

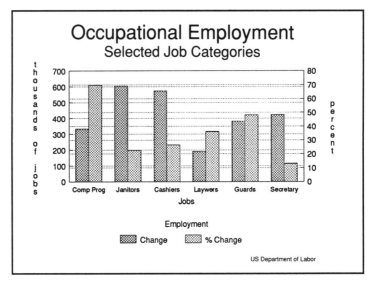

Figure 3.15. Chart with selected data series displayed

Return to the options screen by pressing:

[Esc]

Labeling Bars

Someone not familiar with the structure of the chart with two Y scales will find it impossible to determine which bars are represented by which Y scale. One way to clarify the chart's meaning is to place a value label above each bar. A value label is simply the values show in the series column. In this example, you might choose to place the values in the series 4 column above the series 4 bars. This would then make it clear which bar represented percents.

There are two settings needed to accomplish this task:

Value Labels In a bar chart, none of the data series have value labels. The **Value Labels** option, found on page 2 of the options screens, allows you to activate bar labels in two ways. The **All** option displays value labels for all of the displayed series. The **Select** option works in conjunction with the **Y Label** setting—on page 4 of the options screen—to display labels for specified data series.

108

Y Label   The **Y Label,** found on page 4 of the Bar/Line options screens, changes the format of the chart so that the actual values are displayed above each bar. It works in conjunction with the **Value Labels** option found on page 2 of the options screens. If **Value Labels** is not set to **Select,** the **Y Label** option has no effect on the chart.

In this case, display labels for data series 4 only. Change the **Value Labels** setting from **None** to **Select** by pressing:

[Pg Dn]
[⇓] *(7 times)*
s

Next, move to page 4 of the options screens by pressing:

[Pg Dn] *(2 times)*

In the bottom half of the screen there is a list of series options, shown in figure 3.16. The Y label settings, all **No** by default, control which series display value labels.

Legend Title: Employment	Cum Yes No	Y Label Yes No
1 Year 1986	No	No
2 Year 2000	No	No
3 Change	No	No
4 % Change	No	No
5 Series 5	No	No
6 Series 6	No	No

Figure 3.16. Series options table

Change the display setting for series 4 by pressing:

[⇓] *(13 times)*
[Tab] *(2 times)*
y

Changing Scale

The range of values shown on either the Y1 or Y2 scale is determined by the range of values included in the data series assigned to the axis. However, in some cases you might want to specifically control the range of values covered by an axis. For example, it is common understanding that percentages range between 0 and 100. However, the scale generated by Harvard Graphics for series 4 runs only to 80 because that is the range required by the actual values in the series. It might make more sense to specify a 0 to 100 scale for these value despite the fact that there are no actual percentages above 70 in the series.

Move the cursor to page 3 of the **Bar/Line** option by pressing:

[Pg Up]

This page lists options that effect the axes of the chart. The first section controls the axis labels, the second section controls the grid lines drawn from the axis, and the third section controls the tick marks that appear on the axis when a label is displayed. At the bottom of the screen is a table (figure 3.17) that contain the options which control the scale of the X, Y1, and Y2 axes. There are five options for each axis.

Scale Type	The scale type can be either **Linear** or **Log.** A **Linear** scale is the normal scale used with most charts. The **Log** option is used in scientific and engineering applications when the data points are plotted against a logarithmic scale.
Format	Controls the appearance of values. The format entry uses special symbols, discussed in chapter 2, which alter the appearance of the values.
Minimum Value	Sets the lower end of the scale.
Maximum Value	Sets the upper end of the scale.
Increment	Determines how often a value label and grid line will appear on the axis.

	X Axis	Y1 Axis	Y2 Axis
Scale Type Format Minimum Value Maximum Value Increment	▸Linear Log	▸Linear Log	▸Linear Log

Figure 3.17. Options table controls axis scaling

Keep in mind that manually controlled scales must include all of the values in a series. If you enter a maximum or minimum value that would leave out values in the series, Harvard Graphics ignores the scale specifications and uses the automatic scaling method.

Change the scale of the Y2 axis. Press:

[End]
[⇑] *(3 times)*

The cursor should now be positioned in the **Format** option for the Y2 axis. In this case, add a % to the values. Press:

|% [↵]

Enter zero as the minimum value and 100 as the maximum value:

0 [↵]
100 [↵]

You can use the increment option to increase or decrease the frequency of labels and grid lines on the axis. In this case, set the increment at 25 so that there will be three grid lines drawn from the Y2 axis. Press:

25

It might also be useful to create a simpler scale for the Y1 axis. In this example, the largest value in series 3 is 604. However, it might make the chart more symmetrical if the scale was expended to 1000. By setting the increment at 250, you would establish the same set of grid lines for both scales making the bar values much easier to estimate and reducing the clutter on the chart. Note that the key concept is to make the two Y axes proportional to one another. In this case, the Y1 axis is simply 10 times the value of the Y2 axis. Press:

[⇑] *(2 times)*
[Shift-Tab]
0 [↵]
1000 [↵]
250

Display the chart by pressing:

[F2]

The chart is displayed with the manually controlled scales of both the Y1 and Y2 axis and the value labels displayed above each bar in the **% change** series (figure 3.18). The proportionally scales cause the grid lines divide the chart into sections that are 1/4 of the overall scale. This makes it easy to spot the fact that only computer programming shows a growth rate of over 50%.

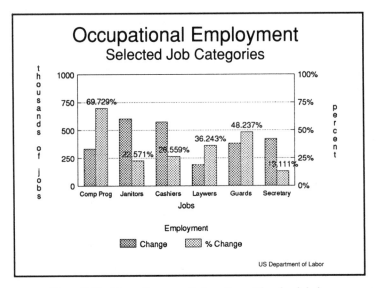

Figure 3.18. Manually controlled scaling with value labels

Save this chart as BAR-02 by pressing:

[Esc] [F10] 4 2
bar-02 [↵]
[Ctrl-Del]
Y1 & Y2, manual scaling [↵]

ARRANGING THE BARS

The bar charts that you have created and stored as BAR-01 and BAR-02 use the default method of displaying bars; all of the bars for each item on the X axis are grouped together with a space between each group of bars. In order to accommodate additional data series, the width of the bars are reduced each time a series is added to the chart. Harvard Graphics provide alternative ways in which bars can be displayed on a chart.

112

3-D Bars   A 3-D bar chart displays the bars as columns in perspective giving the chart a three-dimensional appearance.

Overlapping Bars Overlaps the bars in a series instead of placing each bar next to each other.

Two of the bar options fit the type of data used in BAR-01. Load a copy of the BAR-01 chart back into Harvard Graphics by pressing:

1
bar-01 [↵]
[Esc]

Overlapping Bars

Overlapping bar charts are useful in charts which contain ascending values in consecutive series. This means that the first bars are always shorter than the bars behind. Thus, the front bar will not obscure the next bar in the series. For example, the values in series 1, the 1986 employment values, are smaller for each occupation than the projected values for 2000. You could make the increases in jobs more dramatic by allowing series 1 to over lap series 2. The values in series 3, the change between 1986 and 2000 are not ideal for overlapping because the values in this series are smaller than the preceding series. To see how the overlapping affects the appearance of the chart activate the second page of the Bar/Line options screens, press:

[F8] [Pg Dn]

The first option on this page is **Bar Style.** Change the style of the chart from **Cluster** the normal display of bars, to **Overlap** by pressing:

[Spacebar]

The next section of the options menu shows an option labeled **Bar overlap.** This option controls the percentage of overlap among the bars. The default value 50 means that each bar will overlap the following bar by 50%. Using a value greater than 50 will increase the amount of overlapping while a value less than 50 will show more of each bar. Change the overlap value to 33 so that only 1/3 of each bar is overlapped:

[Tab] *(4 times)*
33

Display the chart by pressing:

[F2]

The chart, shown in figure 3.19, displays the bars in an overlapping pattern.

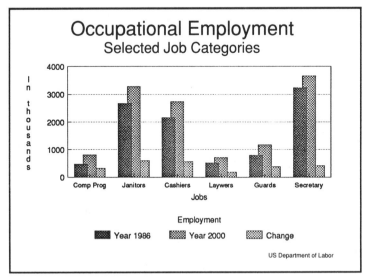

Figure 3.19. Chart with overlapping bars

Return to the options screen by pressing:

[Esc]

3-D Bars

In a *3-D* chart the bars and the chart grid are projected in space to create a three-dimensional look. You can add 3-D to any type of bar chart. In this case, you will combine 3-D with overlapping. Press:

[⇑] *(3 times)*
3
[F2]

The graph combines overlapping bars with 3-D (figure 3.20). The chart does a good job at comparing series 1 values to series 2, but because the values in the third series are smaller than the preceding series, the overlapping causes them to be hidden from view.

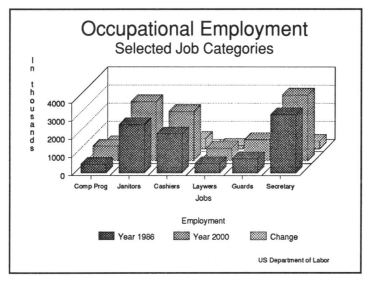

Figure 3.20. Overlap combined with 3-D

Return to the options screen and remove the overlap effect by pressing:

[Esc]
[⇧] c
[F2]

With the **Cluster** option selected, all of the bars in the chart are displayed in 3-D, shown in figure 3.21.

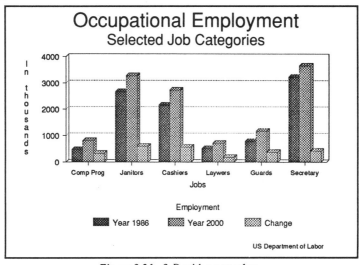

Figure 3.21. 3-D with no overlap

Return to the options screen by pressing:

[Esc]

However, in changing from 3-D/Overlap to 3-D cluster, part of the depth of the chart is lost. You can increase the depth of the bars by using the **Bar depth** option. You can enter values 1-100. The default is 25. Press:

[⇓] *(5 times)*
75
[F2]

The chart increases the depth of the chart, increasing the 3-D effect.

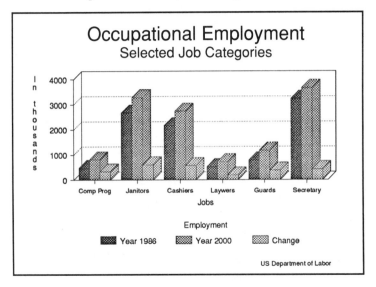

Figure 3.22. Depth of 3-D bars increased to 75

Save this chart as BAR-03 by pressing:

[Esc] [F10] 4 2
bar-03 [↵]
3-D bar chart [↵]

116

PAIRED SERIES BARS

A *paired series* bar chart is a variation on the basic bar charts that you have been working with thus far. This format is designed to sharply contrast the values in a chart. While this type of chart can be created with more than two data series, it usually works best data series.

The most obvious difference between a paired-bar chart and other bar charts is that the axes are rotated 90 degrees. The X axis is vertical while the Y axes are horizontal. In addition, the vertical X axis is drawn in the center of the chart and he bars are drawn horizontally from the X axis. The series assigned to Y1 are drawn to the left while the series assigned to the Y2 axis are drawn to the right.

Return to the chart editing screen by pressing:

[Esc] 2

Display the options screen:

[F8]

In order to prepare the data series for a paired bar chart you must suppress the display of the third series (*change*) and assign one of the series (series 2) to the Y2 axis. Press:

[⇓] *(11 times)*
[Tab] *(3 times)*
[Spacebar]
[⇓] [Shift-Tab] [Spacebar]

You have now limited the display of data to the first two series and assigned each of those series to a different Y axis.

Display page 2 of the Bar/Line options screens by pressing:

[Pg Dn]

Change the **Bar style** to **Paired** by pressing:

p

When feasible, it is also useful to make the Y1 and Y2 axis scales the same. This enables you to easily compare magnitudes among any of the bars on the chart. In this case, set the axis scales at 0 to 4000 with 1000 increments. Move the cursor to the third page of the options screens by pressing:

[Pg Dn]

Adjust the scales for the Y1 and Y2 axes:

[End]
[⇑] *(2 times)*
[Shift-Tab]

0 [↵]
4000 [↵]
1000
[⇑] *(2 times)*
[Tab]
 0 [↵]
4000 [↵]
1000

Display the paired bar chart by pressing:

[F2]

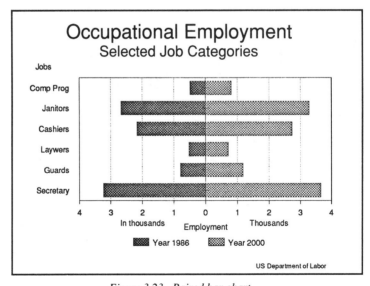

Figure 3.23. Paired bar chart

Save this chart as BAR-04 by pressing:

[Esc] [F10] 4 2
bar-04 [⏎]
paired bat chart [⏎]

CUMULATIVE VALUE DATA SERIES

In chapter 2 you looked at how pie charts could be used to compare individual parts to the whole to which they belong. The example of the federal governments projected 1990 budget was used as the subject of the charts.

Figure 3.24 shows the amount spent by the federal government in various years since 1900 in three categories: defense, interest on the national debt, and all other expenditures.

Year	Defense	Interest	All others
1900	191	40	290
1950	9,919	750	23,875
1960	43,969	9,180	39,075
1970	78,360	19,304	9,824
1980	136,138	74,860	368,013
1990	303,000	170,000	678,000

Figure 3.24. Federal expenditures in selected years since 1900

This information has characteristics of both pie and bar charts. Like a pie chart, for each of the three items represent the parts of a whole (the federal budget for that year). However, if you wanted to look at the chart across years in one particular category—such as the expenditures for defense from 1900 to 1990—the data would be best represented as a bar chart.

The problem is resolved by the use of a *stacked bar* chart. In a *stacked* bar chart, each bar is composed of several sections stacked on top of one another. Each section represents a bar from one of the data series. When stacked one on top of the other, the accumulated bar represent the total of the values from all the data series in one category. Stacked bars are similar to the column format used with pie charts in chapter 2. Of course, because the chart is basically a bar chart, there is one stacked bar for every item on the X axis. In this way a stacked bar chart can represent a table of information that requires a display that combines the characteristics of a pie and a bar chart.

Creating a Stacked Bar Chart

To create a stacked bar chart, press:

[Esc] 1 3 [F10]

Note that even though the X axis items will be expressed in years, you would not use the **Year** option because you are not working with an regular series of years, but years picked at random.

Enter the Title and Footnote for the chart. In this case, skip the subtitle:

Government Spending [↵]
[↵]
US Dept of Treasury [↵]

Enter the years shown on the chart on the X axis:

1900 [↵]
1950 [↵]
1960 [↵]
1970 [↵]
1980 [↵]
1990

Move the cursor to the top of the next column and enter the values for defense expenditures and press:

[⇑] *(5 times)*
[Tab]
191[↵]
9919[↵]
43969[↵]
78360[↵]
136138[↵]
303000

Move the cursor to the beginning of series 2 and enter the data for interest on the national debt:

[⇑] *(5 times)*
[Tab]
40 [↵]
750 [↵]
9180 [↵]
19304 [↵]
74860 [↵]
170000

Finally, enter the data for series 3, all other government expenditures:

[⇑] *(5 times)*
[Tab]
290 [↵]
23,875 [↵]
39,075 [↵]
9,824 [↵]
368,013 [↵]
678,000

The data entry screen should now look like figure 3.25.

Pt	X Axis Name	Series 1	Series 2	Series 3
1	1900	191	40	290
2	1950	9919	5750	23875
3	1960	43969	9180	39075
4	1970	78360	19304	9824
5	1980	136138	74860	368013
6	1990	303000	170000	678000

Figure 3.25. Data entered for stacked bar chart

Once the data has been entered you can use the **Bar style** option to select the **stacked** bar format. Press:

[F8] [Pg Dn] s

Display the chart by pressing:

[F2]

Figure 3.26 shows how the data series are represented in the stacked-bar format. Each bar consists of three sections, one for each data series in the chart. The entire bar represents the total of all three data series.

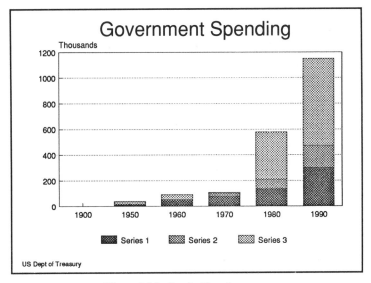

Figure 3.26. Stacked bar format

Return to the options menu by pressing:

[Esc]

Note that the data series are still labeled Series 1, Series 2, and Series 3. Return to the first page of the options screens and enter descriptive names for the series:

[Pg Up]
[Tab] *(7 times)*
[Ctrl-Del] Defense [↵]
[Ctrl-Del] Interest [↵]
[Ctrl-Del] All Others

The chart deals with such radically different values that the first several bars of the chart seem to display no information at all. You can overcome this problem in part by using the 3-D feature. Press:

[Pg Dn] [⇓] 3

Change the depth of the 3-D bars to 50 by pressing:

[Tab] *(4 times)*
50

Display the 3-D stacked bar chart by pressing:

[F2]

The chart, shown in figure 3.27, improves your view of the smaller bars because the perspective use in the 3-D display shows what appears to be the *top* of the bars which is the same size regardless of the height of the bar.

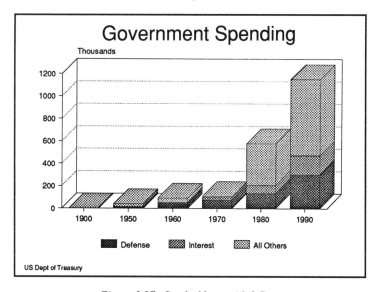

Figure 3.27. Stacked bars with 3-D

Return to the options screen by pressing:

[Esc]

Linked Bar Segments

A variation on the basic stacked bar layout is called a *linked-segment* display. In this display, Harvard Graphics adds lines that are drawn between the same data series segments on different bars. This option is found on the **Bar enhancement** menu under **Link.** Note that this is the same option used for 3-D. This means that linking and 3-D displays are incompatible. Selected a linked stacked bar display by pressing:

[⇑] *(4 times)*
I
[F2]

The chart returns to the standard two-dimensional bars, as shown in figure 3.28. However, this time lines connect the segments on various bars. The lines illustrate the degree of change in a given segment from bar to bar. For example, if a line between two bar segments is steep, the change between the value of that item on the two bars is significant.

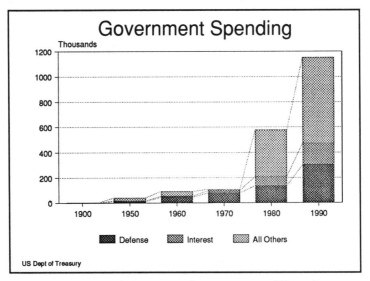

Figure 3.28. Lines link corresponding segments on different bars

Return to the options menu by pressing:

[Esc]

100% Area Charts

The total size of each stacked bar is proportional to the total value of all of the segments added together. In the chart shown in figure 3.28 you can see not only that individual segments change from year to year, but the total bar size (the total federal budget) increases dramatically.

However, another way to analyze the same information would be to try to determine the relative weight of each of the segments in each of the years. This would display information in a similar way provided in a pie chart. In a pie chart, all of the pies are circles of the same size. What is important is the relative size of the slices.

Harvard Graphics includes a special option in which the segments in a stacked bar chart will be displayed as percentages. This means that all of the bars will be the same size: 100%. What will vary from bar to bar is the relative size of each of the segments. In this way a 100% chart allows you to analyze the relative proportions of each segment in different bars.

You can change a stacked bar chart to a **100%** bar chart using the **Bar style** option. Press:

[⇧]
1

Add the 3-D effect to the chart by pressing:

[⇩]
3

Display the chart by pressing:

[F2]

The 100% stacked bar display (figure 3.29) reveals that the percentage of the federal budget spent on defense was greater in 1900 than in 1980 although the overall budget in 1900 was tiny compared to the 1980 budget.

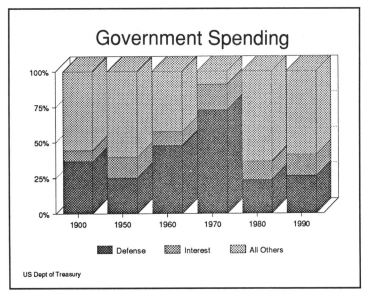

Figure 3.29. 100% stacked bars show relative percentages of segments

Save this chart as BAR-05 by pressing:

[Esc] [F10] 4 2
bar-05 [⏎]
[⏎]

AREA CHARTS

An *area* chart is related to stacked bar charts in that the values from various data series are stacked on top of each other. The difference is that instead of displaying individual bars at each X axis item, the area chart draws lines between the points of each segment and fills in all of the space. The result is similar in meaning to the linked stacked-bar chart (figure 3.28), but without distinct vertical bars.

Changing Chart Types

When logical, Harvard Graphics allows you to change the type of chart you are working with while retaining the data and chart options. For example, while it is true that Bar/Line and Area charts are separate menu items, they use many of the same

126

elements and options. A Bar/Line chart can be converted to an area chart by using the **Create new chart** command while the Bar/Line chart is still in memory. Press:

[Esc] 1 4

Harvard Graphics displays a menu box that asks **Keep current Data: Yes No.** If you select *Yes* the new chart is automatically set up with the same data and options as the existing chart. Press:

[↵]

The **Area Chart Data** screen appears with the data from the Bar/Line Data screen automatically filled in. Display the area chart by pressing:

[F2]

While area chart 1, shown in figure 3.30, looks quite different from the stacked bar chart, it tells much the same story. The primary difference is that by drawing lines between the X axis points and filling in the area between them, the display implies continuous, smooth transitions from one period to the next. In reality this was not actually the case. For example, the chart seems to show that between 1900 and 1950 there was a small, gradual decrease in defense spending. However, if the defense spending during the years of World War II was included in the data series, the chart would look much different. Nonetheless, the chart does give a good picture of the rise in defense spending during the Vietnam era and its decrease following the war. Keep in mind that charts can be manipulated, like statistics, to place emphasis on certain aspects of the information. No one chart tells the complete story, but a variety of chart types can highlight different aspects of the same basic data.

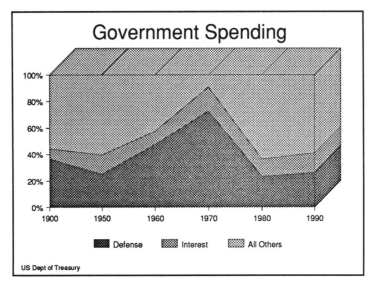

Figure 3.30. 100% style area chart

Return to the data entry screen by pressing:

[Esc]

3-D Area Charts

Note that the area chart in figure 3.30 was a 100% type display because the Bar chart from which it was created as a 100% type bar chart. Change the area chart to a normal 3-D area chart by pressing:

[F8] [Pg Dn]
s

Display the chart by pressing:

[F2]

The normal 3-D area chart shows that the charted data is based on its actual magnitudes. This chart, shown in figure 3.31, dramatically shows a vast increase in government spending since the beginning of 1970s. The area chart tends to imply trends by connecting the various data points into a continuous area.

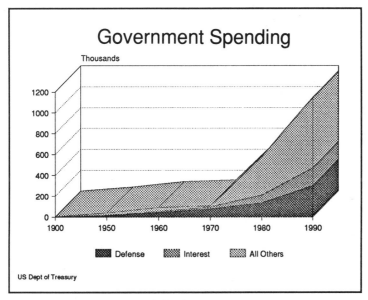

Figure 3.31. 3-D area chart

Save this chart as AREA-01 by pressing:

[Esc] [F10] 4 2
area-01 [↵]
[↵]

SUMMARY

The charts discussed in this chapter were used to compare the magnitude of various items using bars to represent the items.

Bar Charts. Bar charts are displayed within a rectangular grid. The bars are solid columns of varying size that reflect the magnitude of the value it is representing. Bar charts can be used to represent any series of values. They allow you to easily compare the values for each item in the series by comparing the size of the displayed bars.

X Axis. In a bar chart, the X axis is used to list the items for which value bars will be displayed. In most bar charts the X axis is the horizontal axis. The names of the items are written from left to right across the bottom of the chart. The items can be listed in any order.

Y Axis. The Y axis is used as a scale by which the magnitude of the bars can be measured. The program will automatically create a Y axis scaled to contain the smallest and largest values in any of the activate data series. At each label position on the Y axis a grid line is drawn across the chart to make it easier to judge the value of the bars. A chart can have two different Y axis scales (one on the left and one on the right) to accommodate data series with vastly different size values on the same chart. The scale of the second Y axis is determined by the values in the series assigned to that axis.

Bar Clusters. If more than one series of data values is entered into the chart data entry screen, the program will display one bar for each data series for each item on the X axis. All of the bars at any given X axis item are called the bar *cluster.* Clustered bars are the default bar chart style.

Overlapped Bars. You can select to have the bars within a cluster overlap each other by a percentage. The default overlap style causes the bars in each cluster to overlap the bar from the next series by 50%. Overlapped bars emphasize difference in values between bars in the same cluster. They work best when each successive bar is larger than the preceding bar.

Size and Place. The titles that appear on a bar chart can be changed in size and alignment using the [F7] key. The titles for Y axes have the unusual option of vertical or horizontal display. Vertical display of a Y axis title causes the text to be written vertically, parallel to the Y axis.

3-D Bars. The 3-D option causes the bars in the chart to be displayed in 3-D, giving the appearance of three-dimensional columns. This option can be used with normal or overlapped bars. Note that using the 3-D effect with overlapped bars can result in some bars being hidden if they are smaller than the preceding bar. You can control the depth of the bars, set at 25 by default, with the Bar depth option.

Paired Series Bars. A paired bar chart rotates the standard bar chart 90 degrees so that the X axis is vertical and Y axes are horizontal. The Y axes are plotted in opposite directions: the Y1 axis is plotted to the left of the X axis while the Y2 axis is plotted to the right. The **Paired** bar option is typically used to contrast paired values entered in two data series by assigning each series to a different Y axis. However, you can use a single Y axis paired bar chart to rotate bar chart 90 degrees.

Stacked Bars. Stacked bar charts display only a single bar at each X axis item no matter how many data series are used. Instead of generating individual bars for each data series value, the stacked bar chart shows each series as a segment of a single bar that appears at each X axis item. The total value of all data series values for each X axis item is reflected in the overall height of the stacked bar. These charts show part to whole relationships (similar to pie charts) for each X axis item in the chart.

Linked Stack Segments. The link option causes the program to draw lines between the tops of all segments of the same data series.

100% Stacked Bars. A variation on the stacked bat chart is the 100% bar chart. In this type of chart each of the segments in a stacked bar represents the percentage of the whole bar represented by the segment's value. This in this chart all bars have the same overall height (they all total 100%). The display is used when you want to compare the relative magnitude of each segment for different X axis items.

Area Charts. Area charts are an alternative way to display the same information that you would display in a stacked bar or 100% stacked bar chart. The difference between a stacked bar chart and an area chart is that the area chart does not draw vertical bars but lines between points that represent the values of the various segments. The area chart displays the stacked bar information as if there were straight line growth or decline in the periods between the data points. Area charts are related to both stacked bar, pie, and time series charts (explained in chapter 4).

Chart Conversion. Bar/Line charts and Area charts have basically the same data entry and option screens. You can convert an existing bar or area chart to the other type by using the **Create** command from the main menu. When you select the Bar or Area option, Harvard Graphics asks if you want to retain the existing data. If you answer *Yes,* the new chart is automatically set with the applicable data and options used in the existing chart.

Chapter 4

Time Series Charts

The bar and area charts discussed in chapter 3 represent the type of chart that illustrates the relative magnitude of a group of items. The data displayed in a pie chart is used to represent part of a whole. These charts all lack one element that is important in charts used to analyze business transactions: the element of time.

All financial transactions have two basic values which can be used to analyze the activity. The first value is the monetary or numerical magnitude of the transactions. For example, a check is written $1,000 or a share of stock is sold for $100. The second value is the time the transaction took place. If the activity takes places on a regular basis—for example, daily, monthly, or yearly—the values and the time they occurred form what is called a *time series*. For example, the price of a share of stock may fluctuate over a three day period, as shown in table 4.1.

Table 4.1 Stock price table for May 1, May 2, and May 3

Date	Price
May 1	$95
May 2	$90
May 3	$100

You can use the prices of the stock and the date the price was valid to create a chart. The dates form the *time* component of the chart. In mathematical terms this component is referred to as the *independent* because the series of dates (May 1–May 3) would exist even if there were no stock to be sold on those dates.

The prices form the *value* component of the chart. The value is referred to as the *dependent* component because the price of the stock may vary from day to day.

You can use the components to define points on a two-dimensional grid. Traditionally, the independent component (usually time) is measured on the horizontal line of the grid (the X axis), increasing from left to right. The dependent components are displayed on the vertical line of the grid (the Y axis), beginning with the largest value at the top of the scale.

The terms X axis and Y axis are more precise than horizontal and vertical because they refer to the type of information they display (independent and dependent values); the terms horizontal and vertical refer merely to the orientation of the graph paper.

The data in table 4.1 can be converted into a chart by plotting points at the intersection of the dates on the X axis and the prices on the Y axis. Figure 4.1 shows the three points plotted as a chart.

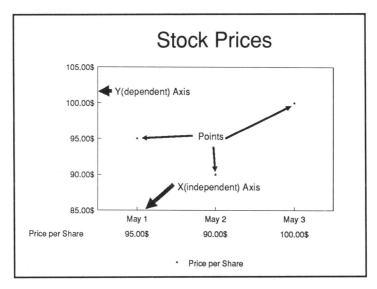

Figure 4.1. Data points plotted on a time series chart

Note that unlike a pie chart where the sequence of the slices was arbitrary, the values on both the axis on a time series chart are arranged in a specific order: chronological for the X axis and numerical for the Y axis. To make the relationship between the points more clear, lines are drawn between the points as shown in figure 4.2.

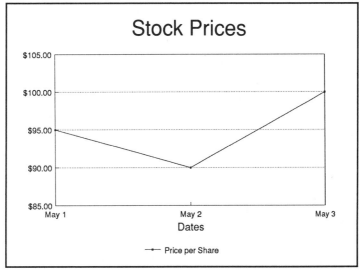

Figure 4.2. Line chart shows relationship between points

The events in a time series lend themselves to analysis since the past is often a guide as to what might happened in the future. Often the points will follow a general pattern of some kind. This pattern can be analyzed mathematically to produce a *trend* line. Figure 4.3 shows a chart which has a *trend* line added. The trend line is used to project the series further into the future. In this case, the trend line shows that the price of the stock will be $105 per share on May 6th. Of course, trend lines can rarely predict the future this accurately, but they can be useful in summarizing a general direction.

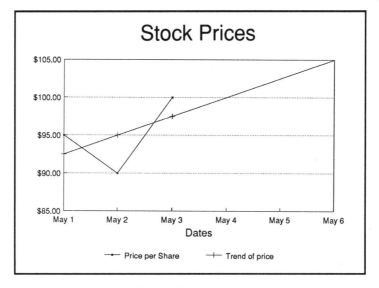

Figure 4.3. Trend line added to chart

Time series charting is a good deal more sophisticated than pie or bar charting. The plotting of trends and other analytical data series requires complex calculations. In order to make these tasks simpler, Harvard Graphics has built in mathematical functions that calculate the values needed to trend and other analytical data series.

BUILDING A BASIC TIME SERIES CHART

Begin this section by loading Harvard Graphics in the usual manner. You should be at the main program menu when you begin.

The most obvious characteristic of a time-series chart is that the items placed along the X axis are not merely arbitrarily selected categories, as is the case with bar charts, but are a logical sequence of values. In most cases the values are a chronological series. In scientific and engineering applications X axis values can be numeric.

Harvard Graphics automatically generating the time series values for the X axis. You only need to specify the beginning and ending values in the series and Harvard Graphics will fill in all the values in between.

Begin the creation process by pressing:

1 3

Harvard Graphics displays the **X Data Type** menu. This menu, shown in figure 4.4, lists a variety of time series that you can select for the chart. The default setting is **name.** This setting is used with bar charts in which the X axis does not represent a chronological or numeric sequence, but instead simply a listing of categories.

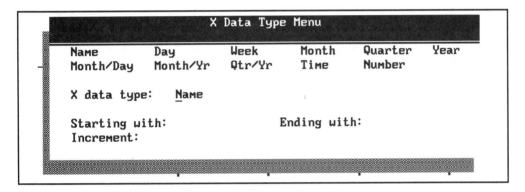

Figure 4.4. X Data Type menu

Harvard Graphics lists nine different types of chronological sequences that can automatically generated for time series charts. To generate X axis values with these series you must enter a starting and ending value. The chronological sequences are as follows:

Day	Generates days of the week. You can enter the days as SUN or Sunday.
Week	Generates numbers for the weeks. Week numbers are entered as 1, 2, etc.
Month	Generates the names of the months. You can use *JAN, January,* or *1* as month names.
Quarter	Generates quarters. You can use 1, first, or Q1 for the quarter names.
Year	Generates years. You can use 1990, 90, or '90 as year names.

Month/Day   Generates day and month series. This series can be extended over periods longer than a single month. You can enter Jan 1, 1/1, or January 1 as day/month names.

Month/Yr   Generates months with years over periods longer than a single year. You can enter JAN 90, January 90, or 1/90 as month/year names.

Qtr/Yr   Generates quarters with years over periods longer than a single year. You can enter 1/90, 1/1990, or first 90 as quarter/year names.

Time   Generates an hourly series. You can use 12:00 at the time name. Increment values in this case are minutes. For example, an increment of 30 would generate times on the half hour.

You can select the time series type you desire by using the [Spacebar] to change the **X data type** entry. You can also select a time series by entering the first letter of the option. If more than one option begins with the same letter, the next item with that letter is selected.

You can also enter an optional *increment* value. By default, Harvard Graphics increases the X axis value one unit at a time until the end value is reached. If you want to increment each value by a different number of units, you can enter that value at the time you define the time series.

In this example, the time series will be a yearly series. Generate years from 1970 to 1986 by pressing:

y [↵]

The next items to enter are the starting and ending values. Press:

70 [↵]
86 [F10]

When the data entry screen appears, the **X Axis** column is filled with the values 70 through 81. To see the remainder of the data series display the next set of data points, press:

[Pg Dn]

The second screen shows the values 82 through 86, a total of 17 data points.

Fill in the title, subtitle and footnote for the chart by entering:

Factory Sales of Cars [↵]
From US Plants [↵]
US Dept of Commerce

To enter the values that correspond to the years, display the first set of years by pressing:

[Pg Up]

Place the cursor in the series 1 column by pressing:

[Tab] *(2 times)*

Enter the following values:

6.5 [↵]
8.6 [↵]
8.8 [↵]
9.7 [↵]
7.3 [↵]
6.7 [↵]
8.5 [↵]
9.2 [↵]
9.2 [↵]
8.4 [↵]
6.4 [↵]
6.2 [↵]
5 [↵]
6.7 [↵]
7.6 [↵]
8 [↵]
7.5

Display the chart by pressing:

[F2]

Recall that by default, all Bar/Line charts are plotted as bar type charts, as shown in figure 4.5.

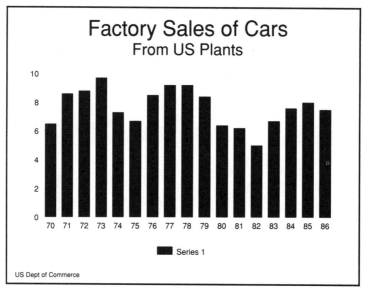

Figure 4.5. Default values display time series as bar chart

Return to the data entry screen by pressing:

[Esc]

LINE CHARTS

The bar chart, generated by the default settings, is designed to help you compare the magnitude of each bar to the others. However, in the case of a time series, the magnitude of the individual bars is less significant than the pattern or trend formed by the variation of the values over time. This is best expressed as a line chart. To change the displays from bar to a line chart display the options screen by pressing:

[F8]

Move the cursor to the options for series 1 by pressing:

[Tab] *(7 times)*

Change the name of the series by typing:

Car Sales

Place the cursor in the **Type** column by pressing:

[Tab]

The type column is automatically set to **Bar** for all of the data series. However you have four other options available, all related to time-series analysis. These options are **Line, Trend, Curve,** and **Pt.**

Line   Displays the values entered in the data series as points on the graph, directly above the X axis. The height of each point is determined by is value. All of the points are connected by straight lines.

Trend   Plots trend lines as calculated by statistical methods, such as *linear regression analysis.* The trend line is closest straight line that fits the pattern established by the zig-zag line created by connecting points. Trend lines can be extended past the last data point in order to project possible further values. Trend lines will rarely pass directly through a data point.

Curve   Plots a curved line. Straight line trends are often too inflexible to take into consideration natural peaks and valleys that are indicated by the line chart. A curve chart is useful when you are attempting to plot a trend that smooths the pattern of the line chart. Curve-chart lines will touch some, but not all, data points.

Pt   This stands for a *point* chart. This chart consists of only the data point markers with no line drawn between them. The chart created by this type of display is called a *scattergram.* It is typically used in scientific charting when both the X and Y scales are numeric.

In this example, the series that you want to display consists of the *raw* statistical data (the actual yearly figures for car sales) so you should select **Line** chart. Press:

[Spacebar]

The **Type** option for series 1 is now **Line.** Display the information charted as a line by pressing:

[F2]

The line chart, shown in figure 4.6, shows the pattern of peaks and valleys taken by U.S. car production much more clearly than the bar chart. The chart indicates peak years in 1973, 1978, and 1985 and low years in 1975 and 1982.

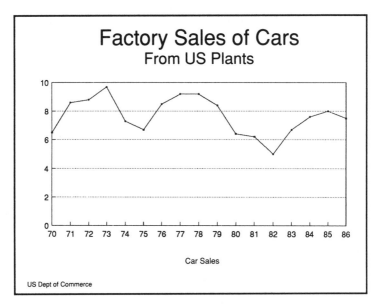

Figure 4.6. Time series values displayed as a line chart

Return to the options screen by pressing:

[Esc]

Focusing on the Pattern

The purpose of time series analysis and the line charts with which they are displayed is to search for patterns and trends in the data. Where as pie and bar type charts are informational in nature (they simply present values); line charts are primarily analytical.

In the current example, the line chart that shows the up-and-down trend in the US car industry is drawn in the upper half of the graph frame. This is because Harvard Graphics begins the Y axis scale at zero by default. While the U.S. auto industry may be having some hard times, it is unlikely that you will need to plot points near zero. Keep in mind that in time-series analysis, the actual magnitude of the points (how high up on the Y axis each point falls), is much less important than how that point compares to the other points in the series. Since the data series contains no values less than 4 million, all of the space taken up on the chart from zero to 4 million is wasted.

You can focus the chart on just the range of values the contain the actual data points entered in the data series, thereby enlarging the portion of the chart which is most important and focusing attention on the line. To do this, use the options screen to specify the values for the Y scale. Move to the third page of the options screens by pressing:

[Pg Dn] *(2 times)*

The bottom section of this screen contains options for setting the maximum and minimum values for the Y axis scale. Set the scale of the current chart to a low of 4 and a high of 10 by pressing:

[Tab] *(10 times)*
[⇓] *(2 times)*
4 [↵]
10

Display the chart by pressing:

[F2]

Figure 4.7 shows the chart with the modified scale shows a larger, more detailed illustration of the changes in the values of the data series. By eliminating the unused space at the bottom of the scale, the chart more clearly displays the significant section of the chart.

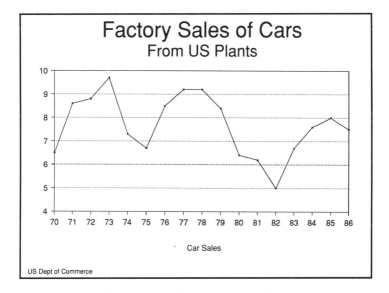

Figure 4.7. Line chart focused on the significant area

The current chart is an example of the basic line chart used in time series analysis. Save the current chart as TS-01 (time series 1) by pressing:

[Esc] [F10] 4 2
ts-01 [↵]
[↵]
[Esc]

Intensifying the Line Chart

The line chart that you have created illustrates the changes over time in the sales of U.S. cars. However, this line chart lacks the visual impact of a bar or pie chart. In large part, this is because a line drawn between points is not a solid block of color like those used in bars and pie slices. By its very nature, lines make a smaller visual impact because they are physically smaller than bars or slices.

You can overcome this problem, at least in part, by using some of the special effects. Return to the chart's options screens by pressing:

2
[F8] [Pg Dn]

These special effects are listed under **Bar style** and **Bar enhancement.** Despite the names of the options, they will have an effect on the display of a line chart as well as a bar chart. In this example, change the line chart from a simple line into a ribbon by using the **Overlap** and **3-D** effect. Used with a line chart, these options will tilt the ribbon so its width is visible on the chart.

Change the **Bar style** to **Overlap** and the **Bar enhancement** to **3-D.** Note that you *must* use both options together in order to get the ribbon effect. Press:

o *(the letter O)*
[⇓]
3

In order to make the ribbon effect as dramatic as possible increase the **Bar width, Bar overlap,** and the **Bar depth** to the maximum value, 100. This will ensure the most visible possible ribbon. Press:

[⇓] *(2 times)*
100 [↵]
100 [↵]
100 [↵]

Display the ribbon chart by pressing:

[F2]

The use of the overlap and 3-D options changes the line chart to a dramatic ribbon chart, shown in figure 4.8. The ribbon chart is especially good for pointing out the peaks and valleys in the data series.

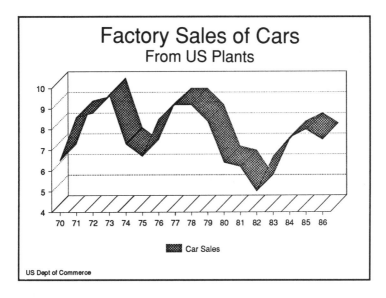

Figure 4.8. Line displays in ribbon style

Save the ribbon chart by pressing:

[Esc] [F10] 4 2
ts-02 [↵]
[Ctrl-Del]
Ribbon Chart [↵]
[Esc]

ANALYTICAL DATA SERIES

The time series charts that you have created so far show only the raw data entered into the time series. As mentioned previously, time series charts can also be used to show information which analyzes the patterns and trends indicated by the raw data. For example, it might be useful to analyze the amount of change from year to year in car production. For example, in 1970 production was 6.5 million cars. In 1971, production rose to 8.6 million cars, an increase of 2.1 million. If you carried through that calculation for each pair of years, you would get a data series that showed the magnitude of increase and decrease each year.

You can get the program to automatically calculate this series of values by using the *@DIFF()* function in a series calculation formula. The @DIFF() function is one of several functions included in Harvard Graphics. These functions perform complex or tedious calculations that generate the data required for different types of time-series analysis. The @DIFF() function generates a series of values by finding the difference between consecutive values in a specified data series.

To calculate the amount of change from year to year in the time series, return to the data entry screen by pressing:

2

Move the cursor to data series 2 by pressing:

[Tab] *(2 times)*

Create a formula for the series by pressing:

[F4]
Yearly Change [↵]
@DIFF(#1) [↵]

The column fills with values. Note that in this example some of the values are *negative*, indicating a *decrease* in sales from the previous year.

Use the options screen to specify a line type for this data series. Press:

[F8]
[Tab] *(7 times)*
[⇓]
[Tab]
I

146

In order to make as clear a presentation as possible you might want to suppress the display of the first data series so that there will be only a single ribbon displayed on the chart. Press:

[⇑] [Tab] n

Before you display the chart you should make some alterations to the Y axis. Recall that you set the scale to a range of values between 4 and 10 million. The *Yearly Change* series values cover a very different range of values. If you do not adjust the Y axis range settings, Harvard Graphics will automatically expand the range to include the values in series 2. However, this would create a chart where the top section, the values in the 4 to 10 million range, would be empty, wasted space. You can avoid this by removing the Y axis scale values and allowing Harvard Graphics to automatically generate the scale. Because the values in series 2 range from plus 3 to minus 3 million, automatic scaling will produce a Y axis scale that does not waste any chart space. Remove the current Y axis scale range by pressing:

[Pg Dn] *(2 times)*
[End] [Shift-Tab]
[⇑] [Ctrl-Del]
[⇑] [Ctrl-Del]

Display the chart by pressing:

[F2]

The chart produced by data generated by the @DIFF() function creates a ribbon chart that exaggerates the high and low points of the raw data series, as shown in figure 4.9. The chart seems to indicate that the auto industry tends to have several consecutive years of declining sales followed a quick upturn. However, the peaks in the chart are not sustained for very long and are soon followed by several more years of decline.

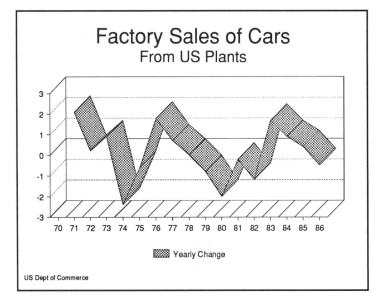

Figure 4.9. Ribbon chart displays values calculated with @DIFF() function

Save this chart as TS-03 by pressing:

[Esc] [F10] 4 2
ts-03 [↵]
[Ctrl-Del]
Yearly Change [↵]
[Esc]

CHARTING CUMULATIVE VALUES

Another way to attempt to analyze a time series is to display the values in the series in a *cumulative* manner. A *cumulative* display is one in which point is the accumulated total of the previous raw data. For example, if the first three data values are 6.5, 8.6, and 8.8, the chart would begin with 6.5. The second value would be 8.6 plus the first value in the series 6.5 to make a total accumulated value of 15.3. The third data point, 8.6 would be added to the previous total making the accumulated value 23.9.

The purpose of a cumulative series is to display the peaks and valleys that occur in a series in a different manner. In a cumulative series the line chart is always rising. The peaks and valleys show up as changes in the rate of increase: peak periods create a steeper rise while a valley slow the rise. A cumulative display tends to smooth out the zig-zag pattern of the line chart. For the cumulative series to show significant up or down changes, the change from year to year must be a large percentage of the overall value. For example, a rise of 0.1 million over a previous period of 8.8 million would not significantly effect the direction of the line chart. The 0.1 million change would only be a change of 1.1%.

Harvard Graphics allows you to chart any series as a cumulative series using the **Cum** option on the 4th page of the option screens. Press:

[F8]

Change the active display series so that series 1 will display on this chart as well as series 2. Press:

[Tab] *(9 times)*
y

Move to the 4th page of the options screens:

[Pg Dn] *(3 times)*

The **Cum** column shown in the table at the bottom of the page is set to **No** for all data series by default. Change both series 1 and 2 to *cumulative* series by pressing:

[Tab] *(8 times)*
y [↵]
y

Display the cumulative series line chart by pressing:

[F2]

The cumulative series chart shows that when the amounts of change are compared to the total volume of sales there appears to be little growth or shrinkage in U.S. auto sales, shown in figure 4.10.

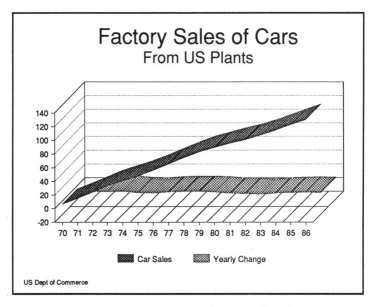

Figure 4.10. Cumulative series shown as a line chart

Save this chart as TS-04 by pressing:

[Esc] [F10] 4 2
ts-04 [⏎]
[Ctrl-Del]
Cumulative series [⏎]
[Esc]

TREND ANALYSIS

Trend analysis refers to the attempt to mathematically analyze the raw values in a data series and arrive at a trend which can be projected into the future as a forecast. The basic tool of forecasting is called *linear regression*. Linear regression analysis seeks to find the closest straight line that fits the data points on the chart. The most common way to find this line is to use the *least-squares* method. This method was developed in 1791 by the great German mathematician Carl Friedrich Gauss. Gauss first applied the *least-squares* method to tracking the path of celestial bodies. However, today it is used in many different fields as a basic statistical method. The calculation behind the *least-squares* method is quite complicated; fortunately Harvard Graphics has a built in function, *@RLIN()*, that will calculate it automatically.

Suppose that you want to apply the statistical techniques of linear regression to the data contained in the time series. Begin by loading the original line chart, TS-01. Press:

4 1
ts-01 [↵]
[Esc]

In Harvard Graphics there are two ways to display a trend line.

Trend This will cause Harvard Graphics to display the data in a special form that shows the data values as a *scattergram* of points and the trend line drawn though those points, as shown in figure 4.11.

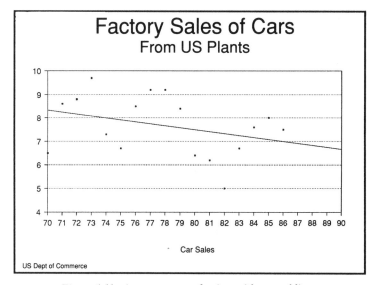

Figure 4.11. A scattergram of points with a trend line

Calculated This method creates a separate data series with the values needed to plot the trend line. The advantage of this method is that you can control the way that the raw data series is displayed independently from the trend line.

Calculating the Regression Values

In order to plot a trend line you must calculate the points for that line. Harvard Graphics makes it simple to find these values by supplying the @RLIN() function which will calculate the values needed to plot the straight-line regression trend. Move the cursor to the series 2 column by pressing:

[Tab] *(2 times)*

Use the [F4] command to enter a formula for calculating the regression values. Press:

[F4]
[Ctrl-Del]
Trend [↵]
@RLIN(#1) [↵]

The values in the series 2 column (figure 4.12) represent the points along the closest straight line that fits the actual values in series 1. You can see that the values are descending starting at 8.333. This indicates that the overall trend in car sales is down. You may have guessed this from the display in chart TS-04 that showed that the low points in the series were more dominant than the high points.

Pt	X Axis Year	Car Sales	Trend
1	70	6.5	8.333
2	71	8.6	8.25
3	72	8.8	8.166
4	73	9.7	8.083
5	74	7.3	7.999
6	75	6.7	7.915
7	76	8.5	7.832
8	77	9.2	7.748
9	78	9.2	7.665
10	79	8.4	7.581
11	80	6.4	7.498
12	81	6.2	7.414

Figure 4.12. Values generated by @RLIN() function

Recall that by default series 2 is formatted as a bar chart. In this example, use the **trend** option to display this line. Press:

[F8]
[Tab] *(8 times)*
[⇓]
t

Display the chart with the trend line by pressing:

[F2]

The trend line (figure 4.13) shows that the general trend of the time series is downward. The trend line does not touch any of the points in the time series; instead it seeks a straight line path through the data fitting as closely as possible to the actual values.

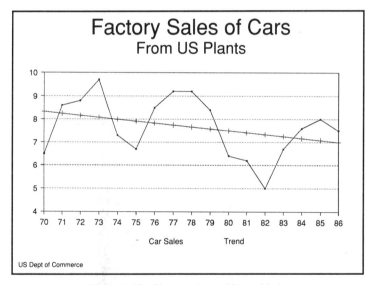

Figure 4.13. Chart with trend line added

Return to the data entry screen by pressing:

[Esc]

Projecting the Trend

The purpose of trends is to attempt to predict what will happen in the future. Selecting **trend** tells Harvard Graphics that the line should be extended past the end of the data series to show where the trend is heading in the future. You can see the projected trend by adding a few years on the X axis.

You can do this manually by simply entering more values in the X axis column or you can use the [F3] command, found on the data entry screen, to recalculate the X axis series. Return to the data entry screen by pressing:

[F8]

Execute the [F3] **Set X type** command by pressing:

[F3]

Harvard Graphics displays the **X Data Type** menu that was used to create the X axis series when the chart was first created. Use this menu to extend the X axis to 1990. Press:

[↵]
70 [↵]
90 [↵]
[↵]

Display the chart:

[F2]

The trend line is extended through 1990 even though the series 1 data stops at 1986. This is shown in figure 4.14.

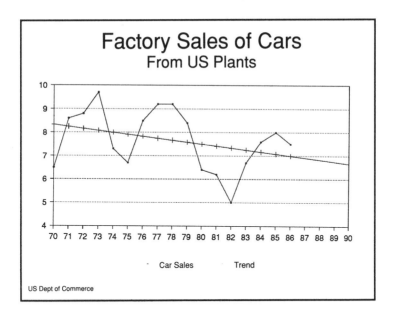

Figure 4.14. Trend line extends beyond last data point

Save this chart as TREND-01 by pressing:

[Esc] [F10] 4 2
trend-01 [↵]
[Ctrl-Del]
Linear Regression [↵]
[Esc]

Curvilinear Regression Models

While the straight-line trend produced by the @RLIN() function is the most commonly used form of trend analysis, there are some problems associated with this approach. In many series the peaks and valleys that occur may be a reflection of natural up and downs that occur on a cyclical basis. On an annual chart you would not be surprised to find seasonal peaks and valleys. Free markets are also subject to the natural rises and falls of the business cycle. When looking at a time series you may want to take into account a certain degree of up and down movement. The goal is to find the peaks and valleys that cannot be accounted for by natural cycles. For example, suppose that a time series has several valleys. Some of these may be simply part of the natural cycle for that business while the deeper valleys may truly indicate a loss of market.

Curvilinear Regression models attempt to incorporate cyclical trends into the regression analysis. This is done by adding factors to least-squares method. The result is a line chart that contains some up and down curves.

Harvard Graphics provides three types of Curvilinear Regression functions: *REXP()*, *@RLOG()*, and *@RPWR()*. All three of these function have in common a technique called *exponential smoothing*. The technique uses statistical methods to vary the *least-squares* values. It is beyond the scope of this book to detail the mathematical differences between these methods. However, you can perform a simple experiment by using these functions to analyze the current data series.

Return to the data entry screen by pressing:

2

Move the cursor to the column for series 2 by pressing:

[Tab] *(2 times)*

You can replace the data in this series by entering a different formula for calculation. In this case, you will replace the @RLIN() function with the @REXP() function. Press:

[F4]
Exp Trend [↵]
@REXP(#1) [↵]

Move the cursor to the series 3 column and enter an @RLOG() formula for that series:

[Tab]
[F4]
Log Trend [↵]
@RLOG(#1) [↵]

Repeat the process for the next column using the @RPWR() function:

[Tab]
[F4]
Power Trend [↵]
@RPWR(#1) [↵]

Note that all three functions produce a series of values that move in the same general direction. However, the exact values produced for each point vary due to a variance in the way that they are calculated.

Display the options screen by pressing:

[F8]

Set series 2, 3, and 4 to the **curve** type of line. Press:

[Tab] *(8 times)*
[⇓]
c [↵]
c [↵]
c

Display the chart by pressing:

[F2]

The chart displays the three curvilinear trend lines produced by the three exponential smoothing functions, shown in figure 4.15. The trend drawn by the @RLOG() function seems to fit the raw data series best because its last point falls almost exactly on the final point of the raw data series.

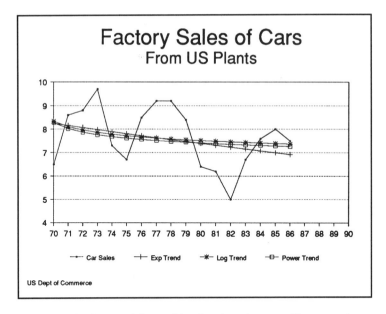

Figure 4.15. Exponential smoothing functions draw curvilinear trends

Save this chart as TREND-02 by pressing:

[Esc] [F10] 4 2
trend-02 [⏎]
[Ctrl-Del]
Exponential Smoothing [⏎]
[Esc]

Moving Averages

The *least-squares* and *exponential smoothing* methods use sophisticated statistical calculations to produce a trend line. Another commonly used method of analyzing trends is the calculation of a *moving* average. Unlike the *least-squares* method, the moving average is a fairly simple calculation. A moving average uses a specified range of values to calculate an average. For example, suppose that the first four values in a series were 5, 6, 6, and 7. In order to calculate a moving average you need to decide how many period should be include in each average. A typical method is to average the current value with the previous value and the following value. Table 4.2 below shows the values you would get with this method.

Table 4.2. Calculation of moving averages

Value	Moving Average
5	-
6	5.67
6	6.33
7	6.50

Of course, the decision to use a single value before and after as the average range is subjective. Based on your judgement about the nature of the data, you may choose to perform moving averaging with a variety of period lengths in order to find one that seems to fit the raw data best.

As an example, create moving average lines that use three different periods: 1 before/1 after, 3 before/1 after, and 5 before/2 after.

Return to the data entry screen by pressing:

2

Move the cursor to the column for series 2 by pressing:

[Tab] *(2 times)*

Harvard Graphics provides the function *@MAVG()* to calculate moving averages. The function can be used in two ways.

@MAVG(series)   In this form you are required to enter only the number of the series for which you want to calculate a moving average. Harvard Graphics automatically sets the period at 1 before and 1 after.

@MAVG(series,b,a)   In this form, **a** stands for the number of periods and **b** stands for the number of periods after. To calculate a moving average on series 1 for a period 5 before/2 after you would enter *@MAVG(#1,5,2)*.

Enter a formula for the current series that uses @MAVG() with the default periods:

[F4]
1-Year Avg [↵]
@MAVG(#1) [↵]

Place a formula for the 3 year moving average in the column for series 3:

[Tab]
[F4]
3-Year Avg [↵]
@MAVG(#1,3,1) [↵]

Repeat the process for the next series making it a 5 year moving average:

[Tab]
[F4]
3-Year Avg
[Del] [↵]
@MAVG(#1,5,2) [↵]

The moving average calculations produce trend lines that have curves as shown in figure 4.16. These curves follow to one degree or another the up and down pattern of the raw data. You can see that the 1-Year average line follows the movement of the raw data very closely. The 3-year line seems to be accurate because its last point matches the last point in the raw data series exactly. The flow of the 3-Year trend line seems to indicate that the first valley in the raw data was a cyclical low that was not indicative of a true decline. However, the dip that began in the last 70's was a true decline from which the industry has made only a partial recovery. The 5-Year line appears less accurate than the others.

Since the best estimate seems to be the 1-Year and 3-Year lines you might want to try moving averages with different combinations of 2 and 3 years periods.

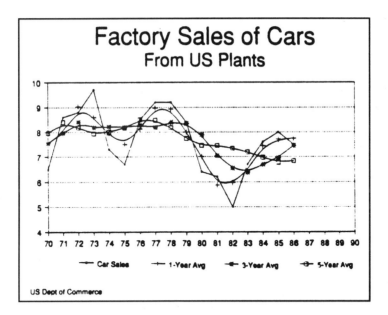

Figure 4.16. Moving averages produce trend lines.

Save this chart as TREND-03 by pressing:

[Esc] [F10] 4 2
trend-03 [⏎]
[Ctrl-Del]
Moving Averages [⏎]
[Esc]

SUMMARY

This chapter has dealt with the use of charts to analyze time series.

Time Series. A time series is a series of values related to a specific chronological sequence. Numeric series, used for scientific or engineering applications, can be used in a similar manner to time series. The main reason for charting time series is to find trends and patterns in the changes that occur in the data over time.

X Data Type. In order to facilitate the creation of time series Harvard Graphics will automatically generate chronological or numeric X axis sequences when supplied with the starting and ending values. By default, the series increases one unit at a time. You can enter an optional increment value to have the series increment differently. Harvard Graphics supports day, week, quarter, year, and time sequences.

Line Charts. Because time series charts are primarily focused on trends and patterns, a line chart display is more appropriate than a bar chart display. A standard line chart plots the values as points on the chart and connects the points with straight lines. In addition, there are trend and curve lines. Trend lines will automatically extend beyond the end of the time series of desired. Curve type lines will draw the closest curve to the points in the series. Curve lines may not pass through all of the point in the series. You can display points without lines to produce a scattergram.

Ribbon Charts. The visual impact of line charts is less than other types of chart because only a thin line connects the points. By combining the **3-D** and **Overlap** effects listed for bar charts with a line chart you can produce a line that looks like a wide ribbon.

Chapter 5

Specialized Charts

T his chapter covers the creation and use of specialized charts supported by Harvard Graphics. These charts are not as widely applicable as the text, pie, bar, and line charts discussed in the first four chapters. Each chart is closely associated with a special type of task, although you may find that you can use a specialty chart for other purposes.

The charts discussed in this chapter are Histograms, High/Low/Close/Open, Organizational, and Multiple.

Histograms
Histograms are usually associated with a form of statistical analysis called *frequency distribution*. These charts are used in statistical analysis for behavior sciences and other statistical based fields.

High/Low/Close/Open
These charts are used to analyze events that cannot be expressed as single numeric value. The events are actually a range of values that occur over a period of time. For example, the price of a stock during one day would be a range event; the high/low/close/open chart would label the data points for the low price, the high price, the opening price, and the closing price set in a day.

Organizational
This type of chart is a special form of text chart in which hierarchical relationships, such as the organization of a company, is expressed by connecting names enclosed in boxes with lines indicating which is in charge of other employees.

Multiple
A multiple-chart display allows you to split the screen in several sections and display a different chart in each section of the screen.

It is doubtful that you will need to create all of these special charts. However, you may want to study each chart in order to learn how complex ideas can be expressed as charts.

Begin by loading Harvard Graphics in the usual manner. The program should display the Main Menu in order to begin.

FREQUENCY DISTRIBUTIONS

With the exception of mathematical charts that generate data from the calculation of equation, the basis of all charts is raw data is drawn from historical records. Historical records can be as simple as a check register as complex as the price/earning ratio of common stocks. In any case, raw data is unorganized. The purpose of charts is to organize the data into a form that can be easily understood.

However, not all raw data is suitable for charting or direct analysis. For example the information stored in a check register would not make a meaningful chart in its raw form. The amounts of the checks would simply make a meaningless zigzag pattern. However, that data could be organized in a form which would make a meaningful chart display. One method of organizing such data is called a *frequency distribution*. This is a fancy name for a common sense method of organizing data. In a frequency distribution you divide the data into a series of categories called *bins*. One bin might contain all checks under $100, the second might contain checks over $100 but under $200, and so on. The number of checks in each of the bins is the frequency distribution.

Frequency distributions are usually displayed in a special type of bar chart called a *histogram*. A histogram is different from an ordinary bar chart in that the bars are displayed with no space between them, so that they form a continuous pattern. This creates a *step ladder* appearance that helps draw attention to the relative frequency of each group. The appearance reflects the fact that each bar represents a range of values that continue with the next bar.

Many events follow a pattern referred to as *normal*. A normal pattern assumes that most events will be closely grouped around a median value. Events of the same type that vary greatly from the median would be rare. A histogram of events that follows a statistically normal pattern would have a bell shape because most of the events would fall in the middle of the range, while few would fall at either extreme.

In a free market it is generally assumed that an item will eventually establish a median market price. One common use of histograms is to try to determine the average or median price of a commodity. For example, suppose you want to determine what the median cost for utilities is for a home in your area in order to know if you are using more or less utilities than your neighbors. Your research into 50 comparable homes turns up the following frequency distribution table:

Utility Bill	# of Homes
80+-100	5
100+-120	7
120+-140	9
140+-160	13
160+-180	9
180+-200	5
200+-220	3

To turn this information into a chart begin by creating a new bar chart. Press:

1 3

The X type data must be the **Name** type x series. Note that even through the names will be numbers such as (80, 100, and 120), you cannot use the **Number** option because it option creates a numeric scale starting at zero on the X axis. This scale is used to plot X-Y coordinate points on a grid. Since a histogram is a type of bar chart, only the **Name** option will yield the correct results. Press:

[↵] *(4 times)*

Fill in the tile for the chart by typing:

Utility Charges
[Tab] *(4 times)*

Enter the the following values down the X axis column:

80 [↵]
100 [↵]
120 [↵]
140 [↵]
160 [↵]
180 [↵]
200 [↵]
220

Fill in series 1 with the following values:

[⇑] *(7 times)*
[Tab]
5 [↵]
7 [↵]
9 [↵]
13 [↵]
9 [↵]
5 [↵]
3

To format the bar chart as a histogram you must select the **stepped** option from the **Bar style** option. Press:

[F8] [Pg Dn]
[⇒] *(4 times)*
[Spacebar]

Display the histogram by pressing:

[F2]

Harvard Graphics displays the bars as a solid block of values with a stepped appearance at the top of the bars. The chart shows that the median bill for utilities falls in the 140 to 160 range. The height of the steps also seems to indicate that variation from that median tends to be more on the lower side than the upper side. This could be interpreted to mean that homes with bills greater than $160 have an unusual characteristic such as poor energy conservation or special energy consuming equipment.

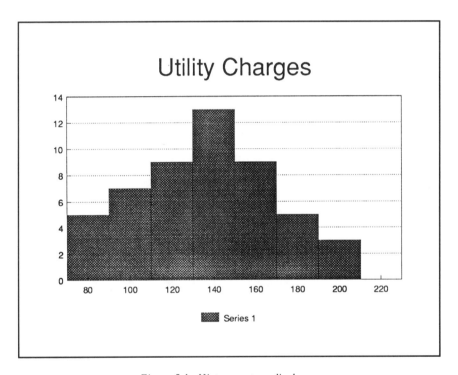

Figure 5.1. Histogram type display

Return to the options screen by pressing:

[Esc]

PERCENTAGE HISTOGRAMS

The distribution of values within a histogram can be expressed a bit more clearly by charting the percentage that each category represents of the total survey instead of charting the raw number of items in each category. This can be done quite simply by dividing each value in the series by the total number of homes surveyed and multiplying by 100. You can make this calculation in Harvard Graphics by creating a calculated series. Return to the data entry screen by pressing:

[F8]

Position the cursor in the series 2 column:

[Tab]

Enter a calculation that will create the percentages:

[F4]
Percent [Del] [↵]
#1/50*100 [↵]

Use the options screen to suppress the display of the values in series 1:

[F8] [Pg Up]
[Tab] *(9 times)*
n

Display the chart by pressing:

[F2]

Note that the basic shape of the histogram is unchanged. All that has been altered is the Y axis scale; it now is scaled in percentages rather than raw numbers. This is the most common way to present histogram information.

Save this chart as HISTOGRAM by pressing:

[Esc] [F10] 4 2
HISTOGRAM [↵]
[↵]
[Esc]

HIGH/LOW/CLOSE/OPEN CHARTS

The High/Low/Close/Open charts (referred to in this text as simply high-low charts) are a specialized form of chart usually associated with the trading of stock, bonds, or commodities. However, high-low charts can also be used in science and other technical fields.

The prime distinction between other charts and high-low charts is that each data point in a high-low chart actually consists or two or more values. This is because high-low charts are designed to express a ranges of values instead of a single summary value. This can tell a much different story. For example, both San Francisco and Boston have similar average temperatures in the spring, as shown in figure 5.2.

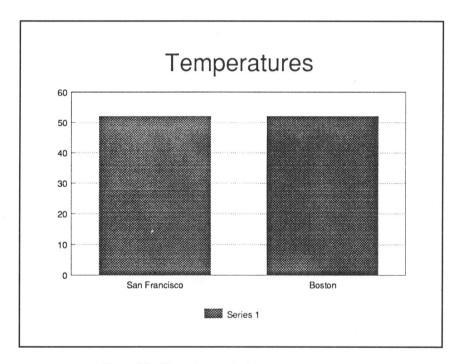

Figure 5.2. Chart shows only the average temperature

However, the average temperature San Francisco is arrived at by a high of 54 and a low of 50, while the average temperature in Boston is arrived at with a high of 60 and a low of 44. Figure 5.3 shows this on a high-low bar chart. The top of the bar shows the high value for the item; the bottom of the bar shows the low value. The result are bars that reflect the range of values in each category rather than a single value, such as the average.

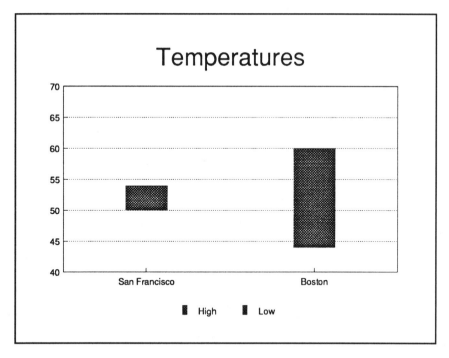

Figure 5.3. High-low format shows the range of temperatures

A high-low chart can also include markers that indicate the opening or staring value in the range and the closing value in the range in cases where they would different from the high and low values. This type of chart is usually associated with the securities markets but it can be used for other types of analysis as well.

As an example of how to use a high-low chart, imagine the LaFish boutique, a small business that is open 7 days a week. The boutique's proprietor, Walter LaFish, is used keeps daily totals that he wants to summarize once a week. A high-low chart will help him do this. The chart will contain four values for each week: sales for Monday and Sunday (the open and close of the period) and the high and low sales days during the period.

Create a new high-low type chart by typing:

1 5
n [↵]

Create an X axis series of four weeks by pressing:

w [↵]
1 [↵]
4 [↵]
[↵]

The data entry menu is the same for a high-low chart as it is for a bar or line chart with the exception that in a high-low chart, the first four data series are preset as high, low, close, and open. Type in the title for the chart:

LaFish Weekly Sales [↵]
[↵] *(2 times)*
[Tab]

Enter the values for the first week:

5.7 [Tab]
3.0 [Tab]
5.0 [Tab]
3.3 [Tab]
[Tab]

Repeat the process for the next three weeks:

6.8 [Tab]
3.8 [Tab]
3.9 [Tab]
3.9 [Tab]
[Tab]

7.2 [Tab]
3.2 [Tab]
5.1 [Tab]
7.2 [Tab]
[Tab]

6.2 [Tab]
3.1 [Tab]
5.4 [Tab]
3.1

Figure 5.4 shows the data entered into the high-low chart.

Pt	X Axis Week	High	Low	Close	Open
1	1	5.7	3.0	5.0	3.3
2	2	6.8	3.8	3.9	3.9
3	3	7.2	3.2	5.1	7.2
4	4	6.2	3.1	5.4	3.1

Figure 5.4. Data entered into high-low chart

Display the chart by pressing:

[F2]

The program displays the default high-low chart layout (figure 5.5). The vertical bars show the range of values for the week. The closing day sales are marked by a tick mark just to the right of the bar. The opening day sales are shown by a tick mark to the left of the bar.

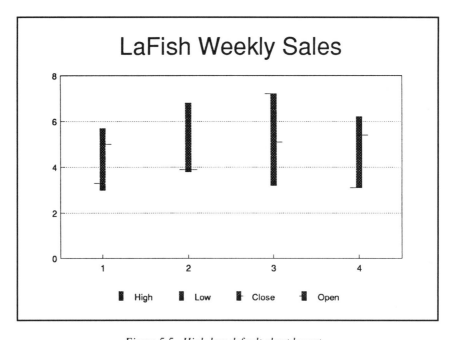

Figure 5.5. High-low default chart layout

Return to the data entry screen by pressing:

[Esc]

High-Low Adjustments

There are two adjustments you might want to make to the basic high-low chart. First, you can use the **Bar width** option to widen the bars displayed for each range. Second, you can use the Y scale options to narrow the focus of the chart to the range of values present in the data series.

Display the options menu by pressing:

[F8]

Note that the chart type column shows types (high, low, close, and open) that do not appear on the option list. These are created automatically when you select the high-low chart from the **Create Chart** menu. You cannot change the type of these series on the options menu nor can you define additional series to those types. Move to the next option screen by pressing:

[Pg Dn]

The **Bar width** setting is blank by default. You can set the width of the range bars by entering a value between 1 and 100. In this case enter a value of 35.

[↵] *(3 times)*
35

Move to the next options screen:

[Pg Dn]

Since the values in all of the data series range between 3 and 7.5 you can narrow the focus of the chart by setting the Y axis range to those values. Press:

[Tab] *(10 times)*
[⇓] *(2 times)*
3 [↵]
7.5

Display the chart by pressing:

[F2]

The modified chart is easier to read because the elements are larger in proportion to the chart frame (figure 5.6).

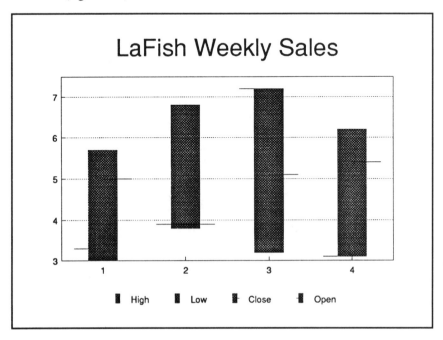

Figure 5.6. Modified high-low chart

Save the chart as HIGHLOW by pressing:

[Esc] [F10] 4 2
highlow [↵]
[↵]
[Esc]

High-Low Styles

There are two options that appear on the High-Low options menus that do not appear on other bar/line chart options menus. They are listed on the item called **High/low**

style found on the second page of the high-low chart options. The options are **Error bar** and **Area.**

The **Error bar** causes the range bar to be displayed as a thin vertical line with horizontal lines drawn at the top and bottom of the vertical line, as shown in figure 5.7.

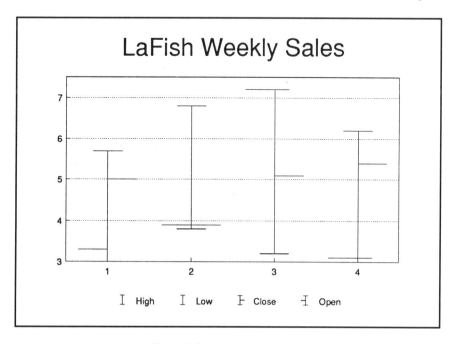

Figure 5.7. Error bar display

This type of display is used in statistical or scientific charting to show statistically calculated values. The high-low format allows the charting of a range of values that represent a margin-of-error factor. For example, suppose that you have a value of 5 with an error factor of + or - .75. You would enter 5.75 as the high value, 4.25 as the low value and use either the open or the close value to hold the actual statistical outcome, 5.

The other display option is **area.** In an area high-low chart only the high and low values are used. The open and close values are ignored. All of the high and low values are connected and the area they enclose filled in to make the high-low area chart, as shown in figure 5.8. The purpose of this chart is to display a field into which the values from the time series fall.

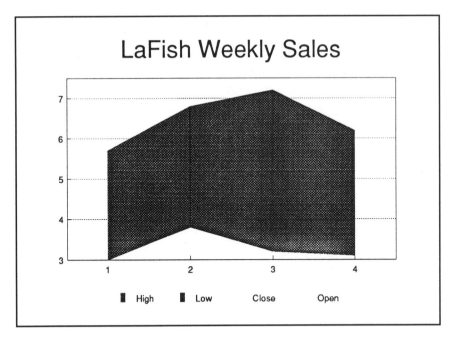

Figure 5.8. High-low area chart

ORGANIZATIONAL CHARTS

Organizational charts are a special form of text chart designed to indicate hierarchical relationships When an organizational chart is used to describe ideas or concepts it is often called a *flow* chart.

Organizational charts are different than normal text charts in that they are created in a series of steps rather than a single data entry screen organized in consecutive pages. Organization charts have the following three basic items.

Managers   A manager is a person in the hierarchy that has some degree of control or responsibility over other individuals in the organization. If the chart is used to organize ideas rather than people the manager would be an idea that encompasses other ideas. Managers are represented as a box with lines that flow to all immediate subordinates.

Subordinates   Subordinates are people who controlled by or responsible to a particular manager. If the chart shows ideas rather than people subordinates are ideas that are subordinate to a main idea. Like managers, subordinates are represented by a box with lines that connect the subordinate to their managers.

Details   Details are a special form of subordinate. Unlike a full subordinate, details are not enclosed in boxes. Instead that are listed in a vertical column below the manager to whom they are responsible. Details can appear only on the lowest level of the organization chart. Because details are not boxed you can fit more details into the same amount of space than you can subordinates.

Organization charts are *inverted tree* structured charts. The structure is called *inverted* because, unlike a real tree, the main trunk is at the top and the branches flow downward. The "trunk" of the organization tree is the top level manager. All of the other subordinates and details branch out from the main manager trunk. A subordinate may in turn have subordinates of their own.

Organization charts, despite their simple appearance, are among the most complex to design because of their tree type structure. In most of the menus used by Harvard Graphics the screens are divided into *data entry* and *options* screens. However, in organization charts, the *data entry* screen is divided into **levels.** The [Ctrl-Pg Dn] and [Ctrl-Pg Up] keys will change the level of the data entry screens down or up one level in the chart.

Creating an Organizational Chart

Create a new organizational chart by pressing:

1 6

The program displays the data entry screen for organization charts, as shown in figure 5.9.

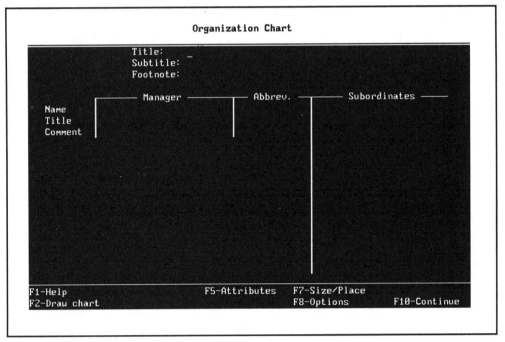

Figure 5.9. Data entry screen for organization charts

The screen is organized a bit differently than other chart screens. At the top are the standard title, subtitle, and footnote lines. However, below those lines the screen is divided into the following three columns:

Manager   The manager column is used for entering the text that will appear within the box for this level of the organization chart. The column allows you to enter text in three categories: name, title, and comments. You can enter up to 22 characters on each of these lines.

Abbrev.   Abbreviations, limited to 11 characters, are used to enter shorter forms of name, title and comments you entered in the **Manager** column. The abbreviations are an alterative way to display the information in the boxes. When there are a large number of subordinates, changing the display from **Manager** to **Abbrev.** will condense the width of each subordinate box. Note that if you know you will be making a complicated chart, entering the minimum amount of text in the **Manager** column will also decrease box size.

Subordinates This column will contain the list of subordinates for the current manager. Each entry in this column can be expended to become a full manager with its own list of subordinates. Harvard Graphics allows up to eight levels of subordinates with a total of 80 names. Keep in mind that complex charts with many levels and subordinates can be difficult to read since the items get crowded into a limited chart frame. Using all eight levels and 80 names will not make a useable chart in most cases.

Create a simple organization chart showing the hierarchical Dewey Decimal system, used by many libraries to organize books by topics. Enter the title for this chart.

Library Classification
[⏎] *(3 times)*

The cursor is now in the **Manager** column. The first manager is the top idea or person to whom all of the other ideas or people are subordinate. In this case the overall manager is the Dewey Decimal System. Enter:

Dewey Decimal System [⏎]
Amherst College 1873 [⏎]
[⏎]

The cursor moves to the **Subordinates** column. In this case you do not need to bother with abbreviations. Since the top level of the organization chart is always on a level by itself, abbreviations are not be needed. Abbreviations are useful on the subordinate levels, where there are more than one manager box on a line.

In the **Subordinates** column you will enter the names of the subordinate classes of books. In this case you will condense the actual Dewey Decimal system (which is normally broken into 10 major divisions) into 6. Enter::

Reference [⏎]
Philosophy [⏎]
Religion [⏎]
Science [⏎]
Art [⏎]
History

The data entry screen for the second level of the organization chart should look like figure 5.10.

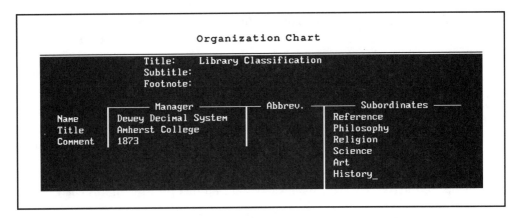

Figure 5.10. Data entered for organization chart

Display the chart as it would appear based on the data entered so far. Press:

[F2]

The chart, shown in figure 5.11, shows the top level manager information enclosed in a box. However, the subordinates, because they are the *lowest* level on the chart, are displayed as *details*.

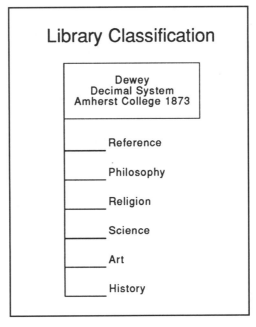

Figure 5.11. Organization chart with a manager and subordinates

Return to the data entry screen by pressing:

[Esc]

Adding Subordinate Levels

You can move to the data entry screen for a subordinate level by positioning the cursor on the subordinate name you want to expand and entering [Ctrl-Pg Dn]. For example, suppose that you wanted to expand the *Reference* topic. Move the cursor to the name of the item by pressing:

[⇑] *(5 times)*

Move to the next level of the chart by pressing:

[Ctrl-Pg Dn]

The program displays a new screen that has the same layout as the main manager screen. Harvard Graphics automatically places the name of the subordinate you had selected, in this case *Reference,* into the manager column, as shown in figure 5.12. The cursor is then positioned in the subordinates column so that you can enter the list of subordinates to this manager.

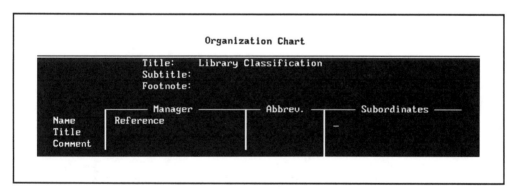

Figure 5.12. Subordinate manager screen

Enter the subordinate topics under *Reference*.

Encycl. [↵]
Periodicals

Display the chart with the new level added:

[F2]

The chart has been changed considerably by the addition of a new level, as shown in figure 5.13. First, all of the subordinates of the main manager level are no longer displayed as details, but are displayed as boxes. The entries under reference, which are now the lowest level on the chart, are displayed as details without boxes.

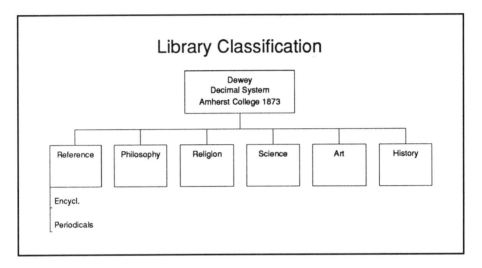

Figure 5.13. Organization chart with multiple levels

Return to the text entry screen by pressing:

[Esc]

Note that when you return to the data-entry screen the reference screen is displayed because it was the level you were working on before you displayed the chart.

If you want to add subordinates to the other topics on the same level you can move through the topics one at a time with the [Pg Up] and [Pg Dn] keys. Move to the data entry screen for *Science* by pressing:

[Pg Dn] *(3 times)*

Create four subordinate topics for science by entering:

Sociology [↵]
Philology [↵]
Physical [↵]
Applied

Deepen the chart by adding a fourth level by creating subordinate for the *Physical* science category. Press:

[⇑]
[Ctrl-Pg Dn]
Physics [↵]
Chemistry [↵]
Biology

Display the chart with all of the current levels:

[F2]

The chart, as shown in figure 5.14, now have four levels of information. You can see that adding the latest level has dramatically reduced the size of the items on the chart. You make take this into consideration when you add new levels.

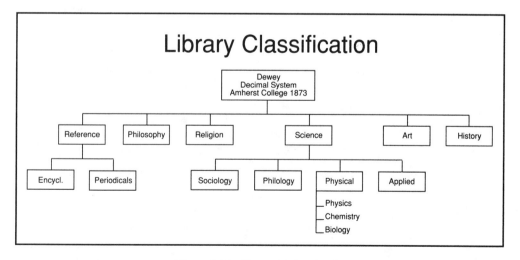

Figure 5.14. Chart with four levels

Return to the data entry screen by pressing:

[Esc]

Suppressing Levels

After viewing a chart you may decide that the addition of a new level reduces the size of the items in the chart too drastically. To solve this problem you could simply delete the subordinate topics from the manager screen. However, if you change you mind again you will have to re-enter that data. An alternative is provided on the organization chart's options menu. On the options menu you can select the number of data levels to be displayed; however, the data is still stored in memory in case you decide to use the chart will all levels.

To change the number of levels displayed on the Dewey Decimal System charts, first display the options menu by pressing:

[F8]

The options menu, shown in figure 5.15, is divided into two sections. The top section contains options that effect each manager defined on the chart. The bottom section that controls the display of the lowest level on the chart. Note that on organization charts the function of the [F5] attributes command is limited to the frame text (title, subtitle, and footnote).

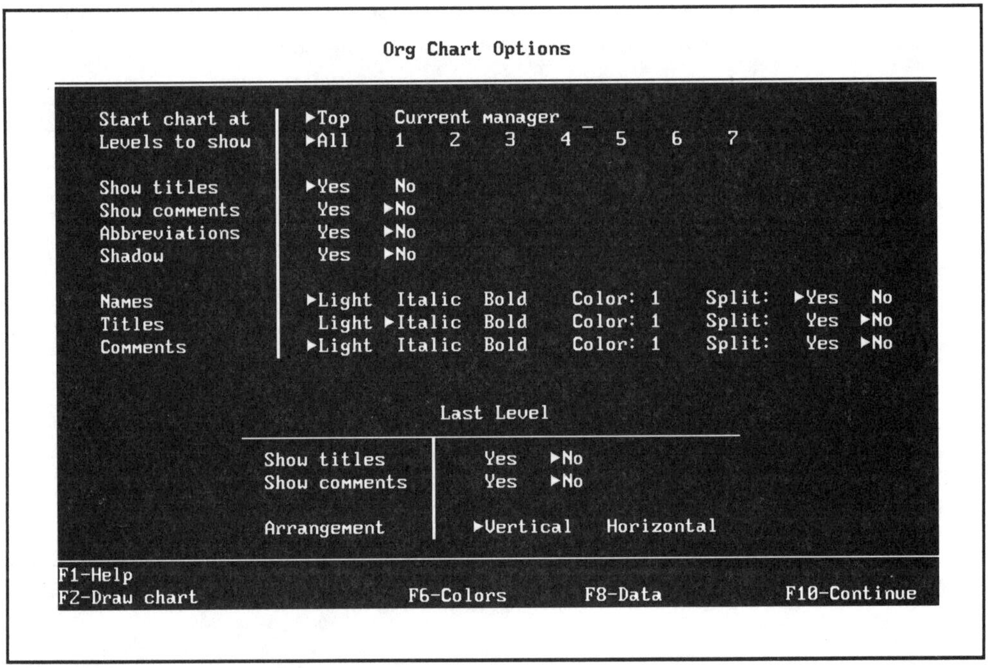

```
                          Org Chart Options

   Start chart at    │ ▶Top    Current manager _
   Levels to show    │ ▶All    1    2    3    4    5    6    7

   Show titles       │ ▶Yes    No
   Show comments     │  Yes   ▶No
   Abbreviations     │  Yes   ▶No
   Shadow            │  Yes   ▶No

   Names             │ ▶Light  Italic  Bold   Color: 1   Split: ▶Yes   No
   Titles            │  Light ▶Italic  Bold   Color: 1   Split:  Yes  ▶No
   Comments          │ ▶Light  Italic  Bold   Color: 1   Split:  Yes  ▶No


                              Last Level

        Show titles        │    Yes   ▶No
        Show comments      │    Yes   ▶No

        Arrangement        │   ▶Vertical   Horizontal

F1-Help
F2-Draw chart              F6-Colors        F8-Data         F10-Continue
```

Figure 5.15. Organization chart options menu

The attributes of the text within the organizational chart are controlled from the options menu under the categories of Names, Titles, and Comments. An attribute, exclusive to organizational charts, **Light,** will also appear on this menu. **Light** prints text with thinner lines than it would normally.

The first two options control what sections of the defined chart are actually displayed. The **Start chart at** option allows you to display the chart as if the current manager was the top level. This option is useful when you have a complicated chart and you want to display it in sections. The second option controls the overall depth of the chart. The default setting **All** displays all of the defined data levels. You can suppress levels by selecting a specific level number for display. In this case, limit the display to 3 levels by pressing:

[⇓]
3

Another option that effects all levels is the **Shadow** option. **This option** draws a drop shadow around each box in the organization chart, giving them a 3-D type of effect. Turn on the **Shadow** option by pressing:

[⇓] *(4 times)*
y

Last Level Options

The bottom section of the options screen effect the last level of the organization chart. By default the last level will show only the **Names** and not the titles or comments. The last option is **Arrangement** which affects the way the last level is displayed. The default of this option is **Vertical.** It produces a vertical list of subordinates on the last level. You can change the last level so that it will also display items enclosed in boxes by selecting the **Horizontal** option. Press:

[End]
h

Display the chart by pressing:

[F2]

The chart will look like figure 5.16. Note that only the first three levels of the chart are displayed.

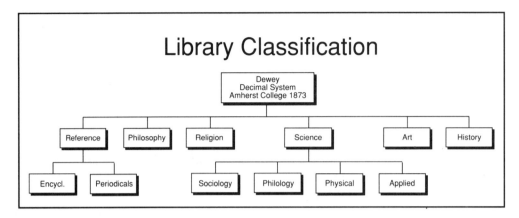

Figure 5.16. Three level chart with shadow boxes

Save the chart as ORGANIZ by pressing:

[Esc] [F10] 4 2

organiz [↵]

[↵]

[Esc]

MULTIPLE CHARTS

Up to this point you have displayed only the current chart. However, Harvard Graphics also allows you to create displays that combine two or more charts. These are called **Multiple Chart** and are created using option 7 from the Create New Chart menu.

Multiple Charts display a split-screen of existing charts. When you select a **Multiple Charts** you select charts stored on the disks for display. You can create a new pie, bar, line or text chart while you are creating a multiple chart.

Begin the process of creating a multiple chart by pressing:

1 7

The selection of **Multiple Charts** displays the Multiple Charts Style menu, as shown in figure 5.17.

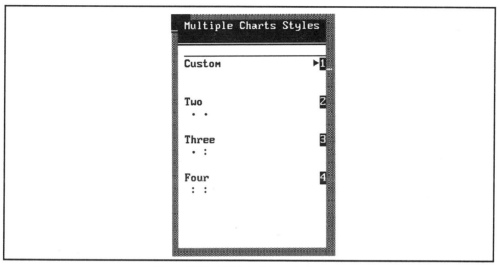

Figure 5.17. Multiple Charts Style menu

This menu consists of five options that refer to the number of charts to be placed on the screen and the style in which they are to appear.

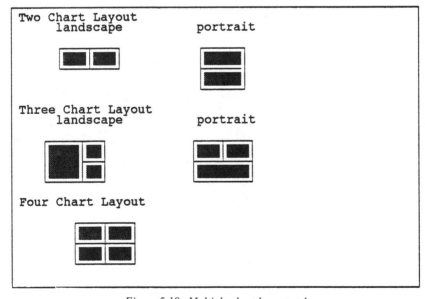

Figure 5.18. Multiple chart layout styles

The **custom** option lets you select between 1 and 6 charts and place then on the page in any way that you desire.

In this case, choose a two chart layout. Press:

2

The program displays the **Edit Multiple Charts** screen, shown in figure 5.19. This screen is not organized like a data-entry screen because you cannot enter data or chart options. All you can do is select charts from those already stored on the disk for placement in position 1 or position 2 of the chart. Note that all of the charts use in a multiple chart display must be stored in the same DOS directory.

The top part of the screen lists a partial directory of the charts stored in the current directory. The bottom section shows the chart you have selected for inclusion in the multiple-chart display. If there are more than 8 charts in the directory, the display will scroll up and down as you move the highlight.

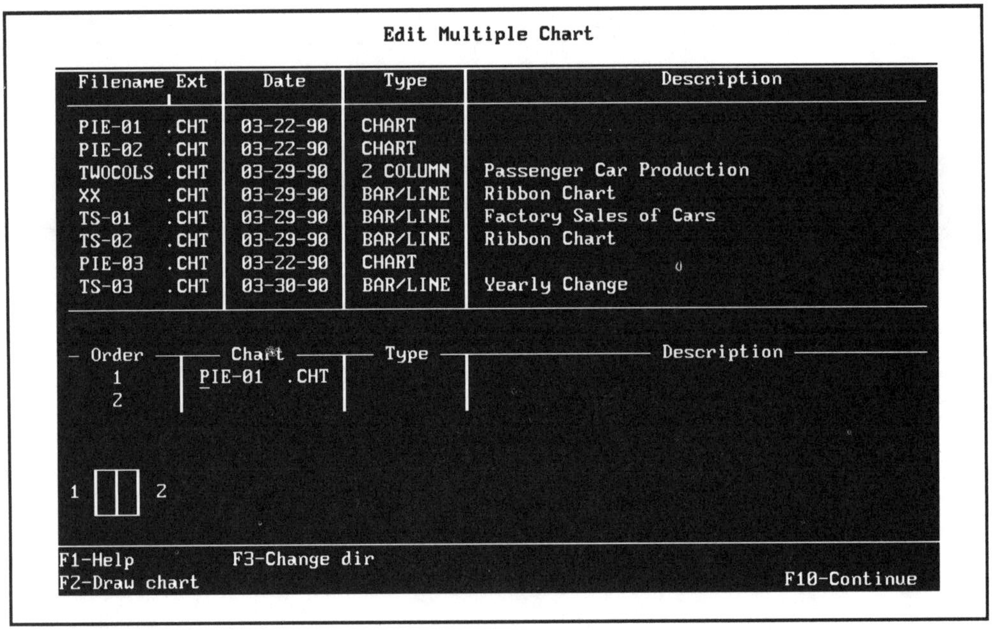

```
                         Edit Multiple Chart

   ┌──────────────┬──────────┬──────────┬───────────────────────────┐
   │ Filename Ext │   Date   │   Type   │       Description         │
   ├──────────────┼──────────┼──────────┼───────────────────────────┤
   │ PIE-01  .CHT │ 03-22-90 │ CHART    │                           │
   │ PIE-02  .CHT │ 03-22-90 │ CHART    │                           │
   │ TWOCOLS .CHT │ 03-29-90 │ 2 COLUMN │ Passenger Car Production  │
   │ XX      .CHT │ 03-29-90 │ BAR/LINE │ Ribbon Chart              │
   │ TS-01   .CHT │ 03-29-90 │ BAR/LINE │ Factory Sales of Cars     │
   │ TS-02   .CHT │ 03-29-90 │ BAR/LINE │ Ribbon Chart              │
   │ PIE-03  .CHT │ 03-22-90 │ CHART    │                           │
   │ TS-03   .CHT │ 03-30-90 │ BAR/LINE │ Yearly Change             │
   └──────────────┴──────────┴──────────┴───────────────────────────┘

   ─ Order ──────┬── Chart ──────┬── Type ──────┬──── Description ────
        1        │ PIE-01  .CHT  │              │
        2        │               │              │


        ┌──┬──┐
      1 │  │  │ 2
        └──┴──┘

   F1-Help         F3-Change dir
   F2-Draw chart                                          F10-Continue
```

Figure 5.19. Select charts for multiple chart display

You can select a chart by using the [⇑] and [⇓] keys to move the highlight in the directory display. Pressing [↵] inserts the highlighted name in the bottom section of the screen. You can also enter the name of the chart manually.

188

In this case, select two charts that were created in this chapter. Press:

HISTOGRAM [↵]
highlow [↵]

The charts shown in figure 5.20 are shown in figure 5.20.

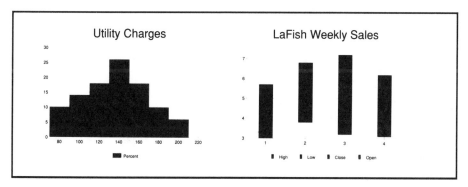

Figure 5.20 Multiple chart with 2 charts

Save the multiple chart by pressing:

[Esc] [F10] 4 2
multi-2 [↵]
[↵]
[Esc]

Custom Layouts

The custom layout option allows you to create a multiple chart display of you own design. Create a custom chart by pressing:

1 7 1

Harvard Graphics asks if you want to keep the current data. In this case that question refers to the selection of the two charts used in the MULTI-2 chart. Keep those charts as part of the new layout by pressing:

[↵]

The custom layout screen is the same as the two layout screen except that the bottom of the screen has room for 6 chart names. The first two names are filled in with the charts selected for the previous chart. Add one more chart to the list by pressing:

[⇓] *(2 times)*
organiz [⏎]

The new chart is added to the list.

Size and Place

When you select a custom layout, Harvard Graphics displays the command **[F7] Size/Place** at the bottom of the screen. However, when working with **Multiple Charts,** the meaning of this command is a bit different then with other charts. In most charts the **Size/Place** command refers to the size of printed text and its alignment. On a multiple chart this command refers to the placement and size of the individual charts within the frame. Press:

[F7]

The size and place display for multiple charts, shown in figure 5.21, shows the selected charts placed within the larger frame of the multiple chart. The charts are sized to 1/6 of the overall frame and placed across the bottom of the screen leaving room for three more charts. A menu on the left side of the screen lists the charts currently displayed so that you can select the chart or charts you want to size or place.

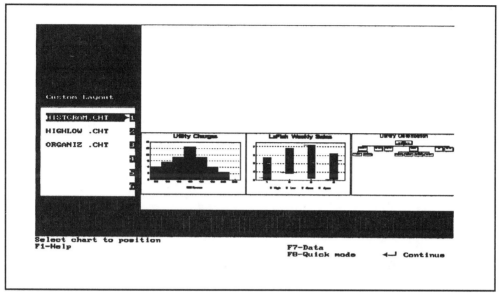

Figure 5.21. Size and place display for multiple charts

You can speed up the process of placing or sizing charts by suppressing the display of the details within each chart. The details slow down your computer because they have to be drawn each time any part of the layout is changed. Press:

[F8]

The charts are changed to boxes that contain the names of the charts. This is called the *quick data* mode.

Changing the Layout

Suppose that you want to change the layout of the HIGHLOW chart. First, select that chart from the menu on the left side of the screen by pressing:

[⇓] [↵]

When you make the selection a cross-bar cursor appears in the center of the screen, as shown in figure 5.22. this is known as the drawing mode. The cursor is used to draw a frame of the size and location you want for chart. There are thee ways to size and place the chart.

Arrow Keys You can use the arrow keys to move the cross-bar up, down, left, or right in the frame.

Mouse If you have a mouse attached to your computer the cross-bar will respond to movement of the mouse in the direction in which you move the mouse. You will learn more about the mouse in chapter 6.

XY You can use the [F3] command to enter a position in the frame using XY coordinates. The lower-left corner of the frame is designated as position 1,1. The frame width is 26,154 dots wide and 20,000 dots in height. You will learn more about these coordinate in chapter 6.

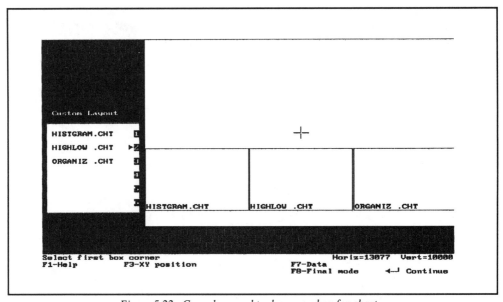

Figure 5.22. Cross bar used to draw new box for chart

In this instance use the XY entry method to position the cross-bar. This is probably not the method you would use on your own, but it is the most accurate way to tell you the exact method with which to write location to place your cursor. Press:

[F3]
[Ctrl-Del] 1000 [↵]
19000 [↵]

This places the cursor near the upper-left corner of the frame. Anchor the chart at that location by pressing:

[↵]

The frame for the HIGHLOW chart is now set. You can draw the frame by using the mouse, the arrow keys, or XY location to set the lower-left corner of the chart frame. Press:

[⇒] *(3 times)*
[⇓] *(3 times)*

The cursor movements draw a small square. If you were to press [ø] at this point the chart would be displayed in that tiny square. You can continue to change the size and shape of the chart frame until you are satisfied. Note that Harvard Graphics allows you to draw one chart over another. If you do not want the charts to overlap you must be careful not to place two chart frames on the same location. Complete the chart by using the XY coordinate entry method. Press:

[F3]
25000 [↵]
[Ctrl-Del]
9000 [↵]

The frame is drawn across the top of the multiple chart frame. Fix the location by pressing:

[↵]

Harvard Graphics uses the frame you have drawn to place the HIGHLOW chart within the multiple chart frame, as shown in figure 5.23. Note that Harvard Graphics does not draw the chart to the exact size frame that you drew. That is because the program maintains the *aspect ratio* of the original chart. The *aspect ratio* refers to the proportions of width to height used to create the original chart. If the program drew the chart to the exact size of your frame the chart would be distorted because the frame did not match the original aspect ration. The arrangement of the charts is the program's best fit for the specified layout.

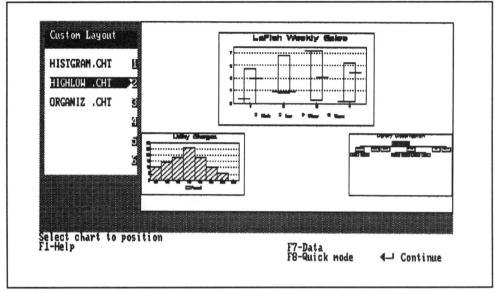

Figure 5.23. Charts rearranged on custom multiple chart

You will learn more about Harvard Graphics drawing mode in chapter 6. Display the chart shown in figure 5.24 by pressing:

[Esc]
[F2]

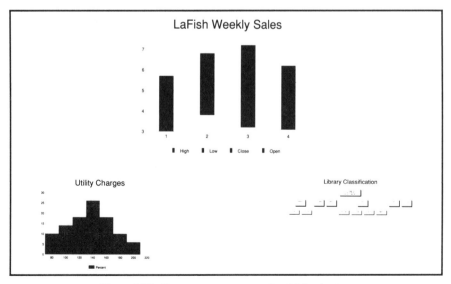

Figure 5.24. Custom arrangement of multiple charts

The chart shows the selected charts in the positions indicated by the frame you arranged within the multiple chart frame.

Save this custom chart by pressing:

[Esc]
4 2
custom [↵]
[↵]
[Esc]

SUMMARY

This chapter covered the creation of four special type of charts.

Histogram. A histogram is a special form of bar chart. Histograms are use to display the data generated by a frequency distribution analysis in which values are grouped together into value bins. The histogram is usually displayed as a stepped bar chart. The stepped chart leaves no open space between the bars.

High-Low. A high-low chart is used to display data points that are not individual values but ranges of values. The high-low chart displays a vertical bar that indicates a range of values from the top to the bottom of the bar. You can also include tick marks to show the opening and closing values in the range. This type of chart is typically used to show changes in the price of securities or in scientific applications to show variations in ranges such as temperatures.

Organization. An organization chart is a special form of text chart which is organized into levels. The chart is used to show hierarchical relationships such as those within a company. The chart can also be used to show the relationship between ideas and concepts such as system of organization in social and physical science.

Multiple. These charts combine existing charts so that more than one chart can appear at a time.

Chapter **6**

Drawing and Annotating

When you work with pie, bar, line, or other charts, the actual creation of the graphics is indirect; you do not actually use commands to draw the lines, bars, slices or other parts of the chart. Instead, you enter raw data into a data-entry screen and select options from menus. The Harvard Graphics program then uses that data and the menu selections to create a chart that corresponds to the selection.

However, you can manually manipulate elements on the chart by *drawing*. Drawing refers to direct manipulation of the physical elements that make up a chart, such as lines, boxes, text, or other shapes that appear within the chart frame. Each of these items is called an *object*. In the drawing mode you have direct control over the size, shape, location, and attributes of each object that you place on the chart.

197

You can use the drawing features to add special graphics objects to existing charts. For example, you can add a special items such a pointing arrows to draw attention to certain features of the chart. In figure 6.1, the text *Oil Embargo* with a pointing arrow is added to the chart to indicate where the effect of that event is located on the chart.

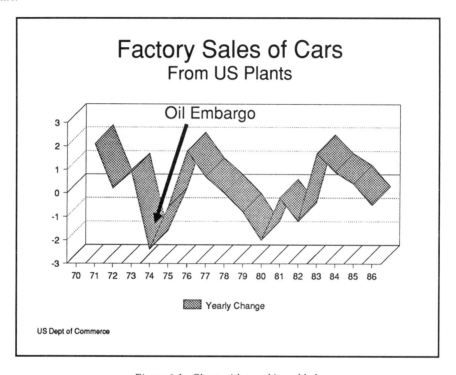

Figure 6.1. Chart with graphics added

You can make drawings using the special drawing features built into Harvard Graphics or you can make drawings from scratch.

From Scratch You can use the drawing features to create a drawing with text, lines, boxes, circles, and polygons. Figure 6.2 shows a logo for the LaFish company created in Harvard Graphics.

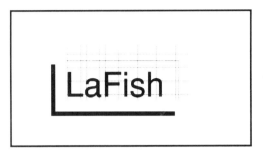

Figure 6.2. Drawing created from scratch

With Symbols In order to help the nonartistic user with their drawings, Harvard Graphics supplies a library of several hundred *symbols*, pictures created with the drawing tools. You can combine several of the symbols and copy them into your drawing to create a finished drawing. Figure 6.3 shows a drawing that uses two symbols, a microscope and a medical symbol, to create a logo for the LaFish company.

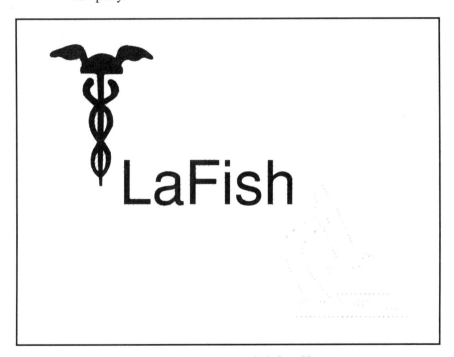

Figure 6.3. Drawing using symbols from library

In this chapter you will look at the use of the drawing features to annotate a standard chart and create a drawing from scratch, with the help of the symbols library supplied with Harvard Graphics.

The drawing mode is activated when you select option 3, the **Draw/Annotate** command, from the main program menu. This mode can be used to modify an existing chart or begin a drawing from scratch.

Begin this chapter by loading the Harvard Graphics program in the usual manner. You should have the main program menu displayed.

ANNOTATING A CHART

The easiest and most common way to use the Harvard Graphics' drawing tools is to annotate an existing chart. Begin by creating a bar chart that shows the *median* income for the average American family. Press:

> **1 3**

Define the X axis as the years 1960 through 1990 in increments of 10 years. Press:

> **y** [↵]
> **1960** [↵]
> **1990** [↵]
> **10** [↵]

Enter the title for the chart and the source as a footnote:

> **Median Family Income** [↵]
> [↵]
> **US Dept of Labor** [↵]

Enter the following values in series 1:

> **[Tab]**
> **5620** [↵]
> **9867** [↵]
> **21023** [↵]
> **31000**

Display the chart as it current exists by pressing:

[F2]

The program displays a basic bar chart (figure 6.4) based on the data entered into the data-entry screen. This is an example of *indirect* drawing since you did not actually draw the lines and boxes that make up the chart.

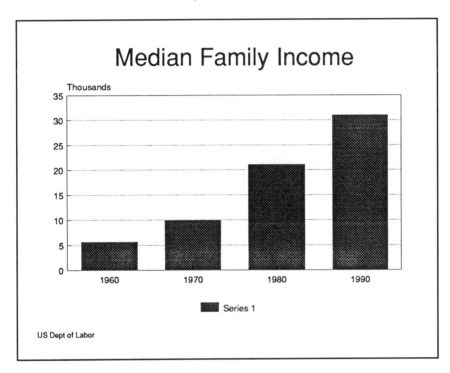

Figure 6.4. Basic bar chart

Because this is the basic chart from which you will create your annotated chart, save a copy of this chart before you begin to make annotations. This allows you to start over again quickly should you maske a mistake. Press:

[Esc] [F10] 4 2
annote-1 [↵]
[↵]
[Esc]

The Drawing Mode

The current chart is pretty straightforward in showing a rise in the median income each decade since 1960. However, you might want to add items to the chart that elaborate certain items. For example, the figures for 1990 are different from those of the previous years in that they are projected estimates rather than actual figures. You can use the drawing mode to add a informational note to the chart that indicates this.

To enter the *drawing* mode, select option 3 (**Draw/Annotate**) from the Main Menu by pressing:

3

When you make this selection the screen display changes drastically. In computer terms you have changed from a *text* mode to a *graphics* mode. Most of the entry and options screens in Harvard Graphics are in the text mode which can display only a standard set of 255 ASCII characters (letters, numbers, and special symbols). Note that in the text mode all of the characters always appear the same size. The advantage of the text mode is that since it is limited to the display of 255 standard characters, it operates very quickly.

In the *graphics* mode is the computer "paints" the screen dot by dot. The advantage of this mode is that the display is not limited to an predefined set of characters; it can show a wide variety of shapes and patterns, different sizes of text, and a number of text attributes, such as italics. Harvard Graphics uses the graphics mode to display the charts when you press [F2]. The disadvantage of the graphics display is that it takes the computer longer to make changes to the display; therefore, Harvard Graphics uses the graphics display mode only when it is necessary for the selected task. (In chapter 5 you encountered the graphics mode when you created the custom layout for multiple charts.)

The drawing mode, shown in figure 6.5, is a graphics mode. In this mode the current chart is shown in its final form in the right side of the screen. To the left of the chart is a menu of options under the title **Draw.** At the bottom of the screen are the function key commands available. In this case, the [F2] key redraws the chart section of the display so that it fills the full screen.

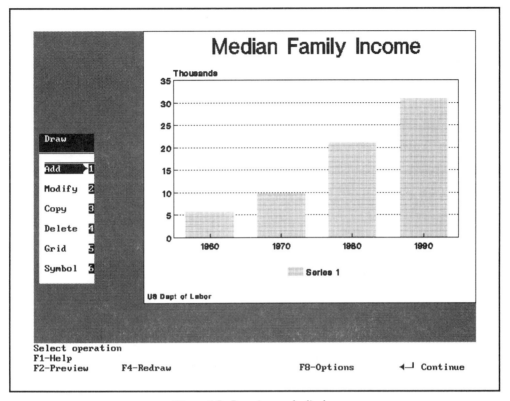

Figure 6.5. Drawing mode display

The Draw Menu

The **Draw** menu, shown on the left side of the draw mode display, lists six commands that can be executed in the draw mode.

Add   Adds a new object, line, box, circle, or text to the current chart or drawing.

Modify   Alters an object currently on the chart.

Copy   Duplicates an object drawn on the chart. This option is useful in drawings since often the same object is used in different places on the same chart. You may find that it is often easier to copy an object and then make modifications with the **Modify** option than to redraw it from scratch.

203

Delete   Deletes an object from the chart.

Grid   Although you cannot see it, Harvard Graphics divides the screen into a grid pattern. The grid pattern can be used to help you draw objects of uniform size and shape by setting the grid size to that you can move only in specific increments of space. If you do not use the grid you can draw in a free form.

Symbol   Accesses for you to the symbol library. You can also use this library to create symbols from your own drawings which can become your own custom-designed symbol library.

Adding an Object

Select the **Add** function to add items to the chart that elaborate on some aspect of the information currently displayed by pressing:

1

The **Add** option displays a second menu that list the types of items that can be added, shown in figure 6.6.

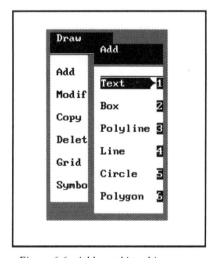

Figure 6.6. Add graphics object menu

Text   Places text at any location on the chart. The text can only be added one line at a time and is always in the same font as the rest of the chart. You can set the size and attributes for each line you add.

Box   Draws rectangles and squares. The boxes can be solid or outlines.

Polyline   Draws curved lines by selecting a series of points along the curve.

Line   Draws straight lines, adds arrowheads to either one or both ends of the lines, and sets the thickness of the lines.

Circle   Draws circles and ellipses.

Polygon   Draws objects with a variety of sides.

Figure 6.7 shows a simple example of each type of object. Keep in mind that the objects can be varied in many ways including size, pattern, and color.

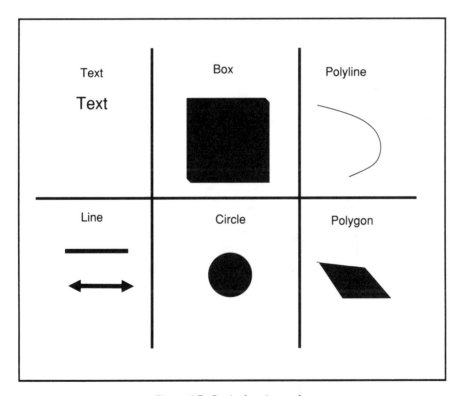

Figure 6.7. Basic drawing tools

Adding Boxed Text

One of the most common ways to annotate a chart is to add text to the chart enclosed in a box. You can also add an arrow to point at the place in the chart to which the text refers. In this example, add boxed text that points out that the 1990 bar is an estimate.

The purpose of boxing text is to cover the existing background so that it will not interfere with the text. By drawing a box for the chart you can create a solid background on which you can place your text.

In working with boxed text, it doesn't really matter in what order you create the box and the text because you can change the size and location of the text and box after the box has been added to the chart. In this case, first add the text and then add the box.

Adding Text

Begin the process of adding text to the chart by selecting the **text** option from the menu.

1

The selection of **text** changes the display in two ways. At the bottom of the screen, just above the function key menu a white bar is displayed with the word *Text:* on the left side (figure 6.8). The bar is called the *text entry* bar. It is here that you actually enter the text you want to add to chart. Below the bar you can see that the [F5] **Attributes** command has been added to the function key menu because you have selected to work with text.

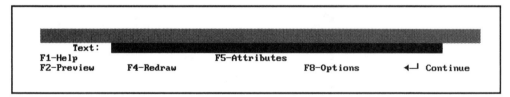

Figure 6.8. Text entry bar

On the left side of the screen, the previous menus have been replaced with the Text Options menu, as shown in figure 6.9. This menu consists of three sections: **Size, Attributes,** and **Alignment.**

Size   The size is a value between .5 and 100. By default the size is set at 5.5 which is the typical the size of a subtitle or column heading.

Attributes   The second section of the menu begins with the **Color** attribute and includes *fill, bold, italic,* and *underline.* In addition two other special effects, *shadow* and *shadow color,* appear. Use can use these options to create a shadow effect by changing the shadow to a different color than the letters. By default the text is white, filled, bold text.

Alignment   The bottom section is used to select the alignment of the text. In addition to selecting the horizontal position (left, center, or right) you can select a vertical position (top, center, base, or bottom). While the horizontal alignment is straightforward, the vertical location may be a bit confusing. The vertical position is related to *text rectangle.* The text rectangle is an area that includes the text plus some additional space above and below the characters. This space, called *leading,* is automatically added to the height of the characters to allocate space between lines of text and for character descenders, (such as the tails on letters like *j, g, and y*) which fall below the bottom of most characters. The default is *base* which aligns text as you would in a word processor.

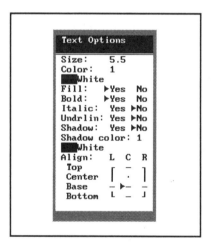

Figure 6.9. Add text menu

You might wonder why the program displays the text attributes in the Text Options menu and also shows the [F5] **Attributes** command. The answer is that the settings in the Text Options menu controls the default attributes of the text. The [F5] **Attributes** command can be used to change the attributes of individual characters or words within a single line of text. For example, if you want to have only one italicized word within a line, use the [F5] **Attributes** command. If you want the entire text line in italics, change the setting in the Text Options menu.

When you add text to a chart the text first appears on the text bar at the bottom of the screen. If you want to enter several lines of text each line must be entered as a separate item. Enter the first line of text:

The value for 1990

As you enter the characters they appear on the text entry bar. Pressing [⏎] causes the program to accept the entry with the options that are currently displayed in the Text Options menu and moves to the placement mode. However, at any time while the text is displayed on the line, you can use the [F8] key to change options. In this example you might want to change the size of the text to something smaller than 5.5. Recall that the title of the chart, *Median Family Income* is size 8 while the footnote is size 2.5. The annotation would probably look better at 4 than at 5.5. To make a change in the text options use the [F8] key to activate the options menu. Press:

[F8]

When you press [F8] the text bar at the bottom of the screen is removed. The highlight moves to the first item in the Text Options menu, **Size**. Erase the current size and replace it with the new size by pressing:

[Ctrl-Del]
4

In addition to changing the size of the text, remove the bold attribute so that the text will be displayed in normal intensity. Press:

[⇓] *(3 times)*
n

To return to the text entry bar, press:

[F8]

Placing the Text on the Chart

When you have entered the text on the text bar and selected the desired options for size, attributes, and alignment, you are ready to place the text onto the chart. To complete the text entry and enter the placement mode press:

[↵]

The text bar is removed from the screen, indicating that the program enters the *placement* mode. A rectangle appears in the lower-left corner of the chart frame, as shown in figure 6.10. The rectangle represents the space occupied by the text that you want to enter. The size of the rectangle is directly proportional to the amount and size of the text that you have entered. Inside the rectangle is a cross-bar. The cross-bar is used as the aiming target for the placement of the text. You might wonder why the cross-bar appears in the center of the rectangle positioned just above the bottom of the rectangle. This is the result of the **Align** options selected in the Text Options menu. Those options are set at **center/base**. The crossbar is positioned exactly in the center of the text and on the *baseline* for the characters.

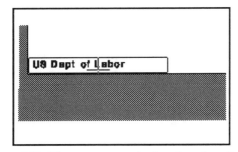

Figure 6.10. Placement rectangle placed on chart display

The text is positioned on the chart by moving the text rectangle to the desired location. For the purposes of drawing, the chart frame is divided into a grid of dots. The lower left corner of the frame is designated as position 1,1. The frame width is 26,154 dots wide and 20,000 dots in height, as shown in figure 6.11. The horizontal (X) and vertical (Y) position of the target is shown by the **Horiz=####** and **Vert=####** displays below the lower-right corner of the frame. As the cross-bar moves these values will change.

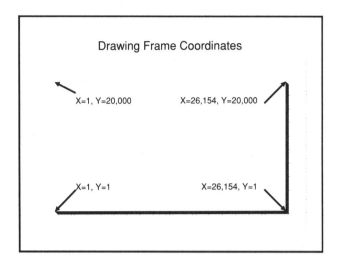

Figure 6.11. Drawing frame coordinate system

There are three ways to change the position of the rectangle: using the keypad, manually setting the XY coordinates, and with a mouse.

Keypad   The keys on the numeric keypad can be used to move the cross-bar and rectangle in eight directions. The [⇐], [⇒], [⇑], and [⇓] keys move the target in the indicated directions. To move in diagonal directions you can use [Home] to move to the upper-left, [Pg Up] to move to the upper-right, [End] to move towards the lower-left, and [Pg Dn] to move towards the lower-right.

When you use the cursor keys the target is moved a fixed length in the selected direction. The movement default is 512 dots, but you can *increase* the distance moved by pressing the + sign on the keypad. Conversely, the - sign on the keypad will *reduce* the amount of space for each keystroke. The * key (on the keypad) will return the movement distance to the original increment.

If you combine the keypad keys with [Ctrl], the target will move to the edge of the chart. Entering [Ctrl-Home], [Ctrl-Pg Up], [Ctrl-End] ,or [Ctrl-Pg Dn] will move the target to the respective corners of the chart frame. Using [Ctrl] with [⇐], [⇒], [⇑] or [⇓] will move you to the left, right, bottom, or top of the frame.

XY   You can directly enter the horizontal and vertical location, in dots, of the location where the target should be placed by using the [F3] **XY position** command. When selected, you can enter values into the **Horiz=####** and **Vert=####**. When you press [↵] the target is moved to that exact location.

Mouse   If you have a mouse attached to the computer, the cross-bar and rectangle will move in the direction in which you move the mouse.

If you hold down the **[Shift]** key the mouse will move only in a straight horizontal or vertical direction. This helps you keep items in alignment.

The **[left button]** on the mouse can be substituted for pressing [↵] in all of the drawing procedures.

In this case, position the text above the 1980 bar. Move the cross-bar to the upper right-hand corner of the chart frame by entering:

[Ctrl-Pg Up]

Move the target to a position above the bar by entering the following keys. (If you have a mouse, use it to move the cross-bar to approximately Horiz= 15,872 Vert=15,840.)

[⇓] *(6 times)*
[⇐] *(12 times)*

With the target position you can place the text into the chart clicking the left mouse button or by entering:

[↵]

The text is placed onto the chart at the specified location, as shown in figure 6.12.

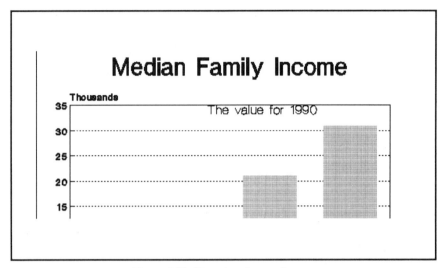

Figure 6.12. Text placed onto chart

Note that placing the text onto the chart does not turn off the text-entry mode. The program displays another text entry bar at the bottom of the screen. You can enter another line of text using the same options which you have selected for the previous line of text. Press:

is an estimated [↵]

When you press [↵] the program displays a text rectangle for the new entry. However, the location for the text entry is immediately below the last line of text placed on the chart. Note that because you have selected center alignment, the text is aligned so that the cross-bar is directly below the cross bar of the previous line. Since this line of text is a continuation of the previous line, place it exactly where Harvard Graphics has positioned the rectangle by pressing:

[↵]

Enter a two more lines of text:

value based on [↵]
[↵]
a projection [↵]
[↵]

When you have completed the entry you can terminate the text entry mode by pressing:

[Esc]

The program returns to the Add menu, shown in figure 6.13.

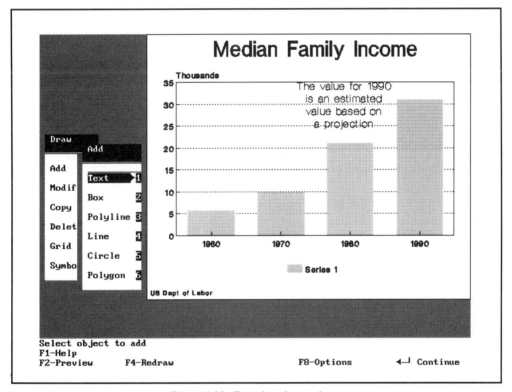

Figure 6.13. Text placed onto chart

Drawing a Box

When text is placed directly on the surface of a chart, you may find that other elements of the chart, such as grid lines, create a difficult background on which to read the text that you have placed. A common solution to this problem is to place the text inside a box. This helps the text stand out by covering the details in the background.

213

To draw a box select the **Box** option from the Add menu, press:

2

When **Box** is selected there are two changes that take place. First, the program displays the cross-bar, without any rectangle, at the last target position on the chart. Second, the program displays the Box Options menu (figure 6.14) on the left side of the screen.

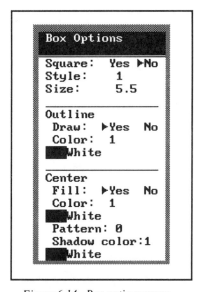

Figure 6.14. Box options menu

Square   If set to *Yes* this option ensures that all four sides of the box are equal in length. The default is *No* allowing you to draw any type of rectangle as a box.

Style   This option selects the style of the box that is to be drawn. Harvard Graphics supports 21 different styles of boxes, shown in figure 6.15.

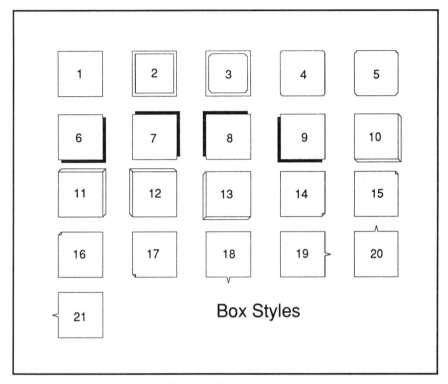

Figure 6.15. Box styles

Size

This size option has a name that may be misleading. This option is not related to the size of the box that is drawn (that is determined by the way in which you move the cross-bar target on the chart surface). In this menu, *Size* refers to the magnitude of the special effect used in the box style (see table 6.1). In styles 2 through 21, the box is enhanced by a 3-D effect, rounded corners, or another special feature. The size relative to the box of that special feature is determined by the **Size** option. The larger the value, the larger the effect will appear. Conversely a small value will minimize the effect. The default is 5.5.

Table 6.1. The Effect of the Size Styles

Style	Effect
2, 3	width of the frame border
4	radius of round corner
5	size cut from corner
6-9	width of shadow
10-13	depth of 3-D
14-17	width of corner
18-21	size of pointer

Outline   Draws if an outline around the box in a specified color. The default is to draw a white outline.

Center   Controls what will fill the box. If *Fill* is set to *No*, the box is transparent. If you select the default, *Yes,* you can select the color and pattern with which the center is to be filled. When *Fill* is *Yes,* the box covers any text it contains.

In this example, draw a box with a shadow, style 7. To do this, first access the Option menu by pressing:

   [F8]

Place the cursor on the **Style** line by pressing:

   [⇓]

You can also change the position of the cursor by moving the mouse in the same direction as the arrow key.

You can select the style by entering the style number. If you are not sure what style you want to select you can display a menu of the box style options by pressing:

   [F6]

The program displays a menu (shown in figure 6.16) that shows all 21 box styles. The first five styles are listed by name. The remainder are shown as pictures indicating the effect that they will have.

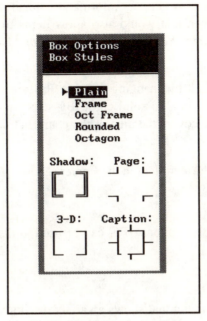

Figure 6.16. Box styles options

Select the style from this menu. Style 7 is a shadow box with the shadow projected from the upper-right corner of the box. Press:

[⇓] *(5 times)*
[⇒]

The highlight is now on the upper-right corner of the shadow section of the menu. Complete the selection by pressing:

[↵]

The program enters the style number 7 into the Box Options menu.

Creating a Background for Text

By default, the outline and fill options are set to *Yes*. The result of the default setting would be a solid white box on screen and a solid black box when printed. Since both the text and the box are displayed in white, you would not be able to read the text inside the box. One alternative would be to set the **Fill** option to *No*. That would create a *transparent* box in which any information already on the chart would show through the box. However, that would also allow items from the chart, such as the grid lines, to show through. You should create a an *opaque* box that contrasts with the text.

You can achieve this result by changing with the **Pattern** command. By default the pattern of the box is set for 0, a solid color. By selecting another pattern you can create a background that covers the area of the chart, but contrasts with the color of the text.

Move the cursor to the **Pattern** item in the Center section of the menu:

[⇓] *(6 times)*

As with the style and color options, [F6] can be used to display a menu of patterns. Enter:

[F6]

The program displays a menu that shows a variety of patterns, shown in figure 6.17, which can be used to fill the box.

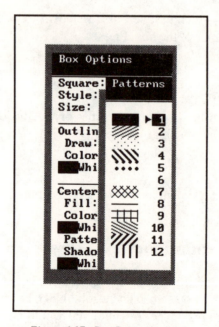

Figure 6.17. Box Pattern options

Pattern 6 is the most useful for creating a background for text because it is always an *empty* pattern. If selected, it will create a black background on screen (white when printed) upon which the text will appear. Keep in mind that an empty pattern is different from a transparent box. With pattern 6, the information below the box, such as grid lines on the chart, will *not* show through. Select pattern 6 by entering:

6 [↵]

You have now made the selections that will draw the type of box you want to use and are ready to place that box in the text. Return to the drawing mode by pressing

[F8]

The Box Options menu is removed from the screen and the cross-bar reappears on the chart.

Drawing a Box

Drawing objects such as lines, boxes, and circles is a two-step process. The first step is to select the *anchor* point. This is the point where the drawing is to begin. In a box, the *anchor* point marks the location of the upper-left or lower-left corner of the box, depending if you are drawing in a downward or upward direction. The anchor point is set by placing the cross-bar at the desired location to start drawing the box and and pressing [↵].

Once the anchor point is set, you can draw the box by moving the cross-bar to the opposite corner of the box. Finalize the box by pressing:

[↵]

In this book you will be asked to use the **XY position** style of positioning the cross-bar because it is easier to give instructions using that method. However, when you are working you will probably find it easier to use the arrow keys and certainly easier to use a mouse. Feel free to move the cross-bar with the cursor keys or the mouse instead of entering the XY coordinates.

Move the cross-bar to the position where the upper-left corner of the box will be placed:

[F3]
11264 [↵]
16896 [↵]

Anchor the box at that location by pressing:

[↵]

With the corner anchored you can draw the box by using the arrow keys or the mouse to Horiz=19968 Vert=12800. Press:

[⇓] *(8 times)*
[⇒] *(17 times)*

Complete the drawing by pressing:

[↵]

The box is drawn on the chart at the specified location, as shown in figure 6.18. But there is a problem: the box not only covers chart information, but the text that you placed on the chart as well. The solution to this problem lies in understanding how graphics *objects* are layered in Harvard Graphics.

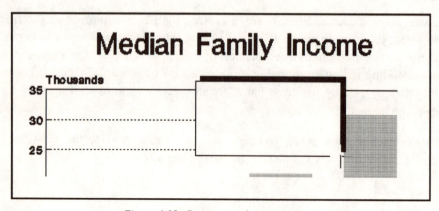

Figure 6.18. Box covers chart and text

Moving Objects Front and Back

When you draw with Harvard Graphics you are creating drawing *objects*, each individual element that can be manipulated individually. In this example, you added four graphics objects to the chart: three lines of text and 1 box.

If the object is transparent, you can see through it to the other object beneath; if the object is opaque, you cannot. It is important to remember when one object covers other, the object underneath is *hidden*, not *erased*. In this example, the box has covered and hidden the text. However, just as in real space, when you place more than one object in the same place they get stacked up on top of each other.

The layer of the object is determined in the order you create them. Each object you create will be placed on top of the previous object. In this example, if you had created the box, you would have been able to read the text on top of the box. However, it is not always logical to create the objects in the sequence in which they should appear. In this example, it would have been difficult to know what size box to draw before you had placed the text onto the chart.

Harvard Graphics allows you to change the arrangement of the objects by moving objects to the front or the back of the stack. (The chart itself is always at the bottom of the stack, below any of the objects that you create). In this case, you can display the text by moving the box to the back or the text to the front. Since there is only one box and there are three lines of text, moving the box is simpler. Exit the *Box* drawing mode and display the main Draw menu by pressing:

[Esc] *(2 times)*

Select the **Modify** option by pressing:

2

The **Modify** menu has five options.

Move	Change the location of object on the chart.
Size	Change the size of objects on the chart.
Options	Change options such as style, color, and pattern.
Front	Move an object to the front of the stack.
Back	Move an object to the back of the stack.

In this example, use the **Back** command to place the box at the back of the stack by pressing:

5

When you choose any of the **Modify** options you must *select* that object that you want to work with by placing the cross-bar on any part of the object that you want to modify. In this case, the cross-bar is still positioned on the box since that was the last operation you performed. To select the object press:

[↵]

When you press [↵] (or click the left mouse button) Harvard Graphics attempts to locate a graphics object at the cross-bar location. If there is more than one object stacked at that location the program takes the first object in the stack. To indicate which object has been selected the program displays small squares at the corners of the object. These squares are called *handles*. The box now has handles displayed on each of its four corners. Since the object that is selected is a box, the program displays the Box Options menu so that you can see the settings that were used to create the box.

In addition to the selection of the object on the drawing area, Harvard Graphics displays a special menu below the drawing area. The menu has three options:

Choose this   This option confirms that the object selected is actually the one that you intended to select.

Select next   This option selects the next object in a stack.

Retry   This option removes all current selections and allows you to start over again with the selection process.

In this example, the object selected is the correct object. Confirm this by pressing:

[↵]

Nothing seems to have changed because the text is still not visible inside the box. This is because, in order to save some of the time it takes to redraw the screen after every change, Harvard Graphics delays updating the screen until you specifically enter a command to do so. To update the screen display press:

[F4]

Harvard Graphics redraws the screen so that it now accurately depicts the chart, as shown in figure 6.19.

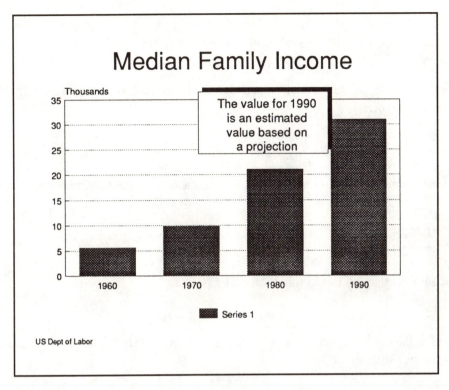

Figure 6.19. Chart with boxed text added

Moving Multiple Objects

Most of the time you will find that after the objects have been placed you need to make adjustments to the locations, size, or options. For example, in looking at the current chart it seems that the boxed text is probably a bit too close to the 1990 bar. It might look better if you moved the boxed text to the left and then used an arrow to indicate that this box is related to the 1990 bar.

It is important to remember that the boxed text is not a single drawn object but rather four different drawing objects: three lines of text and the box. However, Harvard Graphics allows you to select more than one object at a time, enabling you to move a group of objects to a new location as if they were a single item on the chart.

The key to making a *multiple* selection is to place the cross-bar on a section of the chart that does not contain any drawn objects. You can then draw a *selection box* around all of the objects you want to include in the group. When you press [↵] Harvard Graphics will select all of the items within the selection box, allowing you to manipulate them as a single object.

In this example, move the four objects that make up the boxed text. Select the **Move** command by pressing:

1

The cross-bar appears on the screen. Use the XY entry method to position the cursor (or use the mouse to move to the approximate location of the following coordinates).

[F3]
10752 [↵]
17920 [↵]

Anchor the selection box at this location by pressing:

[↵]

Position the cursor so that the selection box will enclose all of the items that make up the text box. Press:

[F3]
20992 [↵]
12288 [↵]

Select all of the items enclosed in the selection box by pressing:

[↵]

The program shows the *handles* for all of the objects that fell within the *selection box* (figure 6.20). At the same time, the program displays the Group Options menu on the left side of the screen to show any common colors or patterns selected for the group. At the bottom of the screen the Selection Confirmation menu is displayed again.

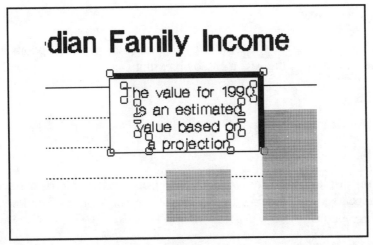

Figure 6.20. Multiple objects selected

Confirm the selection by pressing:

[↵]

The cross-bar appears on the screen again. It is positioned at the upper left-hand corner of the group of objects that have been selected. Moving the cross-bar with the arrow keys or the mouse will have the effect of moving the entire group of objects to a new location. Press:

[⇐] *(10 times)*

As you move the cross-bar, an outline box representing the selected objects moves along with it. The outline box shows you the new location and size of the graphic objects should you choose to place them at the cross-bar location. Note that the original objects are still visible at their current location. You can confirm the move with [↵] or cancel it with the [Esc] key. Press:

[↵]

The text and box have moved to the new location. Note that the location formerly occupied by the box and text is now blank. You can fill in that area by redrawing the screen. Press:

[F4]

Drawing Arrows

You can add pointing arrows to a chart by using the arrow head options on the line drawing menu. Return to the Add menu by pressing:

[Esc] 1

Select line drawing by pressing:

4

The program displays the **Line Options** menu on the left side of the screen. The cross-bar appears in the drawing area at the last cursor location. The line menu has the following options:

Arrows
With this option, you can select to draw a line, or a line with an arrowhead at either end or both ends. The beginning of the line is where the drawing anchor point is placed regardless of the direction in which the line is drawn. The default is no arrowheads.

Width
This option controls the thickness of the line. The default is 5.5.

Outline
Lines, like boxes, have an outline and a center section. On thin lines this makes no difference, but as the line thickness increases you can draw hollow or filled arrows. This option determines the color of the arrow outline. The default is white.

Center
This option controls the color and pattern, if any, that will be used to fill the line. The default is solid white.

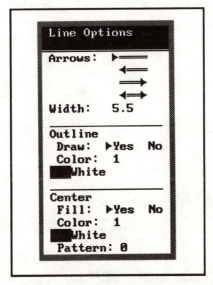

Figure 6.21. Line Options menu

Use the options menu to select a line with an arrowhead at the end of the line. Press:

[F8]
[⇓] *(2 times)*
[↵]
[F8]

Move the cross-bar to the location where you want to start drawing the line. Press:

[F3]
14848 [↵]
14848 [↵]

Anchor the beginning of the line at this location by pressing:

[↵]

Moving the cross-bar with the cursor keys or with the mouse will cause the line to extend in the direction that you move or point. Note that the line will be a simple, thin line even if you have selected a thick line with arrow heads. Those details will not be filled in until you have finished drawing the location of the line. When you are drawing a thick arrow you need to consider the fact that the final line will take up more space than temporary drawing line. Press:

[⇒] *(10 times)*
[⇓] *(3 times)*
[↵]

The arrow is drawn at the indicated location. Display the chart at full screen size by pressing:

[F2]

The chart should look like the one in figure 6.22.

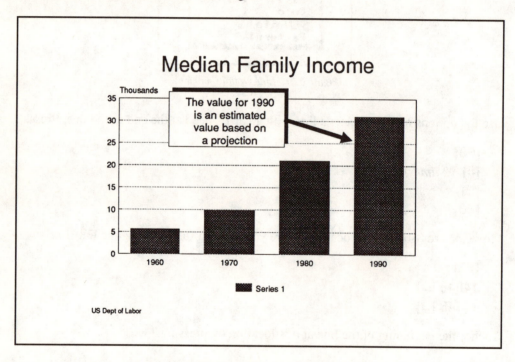

Figure 6.22. Chart with drawn annotations

Save the annotated chart by pressing:

[Esc] *(2 times)*
4 2
[↵] *(2 times)*
[Esc]

USING THE SYMBOL LIBRARY

In addition to being able to annotate standard charts, the drawing features of Harvard Graphics can be used to create almost any type of image. However, most users lack the required artistic skills to create complicated images from scratch. In order to aid user in making drawings Harvard Graphics supplies a variety of *clip art* drawings in the form of a *symbols* library.

A *symbol* is a drawing, stored in a special format on a disk file, that can be added to a current chart or drawing. A single drawing can combine as many different symbols are desired. The symbol libraries supplied with Harvard Graphics contain over 200 different drawings, including maps of major cities, Greek letters, flowchart symbols, and pictures of office equipment.

If you are adept at drawing with Harvard Graphics you can save a drawing that you create as a symbol to be reused at a later time. Note that saving symbols is different than saving charts that include drawings and annotations: Harvard Graphics can only work with one chart at a time; however, you can load as many symbols are you desire into the same chart.

Using Symbols

The drawings stored in the symbols library can be used in any number of ways to enhance your charts and drawings. For example, the subject of the current chart is the amount of money earned by the average American family per year. One way to make clear that the chart represents dollars is to modify the Y axis label to include the word *dollars*. However, you could create a much more immediate impact on the reader by a symbol to convey an idea visually rather than through text. In this example, using a dollar sign will be effective and make the chart visually more interesting.

Return to the drawing mode by pressing:

3

The **Symbol** command is the last one on the Draw menu. Press:

6

The program displays the Symbols menu, shown in figure 6.23. It contains the following options:

Get   Display a symbol file and select a symbol to load.

Save   Save the current selection as a symbol.

Group   Merge a group of selected objects into a single object. All of the drawings in the symbols library are saved as grouped object, This means that although they were created originally with many parts, they will function as a single object when you retrieve them.

Ungroup   Break up a grouped object into its component parts. This option is used when you want to modify a part of a drawing that you retrieve from a symbol library file.

Remove   This option deletes a symbol from the file.

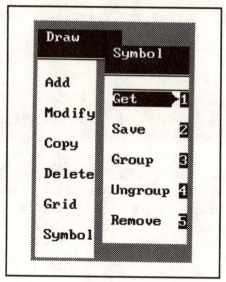

Figure 6.23. Symbol menu

To retrieve a symbol, press:

1

The program displays a list of symbols files with SYM extensions, supplied with the Harvard Graphics program. In this case, select the CURRENCY symbol file. Press:

currency [↵]

The program temporarily erases the chart or drawing from the drawing frame and displays the selected symbols file, shown in figure 16.24. A symbol file may contain any number of stored symbols.

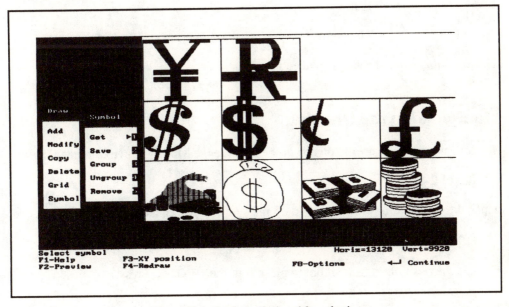

Figure 6.24. Symbols displayed for selection

You can select a drawing to add to the chart by positioning the cross-bar on that symbol and pressing [↵] (or clicking the left mouse button).

In this example, select the *big dollar sign* symbol. Move the cross-bar to the *big dollar sign* drawing by pressing:

[⇐]

Select that drawing by pressing:

[↵]

When you have selected the drawing, the program returns to the drawing screen for the chart or drawing you are working on. However, there is now a outline rectangle and a cross-bar displayed in the center of the drawing area. This rectangle represents the drawing that you have selected from the symbol file. When you load a symbol from a file you are immediately placed into a *sizing* mode in which you can scale the drawing to fit the current chart or drawing.

Reduce the size of the drawing by pressing:

[⇓]
[↵]

The *big dollar sign* drawing is placed into your chart.

Manipulating the Drawing

To move the drawing directly on one of the bars use the **Modify Move** command. Press:

[Esc] 2 1

Since the cross-bar is still positioned on the symbol, you can select it by pressing:

[↵] *(2 times)*

Change the position of the symbol to place it in the 1960 bar. Press:

[F3]
[Ctrl-Del]
4608 [↵]
[Ctrl-Del]
6656 [↵]
[↵]

The $ is drawn on top of the bar.

Copying an Object

One of the advantages of drawing on a computer is that once you have created a drawing you can make as many duplicates of the drawing as desired automatically. To place copies of the $ drawing on each of the bars in the chart to show that they all represent dollars, select the **Copy** command, located on the main Draw menu, by pressing:

[Esc] 3

Select the $ symbol as the object that you want to copy. Press:

[↵] *(2 times)*

When you select an object to be copied, the program displays an outline rectangle. Move the rectangle to the location where you want the copy to be placed. Press:

[⇒] *(11 times)*
[↵]

When you pressed [↵] two things happened. First, the program placed a copy of the object at the indicated location. Second, the cross-bar automatically jumped to the next bar and placed the drawing rectangle at that position. It may seem as if the computer was reading your mind and knew exactly where you want to place the next copy. However, the computer was simply following the pattern you had established. Since you placed the first copy 5,632 dots to the right of the original, the program automatically repeated the pattern placing the outline 5,632 dots from the last copy. Make two more copies by pressing:

[↵] *(2 times)*

Stop the copying process by pressing:

[Esc]

Scaling the Drawings

You have now placed $ in all of the bars. It might be interesting if you changed the size of the $ drawings so that they were proportional to the bars in which they appear. You can alter the size of the drawing using the **Size** command on the Modify menu. Press:

2 2

Select the $ drawing in the 1990 bar by pressing:

[⇐] *(4 times)*
[⏎] *(2 times)*

Expand the outline so that it reaches close to the top of the bar:

[⇑] *(15 times)*
[⏎]

The $ is stretched to fit the height of the bar. Repeat the process for the $ drawings in the 1980 and 1970 bars. Press:

[⏎]
[⇐] *(10 times)*
[⇓] *(15 times)*
[⏎]

Stretch the drawing by pressing:

[⇑] *(9 times)*

Continue with the next bar by pressing:

[⏎]
[⇐] *(10 times)*
[⇓] *(9 times)*
[⏎] *(2 times)*
[⇑] *(2 times)*
[⏎]

Display the chart at full size by pressing:

[F2]

The chart, shown in figure 6.25, displays the $ drawings modified to fit this chart.

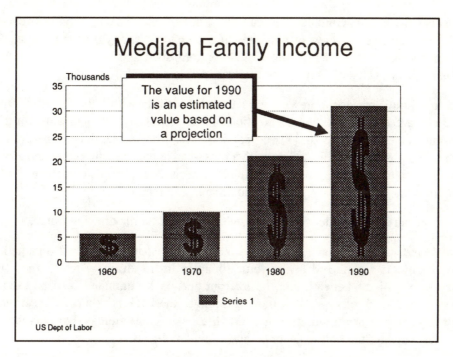

Figure 6.25. Chart with symbols drawings added

Save this chart by pressing:

[Esc] 4 2
annot-2 [↵]
[↵]
[Esc]

SUMMARY

This chapter looked at the basic techniques used to modify charts and create drawings.

Draw. The draw/annotate mode allows you to directly draw on a chart or create a drawing of any kind from scratch. The drawing mode is a full graphics mode in which all of the items on the chart appear exactly as they will when the chart is displayed or printed.

Objects. In Harvard Graphics you can add lines of text, boxes, polylines (curved lines), straight lines, circles, or polygons to any chart or empty drawing frame. You can enhance drawings by utilizing various options such as size, color, pattern, and special effects, such as 3-D boxes or arrowheads.

Position. You can place a drawing object at any position within the drawing frame. Positions are defined by the intersection of horizontal and vertical dots within a drawing frame. There are 20,000 vertical and 26,154 horizontal dots in the drawing frame. The position is indicated by both a cross-bar in the drawing frame and *Horiz* and *Vert* value displays at the bottom of the screen. You can position the cross-bar using the cursor keypad keys, the [F3] command, and a mouse.

Size. You can select or alter the size of objects placed into the drawing frame.

Front/Back. Objects can be drawn and outlines (transparent) or filled (opaque). If opaque objects are placed at the same location in the drawing frame they will obscure the objects beneath them. The front and back commands can be used to rearrange the stack of objects by moving some to the back or others to the front of the stack. If you are annotating a chart, the basic chart items—bars, axes, and grids—are always the bottom layer below all drawn objects.

Symbols. A symbol is a drawing that is stored in a special file format. This format allows the symbol to be copied into other charts and other drawings. Harvard Graphics supplies a library of over 200 symbol drawings that can be used to enhance your charts or drawings.

Copy. You can duplicate an object or group of objects as many times as needed. The copied objects can be manipulated by the **move, size,** and **options** commands.

Chapter 7

Slide Shows

harts and drawings created with Harvard Graphics can be used as individual displays which can be processed on output devices such as printers, plotters or photographic slide recorders. It is also becoming technologically feasible to use output generated directly from a computer to make presentations that would otherwise require the use of photographic slides. Because direct output from a computer is becoming a viable way to make presentations, Harvard Graphics includes the ability to create a *slide show* from the charts that you have created.

The same technology that is used in large screen TVs is used to create projectors that can display images directly from computer output. In addition, simpler and much less expensive LED devices connected to a computer can be placed on an overhead projector allowing screen images to be projected directly from the computer. Special boards such as the VGA TV board from Willow Peripherals can transfer computer output directly to a TV screen or a video recorder.

A Harvard Graphics slide show displays charts, drawings, and images you have created in a specified sequence in a similar manner to the way that photographic slides are used to make presentations. You can use slide shows to make presentations with video projectors or even to be run on individual computers, view by one or two people at a time.

In this chapter you will look at the way in which slide shows can be created and the special effects that can be achieved using Harvard Graphics.

Load the program in the usual manner and begin from the Main Menu.

ELEMENTS OF A SLIDE SHOW

There are three basic elements involved in a Harvard Graphics slide show.

Charts/Images   The basis of the slide show is the charts, drawings, and images that you choose to present and the order in which you present them. You can display any of the charts or drawings created in Harvard Graphics as part of a slide show. In addition, you can also include bit-mapped graphics images stored in the PCX (PC Paintbrush) or CUT (Dr. Halo) formats. These images can be created using painting programs, screen capture programs, or devices such as scanners or video-frame grabbers.

Duration   You can control the length of time each image is displayed. This can be accomplished by setting a specific time duration or maintaining the display until the user presses a key. Harvard Graphics provides advanced options that allow you to display different images depending on what key is entered. You can also create a continuous slide show that will restart each time it is completed.

Transitions   Harvard Graphics provides a variety of ways in which the transition from one image to another can be accomplished. You can even *overlay* one image on another to produce a combined image on the screen.

Creating a Slide Show

If you have been working through this book you have created a wide variety of charts that you can now use to create a slide show. It is important to keep in mind that you can only display information that you have stored in chart files. To begin, press:

7

The slide show menu (figure 7.1) lists tasks which are related to slide shows.

Create slide show Creates a new slide-show file. A slide-show file contains the names of the charts and images to include in the slide show and the options select for transitions. Slide-show files have SHW file extension.

Edit slide show Modifies an existing slide show.

Add Screenshow effects Creates the special transitional effects that can be used to change from one display to another in Harvard Graphics.

Display Screenshow Loads and displays a stored slide show.

Make practice cards Helps you prepare note cards to go along with the slide show. You can enter the text for each slide in the show. The cards can later be printed so that they can function as notes for your presentation.

Select slide show Prints specific slides from the slide show.

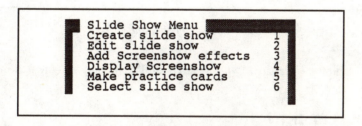

Figure 7.1. Slide Show menu

Begin by creating a new slide show. Press:

show-01 [⏎]
Sample Show [⏎]

The Create/Edit Slide Show screen is displayed, as shown in figure 7.2. This screen is divided into two sections. The top section lists all of the chart files in the current directory and any files with PCX, CUT or SHW file extensions. The SHW (slide show) files are included to allow you to create a large slide show by combining several smaller slide shows.

The bottom of the screen shows the files, if any, that have been selected for this slide show. You can select up to 90 files for each slide show.

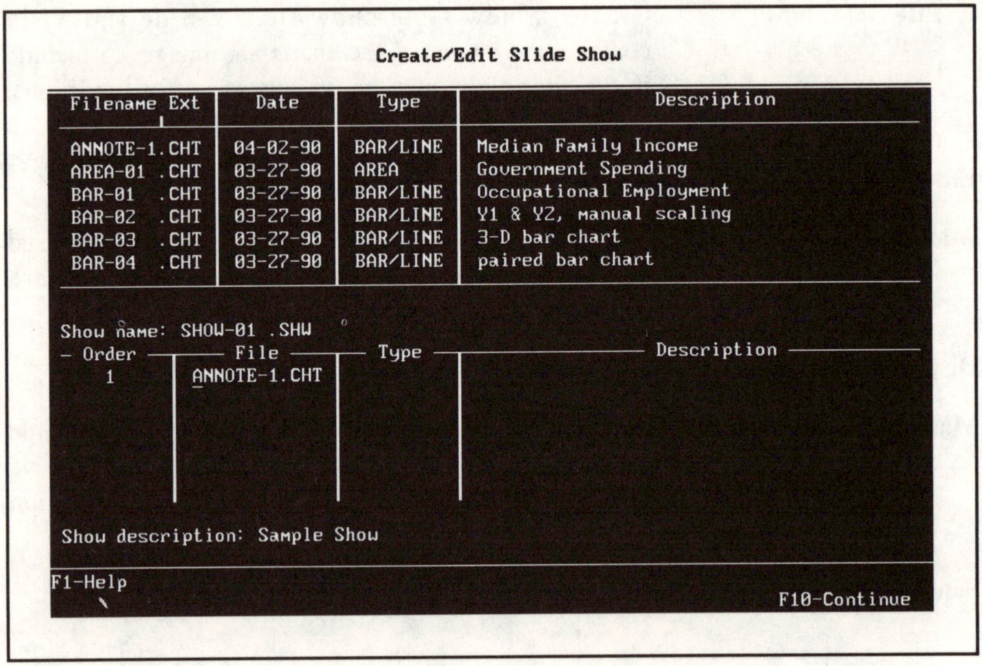

```
                    Create/Edit Slide Show

 ┌─────────────┬──────────┬──────────┬────────────────────────────────┐
 │Filename Ext │   Date   │   Type   │          Description           │
 ├─────────────┼──────────┼──────────┼────────────────────────────────┤
 │ANNOTE-1.CHT │ 04-02-90 │ BAR/LINE │ Median Family Income           │
 │AREA-01 .CHT │ 03-27-90 │ AREA     │ Government Spending            │
 │BAR-01  .CHT │ 03-27-90 │ BAR/LINE │ Occupational Employment        │
 │BAR-02  .CHT │ 03-27-90 │ BAR/LINE │ Y1 & Y2, manual scaling        │
 │BAR-03  .CHT │ 03-27-90 │ BAR/LINE │ 3-D bar chart                  │
 │BAR-04  .CHT │ 03-27-90 │ BAR/LINE │ paired bar chart               │
 └─────────────┴──────────┴──────────┴────────────────────────────────┘

 Show name: SHOW-01 .SHW
 ─ Order ──────── File ──────── Type ──────────── Description ──────────
    1          ANNOTE-1.CHT




 Show description: Sample Show

 F1-Help
                                                          F10-Continue
```

Figure 7.2. Create/Edit Slide Show screen

In this case, begin the slide show with the BULLET text chart you created in chapter 1. Press:

[⇓] **to BULLET.CHT**
[↵]

Note that when you select a chart, Harvard Graphics enters the chart type and the description, if any, in the columns at the bottom of the screen. Next add the PIE-01 chart. Note that because the files may not appear in order you may need to scan up or down the list to find the specified charts. Press:

[⇓] **or** [⇑] **to PIE-01.CHT**
[↵]

240

Next add the TWOCOLS text chart:

[⇓] **or** [⇑] **to TWOCOLS.CHT**
[↵]

Add three more charts:

[⇓] **or** [⇑] **to BAR-01.CHT**
[↵]

[⇓] **or** [⇑] **to ORGANIZ.CHT**
[↵]

[⇓] **or** [⇑] **to TS-01.CHT**
[↵]

[⇓] **or** [⇑] **to TREND-01.CHT**
[↵]

There are now six charts selected for the slide show. Note that Harvard Graphics automatically fills in a 7th name. Keep in mind that this file name is not part of the slide show unless you press [↵]. Save the 6 chart slide show by pressing:

[F10]

The program returns to the slide show menu.

Selecting the Transitions

The primary creative task associated with slide shows is the creation of the transitions between each of the slide. By default the slide show replaces each chart with the next slide. The slide remains on the screen until you press a key. The **Add Screenshow effects** option used to change the transitions between the slides. Press:

3

The programs displays the Screenshow Effects menu (figure 7.3) that lists the charts selected for the slide show.

Filename	Type	Draw	Dir
Default		Replace	
1 BULLET .CHT	BULLET		
2 PIE-01 .CHT	CHART		
3 TWOCOLS .CHT	2 COLUMN		
4 BAR-01 .CHT	BAR/LINE		
5 TS-01 .CHT	BAR/LINE		
6 TREND-01.CHT	BAR/LINE		

Figure 7.3. Screenshow Effects menu

In addition to the file names there are five columns of options that determine how the slide show will appear: **Draw, Dir, Time, Erase,** and **Dir.**

Draw This option determines how the specified chart will be drawn on the screen. Harvard Graphics provides 11 different methods of placing a chart on the screen.

Replace This is the standard way in which to draw a chart. The program displays the entire chart as a single image.

Overlay This option paints the new chart element by element on the screen. In most cases the chart graphics, bars, lines, areas, are painted first followed by the text such as titles. This option will not automatically erase the previous chart. This allows you to combine the appearance of two charts together if desired.

Wipe This effect displays the chart from one side to the other. The effect is as if the chart was already on the screen by hidden by a curtain. The chart image does not move.

Scroll This effect displays the chart by rolling it from one edge to the other. A scroll is different than a wipe in that it moves the image of the chart across the screen.

Fade This effect displays the chart by gradually filling in the detail. The chart begins with a fuzzy image which sharpens to the final image.

Weave The weave effect divides the dots that make up the picture into two screen, one with all the even dots while the other has all the odd dots. The two particle images then scroll onto the screen in opposite directions. When both images have crossed the screen they form the final complete image.

Open   This effect begins the drawing of the image with a line across the center of the screen. The remainder of the images is drawn by wiping up and down from this center line to the edges of the screen. The picture appears to open in the middle and spread out to the sides.

Close   This effect is the reverse of open. In this effect, the images begins as two lines, one at either side of the screen. The images then wipe towards the middle of the screen to complete the image.

Blinds   Blinds are really a multiple open or close effect. The image begins as several lines across the screen that then wipe together to form the image.

Iris   This effect draws the chart from the center out to the edges. This is the effect used with the Harvard Graphics logo when you first load the program.

Rain   The rain effect creates the image by wiping down the screen in a series of staggered lines rather than in a single sweep. The staggered effect is reminiscent of the staggered way that rain drops run down a window.

Dir   This option allows you to choose the direction used by the **Draw** effect. This applies only to those effects that draw the image in one direction or another. For example, the scroll effect usually scrolls in an *up* direction, from the bottom of the screen towards the top. You can select left, right, down, or alternative directions.

Replace   No direction.

Overlay   No direction.

Wipe   Default = right. Options = left, up down.

Scroll   Default = up. Options = left, right, down.

Fade   Default = full screen. Options = down.

Weave	No direction.
Open	Default = up/down. Options = left/right.
Close	Default = up/down. Options = left/right.
Blinds	Default = up/down. Options = left/right.
Iris	Default = center out. Options = edges in.
Rain	No direction

Time This option allows you to specify the length of time for which the image is displayed. If the option is left blank then the image remains on the screen until the user presses a key. If a zero value is entered, the images are flashed on the screen as quickly as possible given the speed of the hardware. Keep in mind that less powerful computers take longer to change screens. Color screens are slower than monochrome. Durations are entered in mm:ss format; for example, 1:30 would be one minute 30 second, :10 would be 10 seconds.

Erase The erase option allows you to select a special effect for removing the chart from the screen. All of the standard drawing effects with the exception of **overlay** will automatically erase the previous image. The erase option is used in two cases. First, if you want to use overlay, but you do not want the image; combined with the previous image or second, when you want to draw attention to the erasing of the current screen. When you select a special effect for erasing the program operates by drawing a blank screen over the current image. For example, if you selected **wipe** as the erase effect, the program would wipe a blank screen across the graph image. Keep in mind that the erasing effect for one screen does not effect the drawing effect for the next screen and that using an erase effect does slow the transition between one screen and the next.

Dir This controls the direction of the erase effect, if any.

At the top of each option column is a row labeled *Default*. The default line is used to establish the default value for items left blank in the column. For example, if you set the Default line for the **Draw** column to **fade,** all of the charts would be drawn with a **fade** effect unless otherwise specified in the column.

In this case, set the default effect for charts as **open.** The [F6] command will display a menu of options. Press:

[F6]
o
o
[↵]

The word open appears at the top of the column indicating the default method.

Change the settings for the first chart so that it uses the **Iris** effect for drawing and erasing. Press:

[⇓]
[F6] i [↵]

To change the direction of the **Iris** from out to in. Press:

[Tab] *(3 times)*
[F6] i [↵]
[Tab]
[F6] i [↵]

Previewing the Show

Once you have established the basic slide show, you can use the [F2] key to preview the your selections. In order to have the show run automatically change the default timing setting to 3 seconds. Press:

[Shift-Tab] *(2 times)*
:03

Display the slide show by pressing:

[F2]

The program displays the slides using the three second delays and the specific effects.

INTERACTIVE SLIDE SHOWS

The slide show that you just created was a *straight line* show. This means that the charts were displayed in exactly the order in which they appeared on the screen. You can create an interactive slide show that will vary the order of the slides based on the keys entered by the user.

For example, suppose that you want to give the person looking at the slide show the option to continue to view all of the detailed slides or to skip to the end of the slide show.

In order to do this you first need to create some simple text charts that display messages to the user. Create a new text chart by pressing:

[F10] [Esc]
1 1

Use the **Title** type chart. Press:

1

Enter a title for the slide show:

Sample Slide Shows
[Tab] *(3 times)*
Time: 2:00
[Tab] *(3 times)*
Press any key to begin [↵]
or E to Exit

Save this chart as TITLE-01 by pressing:

[F10] 4 2
title-01 [↵]
[↵]
[Esc]

Create a second title chart that simply tells the user they have reached the end of the slide show. Press:

1 1 1
The End
[F10] 4 2
title-02 [↵]
[↵]
[Esc]

Adding a Slide to a Show

The next task is to add the slides to the slide show. Return to the slide show menu by pressing:

7

Select the **Edit Slide Show** option by pressing:

2

Add the TITLE-01 and TITLE-02 charts to the slide show list. Press:

[⇓] or [⇑] to TITLE-01.CHT
[↵]

[⇓] or [⇑] to TITLE-01.CHT
[↵]

When you add a new slide to the show list it is *always* placed at the bottom of the list. However, you can rearrange the order of the charts in the slide show after they have been added.

Changing the Order of Slides

In order to change the order of the slides in the show you must first change the operating mode on the screen by using the [Tab] key to change the operational mode. Press:

[Tab]

When you press [Tab], the highlight moves from the top of the screen (where it was used to select files) to the *select files* list at the bottom of the screen. With the highlight in this section of the screen, you can change the order of the charts in the slide show. In this example you want to place the TITLE-01 charts which is currently in the #7 position, to the #2 position in the slide show. This will display the first chart before the user is asked if they want to continue with the slide show. To do this, position the highlight on TITLE-01 by pressing:

[⇑]

With the highlight on the chart that is to be moved, TITLE-01, you can use the [Ctrl-⇑] or [Ctrl-⇓] keys to move the chart up or down in the order. Press:

[Ctrl-⇑] *(5 times)*

Notice that each time you press the [Ctrl-up arrow] combination the selected chart name moves up one line in the chart list. The selected chart is now positioned in slot #2 of the slide show.

Defining a User Option Key

Recall that the TITLE-01 chart tells the person looking at the slide show that they can enter the letter *e* to exit the slide show. To make this command operative, however, you must enter a special instruction that tells Harvard Graphics that the sequence of slide-show display should be altered if the user enters *e*. This type of instruction is called a *User Option Key* which allows you to specify a chart to be displayed when a certain key is entered. In the current example, you want to display the last chart in the show (#8) if the user enters the letter *e*. Harvard Graphics allows you to define up to ten user option keys for a single screen. This allows you to create a menu with up to 11 options (the 11th is what happens if none of the ten specified keys are entered).

To add a user option key to the slide show return to the **Add slideshow effects** screen.

[F10] 3

Move the cursor to the slide for which the option is to be entered. The cursor can be in any of the columns.

[⇓] *(2 times)*

The [F8] key is used to specify user option keys. Press:

[F8]

A menu with two columns will popup in the upper-right corner of the screen. The **Key** column is used to enter the keys, (0–9 or a–z) that the user might enter. The **Go To** column should contain the number of chart to go to when the key is pressed. In this case, you want to set up the option so that if the user enters the letter **e** the slide show will jump to the slide #8. Press:

e
[Tab]
8
[F10]

You can create a *default* goto instruction by leaving the key code blank but entering a slide number in the **Go To** column. The result of this is that the specified slide will be the next one displayed if none of the specified keys are entered.

This approach would allow you to create a continuous slide show if applied to the last chart on the list. Instead of filling in a specific key, the key column is left blank. However, the 1 is placed into the Goto column. The effect of this option is that when ever the slide show reaches the last slide, it automatically returns to the first slide and replays the show endlessly.

Keep in mind that the default setting for time is set at 3 seconds. This means that the program will pause only for three seconds when the #2 chart is displayed. That is not sufficient time to allow the user to decide what key to press. In order to make it seem as if the program has paused indefinitely, enter a long time period (such as 10 minutes) into the time column. Keep in mind that when a time delay is used, the delay is automatically terminated if the user enters a key. This means that impatient users can move though a slide show faster than the specified times if they desire. Press:

[Tab] *(2 times)*
10:00

Return to the **Slide Show** menu by pressing:

[F10]

Display the slide show by pressing:

4

When the second screen is displayed the program is paused for 10 minutes. According to the instructions, the user can exit the program by entering the letter *e*. Press:

e

The slide show removes the current chart and jumps directly to the last chart that displays the words *The End*.

Return to the main menu by pressing:

[Esc]

SUMMARY

The charts that you create in Harvard Graphics can be organized into a slide show presentation.

Slide Shows. A slide show is a list of charts, drawings or images that you want to display in a particular sequence. You can create a slide show by selecting charts files for display. Harvard Graphics will also display bit-mapped graphics files in the PCX format along with the Harvard Graphics charts.

Special Effects. You can add interest to the slide show by selection from 11 different ways in which the charts can be drawn on the screen. You can specify a effect for erasing the chart as well. The charts will stay on the screen until the user enters a key. You can specific a duration in minutes and seconds so that the display of the charts is timed.

User Options. User options allow you to create menus and options within a slide show that can use used by the person watching the show to alter the sequence of slides. The [F8] option is used enter up to 10 different keys and the slide to go to if those keys are entered.

Chapter 8

Advanced Features

As you create more charts with Harvard Graphics you will find that you may be able to take advantage of the some of its advanced features. In this chapter you will learn how to use chart templates and how to transfer charts and data between Harvard Graphics and other applications.

TEMPLATES

You will find that many of the charts you create involve repetition of the same basic designs. For example, you may need to create the same set of charts every quarter, each using the same basic style, options, and in some cases, titles. The only change in each chart is the data.

In order to make this type of repetitive chart easier to create, Harvard Graphics allows you to create a special form of chart called a *template*. The purpose of template is to store in a file all of the settings needed for a particular type of chart.

251

When you want to create that chart, instead of entering all of the options and settings again you can simply load them from the template file. All you need to do to complete the chart is fill in the specific values and save the resulting combination as a new chart.

When you create a template file, Harvard Graphics automatically includes the following items:

Attributes   Attributes are enhancements—such as fill, bold, italics, underline, or color—added to text with the [F5] or [Shift-F5]command. Note that these attributes are saved even if you do not save the text to which they were applied. For example, suppose that you use the [Shift-F5] command to add italics to the title of the chart. When you save the template, the title line will be automatically set in italics. This means that when you use the template to create a new chart the title will automatically appear in italics when the new text is entered.

Size/Place   The size and place alignment of text, controlled by the [F7] command, is also saved as part of the template.

Options   Any options set with the [F8] command will be saved as part of the template.

Drawing   If you use the Draw/Annotate mode to add drawn objects to the chart, they are saved as part of the template.

The data entered into the chart titles, footnotes and data series is optional. The Save Template menu allows you to choose to save the current data along with the other attributes, or to strip the data when the template is saved. Saving the data is useful when the chart titles and X axis information does not need to be changed when the chart is revised.

Creating a Template

You can create a template from any chart. To make a template out of the TREND-01 chart (which you created in chapter 6 to calculate the straight-line regression of a yearly time series), load the chart into Harvard Graphics by pressing:

4 1
trend-01 [↵]

The program loads the chart file and displays the chart on the screen. Exit the display by pressing:

[Esc]

The program automatically enters the Edit Chart mode. You must first decide what elements you want to save as part of the template. Keep in mind that all templates save the attributes, size/place settings, and the chart options. However, in the case of the TREND-01 chart one of the major features is the straight-line regression calculation. You may want to retain that data series as part of the template.

Since you intend to save some of the data as part of the template, you need to clear out all of the data that will not be part of the template. In this case, that includes the chart titles, the X axis data, and the series 1 values.

Move the cursor to the beginning of the screen and delete the frame text:

[Home]
[Ctrl-Del] [↵]
[Ctrl-Del] [↵]
[Ctrl-Del] [↵]

Clearing a Series

The next task is to clear the data series information from the series 1 columns. You could accomplish this task by moving the cursor to each of the points in both series and using the [Ctrl-Del] command to delete the contents. A more efficient method, however, is to use a special function called *@CLR*. This function, unlike most calculation function does not generate values. Instead it removes all values from the current series. Place the cursor in the series 1 column. Press:

[Tab]

Use the [F4] command to calculate a column formula. Press:

[F4]
[Ctrl-Del] [↵]
@CLR [↵]

The column is cleared of all values. Note that the [F4] command also allowed you to remove the series 1 label. This saved you the trouble of having to access the options screens to remove the series name.

Saving a Template

Save the modified chart as a template by pressing:

[F10] 4

This time choose the option instead of the **Save Chart** option. Press:

4

The Save Template menu, shown in figure 8.1, is displayed.

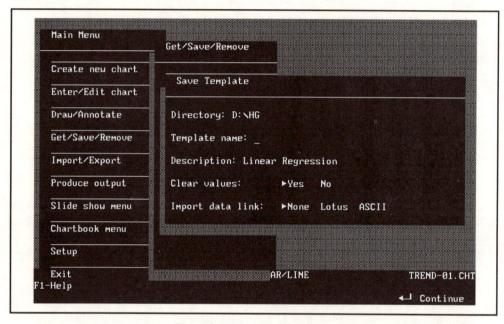

Figure 8.1. Save template menu

Enter the name of the template:

lineregr [↵]

Note that the description of the chart is entered as *Linear Regression*. Harvard Graphics automatically generated that name based on the @RLIN() function left in the data series. Press:

[↵]

The **Clear Values** option determines whether or not the values left in the data-entry screen should be saved along with the template. In this case, you do *not* want to clear the chart values. Change the setting from *Yes* to *No* by pressing:

n

Complete the process by pressing:

[F10]

The template is saved. In order to see how the template works, load the BAR-01 chart to ensure that all of the template settings have been replaced by those of a different chart by pressing:

1

bar-01 [↵]

To create a linear-regression analysis chart using the setting stored in the template file press:

[Esc] [F10] 4

Select the **Get Template** command from the menu by pressing:

3

The program displays the Select Template menu, shown in figure 8.2. All template files use the TLP file extension.

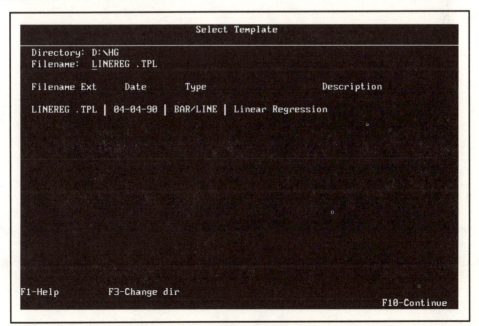

Figure 8.2. Select Template menu

Enter the name of the template that you want to retrieve:

linereg [↵]

The template file is retrieved. Unlike a chart file, the template does not generate a chart display. Instead the program moves immediately to the data-entry screen. Create a simple chart using the template. Enter the title:

Chart Made from Template
[↵] *(3 times)*

Change the X series to 1985 through 1990 by pressing:

[F3] [↵]
1985 [↵]
1990 [↵]
[↵]

The X axis column is adjusted to the new range of years. Move the cursor to the series 1 column and enter the following values:

[Tab]
6 [↵]
4 [↵]
8 [↵]
5.5 [↵]
7 [↵]
6.1

Recalculating Formulas

The chart has new values for the X axis and the first data series. However, the values in data series 2, which were generated by the @RLIN() function, remain as they were when the template was saved. These values are not correctly calculated and will not plot the trend line of the current series of values. To let you correct this easily, Harvard Graphics provides a nonarithmetic function called *@RECALC*. When activated this function will recalculate all of the data series formulas in the current chart. Note that it does not matter what column the cursor is in when you calculate the @RECALC function. Press:

[F4]
[Tab]
@RECALC [↵]

The recalculation process adjusts the values in the trend series to match the current data in the chart. Display the chart by pressing:

[F2]

The chart retains all of the characteristics of the original TREND-01 chart, but the data displayed is new (figure 8.3). Keep in mind that part of the template that you created was a Y axis scale of 4-10.

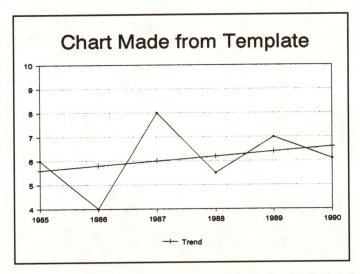

Figure 8.3. Chart created from template

Save this chart as TREND-04 by pressing:

[Esc] [F10] 4 2
trend-04 [↵]
[↵]
[Esc]

The Default Template

Individual templates provide a means by which you can use an established chart layout to quickly create new charts. Harvard Graphics allows you to create templates that function as the *default* layouts for each of the 12 different types of charts that you can create.

Recall that for each type of chart you create, Harvard Graphics has a default set of values. For example, all of the data series in the Bar/Line chart style are set to bars. If you use line charts more than bar charts, you might find that it suits your purposes better if the series were to default to line rather than bar.

You can use templates to establish your own personal default styles for each type of chart. This is done by creating templates with special names. The names must match the one shown on the list in table 7.1 in order to function as templates.

Table 8.1. Template names to personalize defaults

Chart Type	Template Name
Title chart	TITLE
Simple lists	LIST
Bullet lists	BULLET
2 column	2_COLUMN
3 column	3_COLUMN
Free form	FREEFORM
Pie charts	PIE
Bar/Line	BARLINE
Area charts	AREA
High-Low	HLC
Organization	ORG
Multiple	MULTIPLE

Suppose that you wanted to change the default style for the Bar/Line charts to lines instead of bars. Create a new Bar/Line chart by pressing:

1 3
[F10]

Display the options screen:

[F8]

Change all of the series types to line by pressing:

[Tab] *(8 times)*
| [↵] *(Then repeat the* **|** *[↵] 7 more times)*

All of the types should now be set to line. Save this as the BARLINE template. Press:

[F10]
4 4
barline [↵]
[F10] [↵]

To test the effect of this new template, load a pie chart to ensure that you have wiped out the previous chart's settings:

1
pie-01 [↵]

The pie chart is displayed. Create a new Bar/Line chart by pressing:

[F10] 1 3
n [↵]

Display the options screen by pressing:

[F8]

All of the series are set by default to line type series.

Removing the Default Template

You can return to the normal factory set default values by using the **Remove File** command to erase the BARLINE template file. Press:

[F10] 4 5

Enter the name of the file you want to remove. Note that this command requires you to enter the full file name including the file extension. Press:

barline.tlp [↵]
[↵]

Create a new Bar/Line chart:

1 3
[F10] [F8]

The option menu shows that the series now defaults to bar because the custom default template has been deleted from the disk. Return to the main menu by pressing:

[F10]

IMPORTING FILES

To create charts in this book you have entered all of the raw data directly into the Harvard Graphics program . However you may be able to import information entered in other applications into Harvard Graphics, saving you the trouble of re-entering all of the values. It also can eliminate mistakes made during the re-entry of values.

Two popular applications are WordPerfect in the word processing field and Lotus 1-2-3 in the spreadsheet area.

Importing From WordPerfect 5.0

Numeric information, such as that needed as the raw data for a chart, is often entered in table form in word processing documents, such as WordPerfect, the most popular word-processing program for MS-DOS computers. You can transfer the data in such tables directly into a Harvard Graphics chart.

Figure 8.4 shows a typical table entered into a WordPerfect document using tab stops to align the data in columns.

```
                        Boston    Dallas    Seattle
        Model 200          51        53        72
        Model 400          48        64        47
        Model 300X         45        74        64
```

Figure 8.4 . WordPerfect text table

To import this information into Harvard Graphics, you first need to place the table into a document by itself if it is part of a larger document. This can be done using WordPerfect's block highlighting and **Move/copy** commands.

Begin in the WordPerfect document by placing the cursor at the beginning of the table. Turn on the WordPerfect block highlight mode by pressing:

[Alt/F4]

Move the cursor to the end of the table. The entire text of the table should be included in the highlight. Use the **Move/Copy** command to make a copy of the text. Press:

[Ctrl/F4] b c

To place the text into a document by itself switch to Doc 2 in WordPerfect by pressing:

[Shift-F3]

Place the copy of the table into the new document window by pressing:

[↵]

Keep in mind that Harvard Graphics cannot read WordPerfect files. You must convert the WordPerfect document into a ASCII text file in order to be able to load the document into Harvard Graphics. To save the text as an ASCII text file press:

[Ctrl-F5] t s

When you enter the file name it might simplify operations if you placed the file directly into the Harvard Graphics directory. For example, assuming that Harvard Graphics is stored in the \HG directory of the same hard disk on which WordPerfect is stored, you would press:

\HG\table.txt [↵]

You can now exit WordPerfect and load the Harvard Graphics program.

When you have loaded Harvard Graphics, create a new chart to display the data you are going to import. In this case, a bar chart would be appropriate. Press:

1 3

In this case, you will not bother to enter data, but simply return to the main menu:

[F10] *(2 times)*

Choose the **Import/Export** option by pressing:

5

The menu list the import and export options. Text created with the **DOS Save** command in WordPerfect ([Ctrl-F3] d s) is imported using the **Import ASCII data** option. Press:

3

Enter or highlight the name of the text file you have created with WordPerfect.

table.txt [↵]

The data is ready into Harvard Graphics and displayed on the Import ASCII Data screen, shown in figure 8.5.

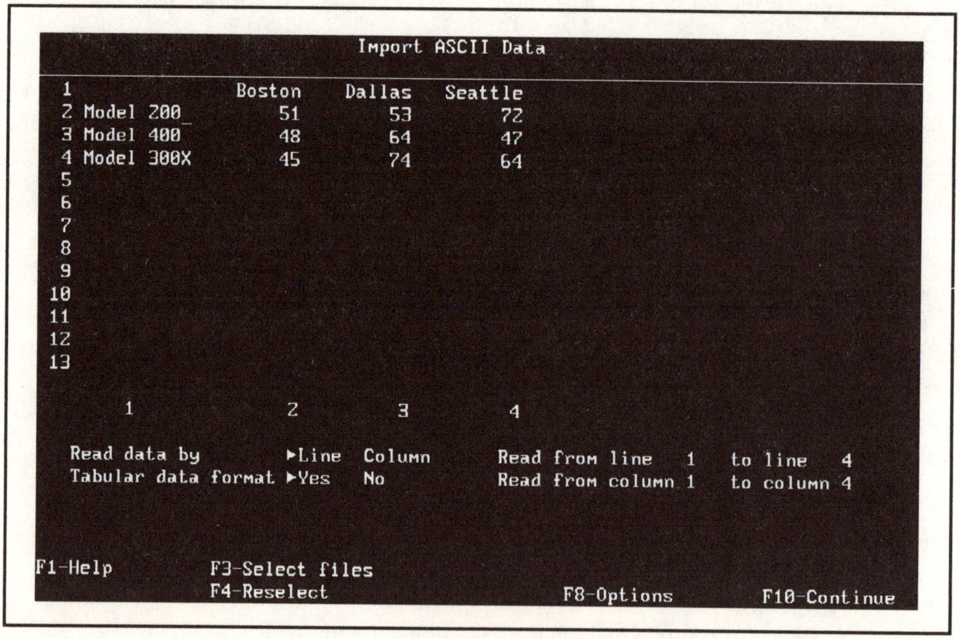

```
                         Import ASCII Data
 1                 Boston   Dallas   Seattle
 2 Model 200_        51       53       72
 3 Model 400         48       64       47
 4 Model 300X        45       74       64
 5
 6
 7
 8
 9
10
11
12
13

        1                2        3        4

   Read data by         ▶Line  Column    Read from line    1   to line    4
   Tabular data format  ▶Yes   No        Read from column 1   to column 4


F1-Help            F3-Select files
                   F4-Reselect                   F8-Options      F10-Continue
```

Figure 8.5. Import ASCII Data

To accept the data as part of the chart you are working with press:

[F10]

The program displays a menu entitled **Import Titles and Legends,** shown in figure 8.6.

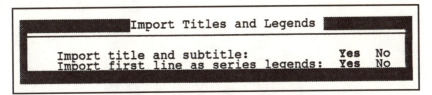

Figure 8.6. *Import Titles and Legends menu*

This menu is used to determine if the imported text contains information such as the chart titles or the series headings. In this case, the data does not contain title and subtitles lines, but it does list the names of the data series on the first line. Press:

n
[⇓]
y
[F10]

The program displays the data-entry screen with the values entered into the series, shown in figure 8.7.

```
                         Bar/Line Chart Data                              ▼

    Title: _
 Subtitle:
 Footnote:


             X Axis          Boston       Dallas      Seattle      Series 4
    Pt       Name

 1      Model 200             51           53           72
 2      Model 400             48           64           47
 3      Model 300X            45           74           64
 4
 5
 6
 7
 8
 9
 10
 11
 12

 F1-Help           F3-Set X type                          F9-More series
 F2-Draw chart     F4-Calculate            F8-Options     F10-Continue
```

Figure 8.7. *Data ready for charting*

When displayed, the chart will look like figure 8.8.

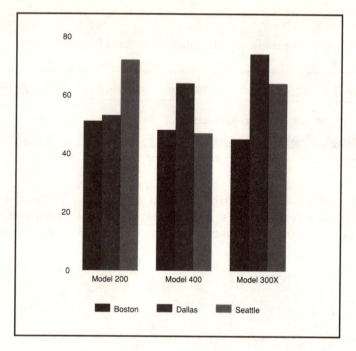

Figure 8.8. Chart with values imported from WordPerfect

Save the chart by pressing:

[F10] 4 2
import-1 [↵]
[↵]
[Esc]

Importing From Lotus 1-2-3

Another popular application in which you might find data for charts is Lotus 1-2-3.

Figure 8.9 shows a Lotus 1-2-3 spreadsheet with data that could be used as the basis of a Harvard Graphics chart.

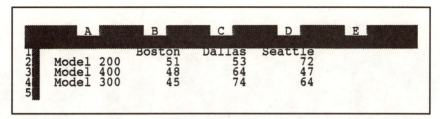

Figure 8.9. Lotus 1-2-3 spreadsheet

When using 1-2-3 it is not necessary to convert the data to ASCII format because Harvard Graphics can directly read information from a Lotus 1-2-3 WKS or WK1 file. Assume that this file is saved on the disk with the name SALES.WK1.

Load the Harvard Graphics program and select the type of chart you want to create with the data. For the data listed in figure 8.9, a bar chart would be most appropriate. Press:

1 3

In this case, you will not bother to enter data but return to the main menu.

[F10] *(2 times)*

Choose the **Import/Export** option by pressing:

5

The menu lists the import and export options. You can access information stored in a Lotus 1-2-3 worksheet file by using the **Import Lotus data** option. Press:

2

Select the worksheet file from which you want to extract data. Note that you mat need to change directories in order to locate the worksheet file, unless you took the trouble to copy it to the Harvard Graphics directory. Press:

sales.wk1 [↵]

The program displays the Import Lotus Data menu, shown in figure 8.10.

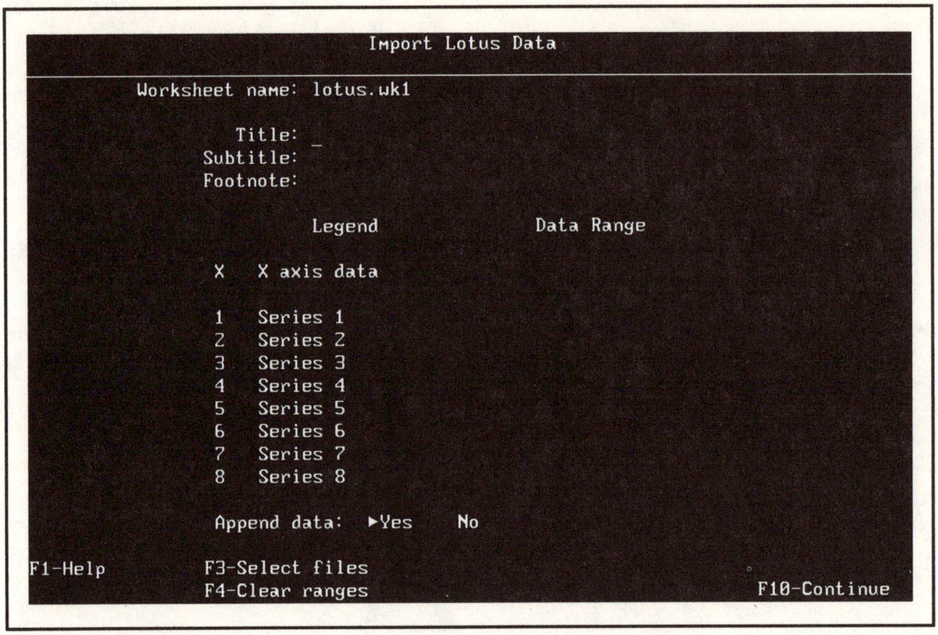

```
                        Import Lotus Data
          Worksheet name: lotus.wk1

                  Title: _
               Subtitle:
               Footnote:


                         Legend              Data Range

               X    X axis data

               1    Series 1
               2    Series 2
               3    Series 3
               4    Series 4
               5    Series 5
               6    Series 6
               7    Series 7
               8    Series 8

               Append data:    ►Yes      No

 F1-Help            F3-Select files
                    F4-Clear ranges                      F10-Continue
```

Figure 8.10. Import Lotus Data menu

This menu allows you to enter spreadsheet ranges that contain the data you want to extract for your chart. Enter the cell range for the X axis data. In this case, press:

   [Tab] *(3 times)*
   a2.a4 [↵]

Enter the cell ranges for the data series values:

   b2.b4 [↵]
   c2.c4 [↵]
   d2. d4

Extract the values by pressing:

   [F10]

The data is imported into the chart data entry screen, shown in figure 8.11.

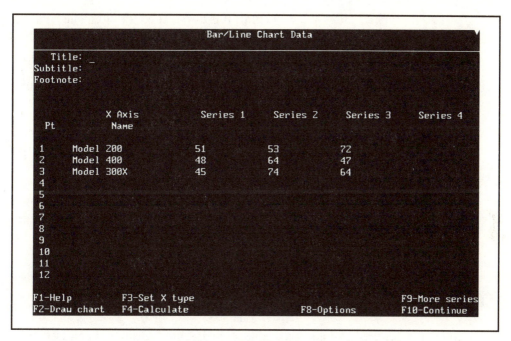

Figure 8.11. Lotus data transferred to Harvard Graphics chart

EXPORTING PICTURES

You can integrate charts created with Harvard Graphics into applications such as Ventura Desktop publisher, Microsoft Word 5.0, and WordPerfect 5.0 by exporting the chart image in one of two ways: *EPS* and *HGPL*.

EPS   EPS stands for *encapsulated Postscript* file format. This type of file can only be used when the output is going to be printed on a Postscript or compatible printer or typesetting machine. The EPS format is a text file that contains commands written in the Postscript language. Note that these types of files do not carry information about the screen image of the chart, only the printer commands needed to print the chart. This means that when you load these files into an application such as Ventura, you will not see an image of the chart. Only when the page is printed on a Postscript printer will the chart appear.

EPS files are created using the **Export picture** option on the **Import/Export** menu. Make sure that you select the **Encapsulated**

Postscript option under **Format.** It is also a good idea to include the file extension EPS. Although this has no effect on the contents of the EPS file, many applications assume that EPS files carry that extension.

If you use the **Standard** quality option instead of the **High** quality option you will create a significantly smaller EPS file with the same quality as the high quality option.

HPGL   HPGL stands for Hewlet Packard Graphics Language. These files contain instructions in the HPGL that will draw the chart image. The HPGL is used extensively for plotters. The advantage of the HPGL format is that it produces a chart that can be printed on a variety of printers. In addition, the HPGL files will display an image on the screen that shows the chart when it is imported into an application. On the other hand, HPGL charts will not display in a landscape orientation.

SUMMARY

This chapter discussed special ways in which Harvard Graphics charts can be organized.

Templates. A template is a special form of chart file that enables you to save commonly used chart layouts so that you do not have to start every chart from scratch. A template file will hold all of the chart's attributes, size, and place and option settings. You can also select to store data along with these settings as part of the template.

@CLR. This function is used to clear out the values in a data series column. When entered into the [F4] formula box, it clears all data from the currency series column.

@RECALC. This function can be entered into any data series column as a formula. It will cause Harvard Graphics to update all of the calculated data series in the chart to conform to the current values in the data series.

Default Templates. Templates can be created to provide custom defined sets of default values for each of the 12 types of charts in Harvard Graphics. Each chart type will automatically load a template with the corresponding name, if one exists, each time a new chart of that type is used. You can return to the original default values for that chart type by deleting the special template from the disk.

Chapter 9

Harvard Graphics Version 2.3

Version 2.3 of Harvard Graphics contains several new features in addition to the functions outlined in previous chapters. The most significant new feature is the addition of a chart *gallery*. The chart gallery allows you to create charts by selecting an already completed chart from a menu of standard text, pie, line, area and bar charts. The value of the gallery is that you do not have to format each new chart from scratch. The gallery feature does not actually change the way Harvard Graphics works. It expands the concept of chart templates, discussed in Chapter 8, that existed in Version 2.0.

This chapter explains, in detail, the new features added to Version 2.3. This information is for users who have upgraded to Version 2.3 or those thinking about upgrading. Table 9-1 lists these features (in addition to chart gallery).

Table 9-1 New features added to Harvard Graphics Version 2.3

Feature	Description
Applications Menu	You can now create an applications menu within Harvard Graphics. This allows you to run another program, such as Draw Partner or Lotus 1-2-3, without having to leave Harvard Graphics.
Compugraphics Metafile (CGM) Support	By installing the VDI memory resident driver, you can directly export your Harvard Graphics charts in a Compugraphics Metafile format. Many graphics applications and desktop publishing programs that cannot read Harvard Graphics chart files can read CGM format. Keep in mind that you must still install and load the VDI driver in the CONFIG.SYS file of the computer, in order to use the CGM features.
Draw Partner	Version 2.3 of Harvard Graphics includes an additional program called Draw Partner. Draw Partner is a separate program that allows you to create or modify the graphics symbols discussed in Chapter 6. Draw Partner operates similarly to the Draw/Annotate feature in Harvard Graphics, except that it contains a wider variety of drawing features, such as circular text, pie wedges, standard polygons and free-hand drawing. Draw Partner images are imported directly into Harvard Graphics without the need to save the drawing as a symbol file.
Excel	Harvard Graphics can now import Excel spreadsheet data (XLS files) and charts (XLC files). Since Excel is the leading spreadsheet product operating under Windows, this feature provides a useful link between the current non-windows version of Harvard Graphics and the leading Windows application. Importing Excel charts or data follows the same basic procedure as importing data or charts from Lotus 1-2-3.
Hypershow Buttons	You can now create mouse sensitive areas on charts used in the slide show displays discussed in Chapter 7. In Version 2.0 you could respond to slide show display only with the keyboard. In Version 2.3 you can designate areas

continued...

...from previous page (Table 9-1)

Feature	Description
	on the screen that, when clicked with the mouse, will jump to specific parts of the slide show.
New Font	Harvard Graphics has added a new font called Traditional to its list of fonts displayed on the Setup menu.
Palette	The Color Palette feature found on the Setup menu has been improved. You can now load and modify any of the 33 palettes supplied with the program. You can also create your own palette files based on existing palettes, or from scratch. In addition, palette selection is integrated with the Gallery feature.
Showcopy	When you create a Harvard Graphics slide show, you create a slide show file with a .SHW extension. However, this file does not contain all the information needed to run the slide show. The .SHW file contains instructions that coordinate and control the display of the charts included in the slide show. This means that if you want to transfer a slide show to another disk or computer, you must remember to manually copy all the files (charts, templates, palettes, etc.) used by the main slide show file. Otherwise, the slide show will not operate properly. Version 2.3 includes a utility program called SHOWCOPY that will read the contents of the slide show file and automatically copy all the required files to a different disk.
Speed Keys	Harvard Graphics Version 2.3 supports the use of special "speed keys" to execute common operations:

[Ctrl-g]   Get file

[Ctrl-s]   Save file

[Ctrl-p]   Print current chart

[Ctrl-r]   Draw/annotate chart

[Ctrl-d]   Activate Draw Partner

[Ctrl-l]   Import Lotus 1-2-3 data

[Ctrl-x]   Import Excel data

THE CHART GALLERY

In Chapter 8 you learned how to create a chart *template*. A chart template is a chart that you store for the purpose of using it as a starting point for new charts sharing the same basic characteristics. Templates are handy because they allow you to avoid creating each and every chart completely from scratch.

This template concept is expanded in Version 2.3 by the chart *gallery* feature. This gallery consists of 76 predefined charts. These charts are designed to be used as chart templates. You can, therefore, begin a new chart by selecting one of 76 gallery charts as your starting point, rather than starting from scratch.

Choosing a chart from among 76 examples can be quite confusing. In order to simplify the selection process, a new option has been added to the **Create new chart** menu, called **From gallery**. This option displays a full screen graphic menu that allows you to select a chart visually, since each chart type is represented by a reduced size display of the actual chart, rather than simply the name of the chart file (which is the case when you select a chart template). The graphic menu used by the **From gallery** is the most important difference between using chart templates and the chart gallery.

It is interesting to note that the entire Gallery feature is composed of standard Harvard Graphics features, such as templates, charts and slide shows. In fact, you can modify the Gallery by editing the charts, templates and slide shows used to create the Gallery.

The Gallery Menu

The Gallery menu is displayed when you select the **From gallery** option on the **Create new chart** menu. Assuming that you are starting from the Main Menu, select the **Create new chart** option by entering

1

Option 8 on this menu is the **From gallery** option. Select this option by entering

8

The display will change from normal text to a grid of 9 boxes, each representing a different style of chart, (see Figure 9-1).

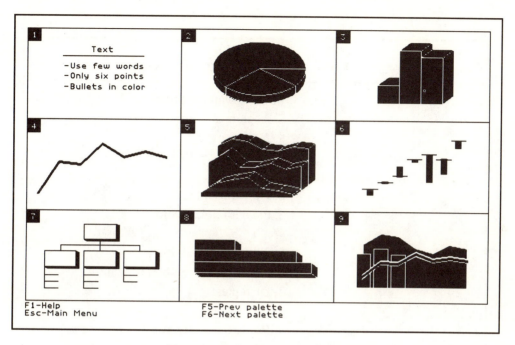

Figure 9-1. Chart gallery main menu

The 76 charts available through the gallery are divided among the nine major chart groups, indicated by a number on the gallery menu. Each number on the main gallery display is linked to a submenu display on which the charts contained in the gallery are shown. Table 9-2 lists the charts available under each number. Note that the gallery will use about 900K of hard disk space to store its 104 files. All files are required for the gallery feature to function.

Table 9-2. Charts available from the gallery

Menu Number	Chart Type	Charts Available
1	Text Charts	1. One column bullet 2. One column bullet with subtitle 3. One column build with subtitle 4. One column, no bullets 5. Title chart

continued…

...from previous page (Table 9-2)

Menu Number	Chart Type	Charts Available
		6. One column numbered
		7. 2 columns
		8. 3 columns
		9. Free form, with 4 columns
2	Pie Charts	1. Pie
		2. Pie with subtitle
		3. Pie with linked column
		4. 3D Pie
		5. 3D Pie with subtitle
		6. 3D Pie linked with 3D column
		7. Dual pies
		8. Dual 3D pies
		9. Proportional 3D pies
3	Column Charts	1. Bar
		2. Bar with overlap
		3. Stacked bar
		4. 3D bar
		5. 3D bar with overlap
		6. 3D stacked bar
		7. Bar + line, dual Y axis
		8. Bar with highlighted bars
		9. Stepped bar (histogram)
4	Line Charts	1. Line
		2. Curved line
		3. Trend line
		4. Scattergram (points only)
		5. Line on logarithmic scale
		6. Bar plus line
		7. Overlap line
		8. Ribbon line (3D)
		9. Line with data table

continued...

...from previous page (Table 9-2)

Menu Number	Chart Type	Charts Available
5	Area Charts	1. Area 3D overlap
		2. Area 3D stacked
		3. Area 3D 100%
		4. Area with overlap
		5. Area stacked
		6. Area 100%
6	Hi-Lo Charts	1. Stocks by day
		2. Stocks by hour
		3. Stocks by day, with area
		4. Moving average curve with lines
		5. Moving average curve with points
		6. Actual vs. projected with error
7	Organization Charts	1. Two full with boxes, one abbrev.
		2. Two full with shadow boxes, one abbrev
		4. Three full levels with boxes
		5. Three full levels with shadow boxes
8	Horizontal Charts	1. 3D bar
		2. 3D stacked bar
		3. Stacked bar
		4. Bar with overlap
		5. Bar, area and line
		6. Area with overlap
		7. Paired bars
		8. Line with overlap
		9. Line on logarithmic scale
9	Combination Charts	1. Bar with lines
		2. Area, line and bar
		3. Area, line and bar with data chart
		4. X-Y with drop points

When the main gallery menu screen is displayed you can use either the mouse or the keyboard to make a selection.

Keyboard   Since each of the graph images displayed on the menu grid is assigned a number, you can select the desired chart type by entering the corresponding number 1-9. The [Esc] key exits the gallery and returns you to the main Harvard Graphics menu.

Mouse   You can use the mouse to select a chart type by clicking the mouse anywhere within the box on the grid that you want to select.

In this case, select the bar charts, block 3, by entering

   3

The program displays another grid that shows the 9 bar charts supplied in this submenu (see Figure 9-2).

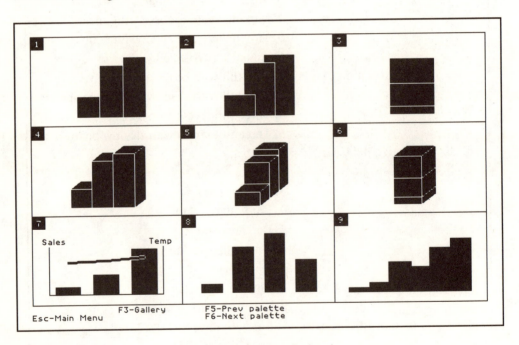

Figure 9-2. Bar charts displayed

The bar chart submenu is organized like the main menu, except you can use the [F3] key to move back to the previous menu. If you have a mouse, you can also move back to the main gallery by clicking the location on the screen where the words **F3-Gallery** appear.

A submenu only displays the chart choices you have under that category. For bar charts, you have a full grid of choices (9 different charts). You can examine the charts more closely by selecting the chart you want to inspect by number or by mouse click. For example, take a closer look at chart 4 by entering

4

The selected chart is displayed at full-screen size, as in Figure 9-3.

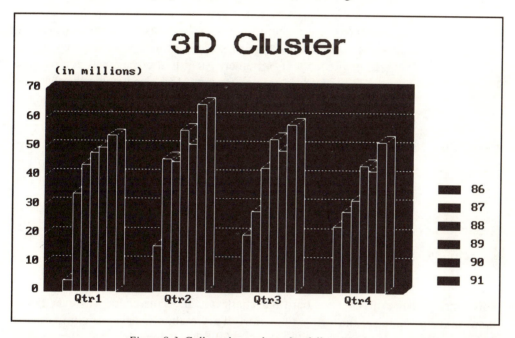

Figure 9-3. Gallery chart enlarged to full-screen size

Displaying the chart at full size displays the details of your selection. In this case, you have selected a 3D bar chart with data series and four items in each series, creating 24 bars grouped into 4 clusters of 6 bars each. It is important to note that in order to actually see the effect of various chart options, the gallery charts **must** contain data as well as template settings. A major disadvantages of the template feature is that the **Get Template** only displays the file menu and text description of a chart. The gallery shows you the complete chart before you decide to load it into the program. From the chart display, you have four options.

Exit Pressing the [Esc] key will cancel the gallery display without selecting a chart. You will return to the main program menu.

Gallery   Selecting Gallery with the [F3] key or mouse click returns you to the previous menu display, in this case, to the bar chart grid menu. You can then select another chart for full-screen display, or press [F3] again to move back to the main gallery menu.

Edit   Selecting the **Edit** option by using the [F9], key or by clicking on **F9-Edit**, will copy **all** the information stored in the gallery chart to the current chart. Keep in mind that this option includes all of the chart text (chart title, etc.) and numeric data used to compose the selected chart, as well as the chart formatting options. The advantage of selecting this option is that you can see how each text or numeric item in the chart was entered into the chart data or options screens. The disadvantage is that you will have to delete any data series or text that does not belong in your version of this chart.

Edit + Clear   Selecting the **Edit + Clear** option by using the [F10] key, or by clicking on **F10-Edit + Clear**, will copy all of the option settings from the displayed chart into a new chart. Note that this option removes all the text and numeric data from the chart.

Return to the bar chart gallery and select a different chart.

[F3]
1

This time the bar chart is a standard bar chart, not 3D. This chart uses exactly the same text and data as the other bar chart. This makes it easy to compare the differences in style between the gallery charts. Edit the current chart by entering

[F9]

The program displays the edit screen for a bar/line chart data, as seen in Figure 9-4. Note that the data displayed is the data used to create the chart as shown in the gallery display, as in Figure 9-4. To turn this chart into your own chart you must type over the existing items with your own data and delete any items you do not replace.

```
┌─────────────────────────────────────────────────────────────────────────┐
│                        Bar/Line Chart Data                           ▼    │
│      Title: Cluster                                                       │
│  Subtitle:                                                                │
│  Footnote:                                                                │
│                                                                           │
│                X Axis        86        87        88        89            │
│       Pt        Name                                                      │
│                                                                           │
│       1      Qtr1            4        34        44        48             │
│       2      Qtr2           16        46        45        56             │
│       3      Qtr3           20        28        43        53             │
│       4      Qtr4           23        28        32        44             │
│       5                                                                   │
│       6                                                                   │
│       7                                                                   │
│       8                                                                   │
│       9                                                                   │
│      10                                                                   │
│      11                                                                   │
│      12                                                                   │
│                                                                           │
│  F1-Help          F3-Save         F5-Set X type                F9-More series │
│  F2-Draw chart    F4-Draw/Annot   F6-Calculate     F8-Options  F10-Continue   │
└─────────────────────────────────────────────────────────────────────────┘
```

Figure 9-4. Data and settings from gallery chart

If you want to start off with a blank chart that has the desired format settings but no data or text, you can return to the gallery, select the same chart, but with the **Edit+Clear** option. Enter

[F10] 1 8

Select a bar chart from the gallery, such as the Bar/line combination chart (**7**).

3 7

This is a bar chart that shows monthly sales, combined with a line chart which plots the average temperature of each month. Such a chart could be used to indicate the relationship between the temperature and sales — you sell more ice cream in August than in January (see Figure 9-5).

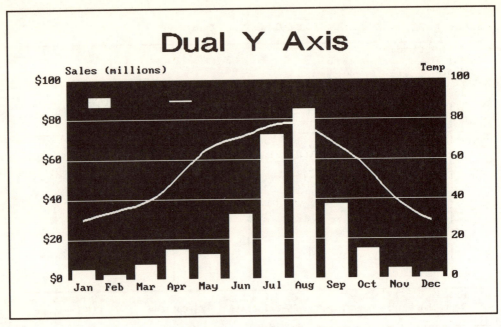

Figure 9-5. Bar /line combination chart

This time, use the **Edit+Clear** option by entering

[F10]

Now, the program takes you to the **Create new chart** entry screen. For a bar/line chart, which is a time/series type chart, you are asked to select the X type series (Name, Day, Week, Month, etc.). **Create new chart** starts a new chart. Select month as the default by entering

[F10]

This time the data entry screen is empty, so display the options screen by entering

[F8]

Note that the Type for series 2 is set as **Curve** instead of **Bar**, which is the usual default when you begin a new chart from scratch. Also note that the Y axis for series 2 is set as Y2. The second Y axis makes this a dual axis chart, as discussed in Chapter 3. Exit the chart by entering

[F10]

Once you have loaded the desired chart from the gallery display, with or without data, you can operate exactly as you would on a chart you created from scratch.

Customizing the Gallery

The gallery feature is a super-set of normal Harvard Graphics features, such as charts, templates and slide show files. Because all the elements that make up the gallery can be modified with existing Harvard Graphics features, it is relatively easy to customize the gallery. If you desire, you can directly access the files that create the gallery, using the standard get chart, template or slideshow commands. All of the files required for gallery to operate are stored the **GALLERY** subdirectory of the **\HG** directory. These directories were created by the Harvard Graphics installation program.

The 3D chart used as the first example in the previous section (see Figure 9-3) contains 6 data series, with values for all four quarters of the years 1986 through 1991. Suppose you frequently prepare a chart similar to the gallery chart, but require the years 1989 through 1992 .

One solution would to be to create a chart template with the format you desire. However, the chart gallery is a more convenient place to store frequently used charts. What would be ideal would be to substitute your 3D bar chart for the one supplied by Harvard Graphics.

You can accomplish this by loading the closest gallery chart and making modifications to it. Then, the next time you select that chart, you will get your customized version, instead of the original chart.

Begin by loading a chart from the gallery. Use the speed key for getting a chart from disk.

[Ctrl-g]

Recalling that all the gallery files are stored in a directory with the path name \HG\GALLERY, change to the GALLERY directory. Note that the following command assumes you have installed Harvard Graphics on drive C in the \HG directory. If you are using a different drive, change the command letter to match your drive.

[Shift-Tab]
C:\HG\GALLERY [return]

The program now displays the charts that make up the gallery. The chart names indicate the type of chart, e.g., AREA505.CHT or BAR505.CHT. The description of the charts provide some details about what the chart files contain. Recall that the chart description is automatically drawn from the chart title if no description is entered. In this case, the chart you are looking for is a BAR chart. Scroll the display down one screen to reveal the rest of bar chart files.

[PgDn]

The file named BAR705.CHT has the description **3D Cluster**, indicating this is the file that matches choice 4 on the bar chart menu. Load that file by entering

[down] *(5 times)*
[return]

The program loads and displays the chart on the screen. Display the data screen for this chart by entering

[return]

As a safety precaution, you can save a copy of the chart under another name. This allows you to recover the original Gallery chart without having to reinstall the program. Enter

[Ctrl-s] *(7 times)*

Change the name of the file to BARORG (bar original) by entering

BARORG [return] [return]

Next, change the data and option features of the chart: change the series names to 1989 through 1992. Enter

[F8]
[Tab] *(7 times)*
89 [return]
90 [return]
91 [return]
92 [return]
[Ctrl-Del] [return]
[Ctrl-Del] [return]

Return to the data entry screen.

[F8]

Delete the last two data series by entering

[F9]
[Tab]
[F6] [Tab] @clr [return]
[Tab]
[F6] [Tab] @clr [return]

Save the modified chart by entering

[F3]
BAR705 [F10] [return]

You have now replaced chart 4 on the bar chart gallery menu, with a modified version of the 3D cluster chart. Select that chart using the gallery menus.

[F10] 1 8
3 4

The chart displayed contains only four data series for the years 89 through 92, as seen in Figure 9-6, because you have substituted your own custom file for the original BAR705 chart. Return to the main menu by entering

[Esc]

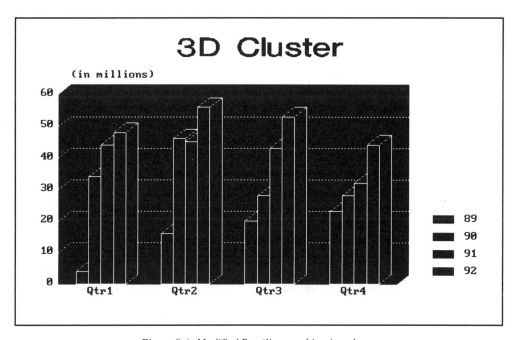

Figure 9-6. Modified Bar /line combination chart

CHANGING THE PALETTES

All Harvard Graphics charts are composed of up to 16 different colors which form the *palette*. Each palette, or set of colors, is stored in a file with a PAL extension. In Version 2.3 of Harvard Graphics the palette feature has been expanded to make it simpler to select, create or modify palettes. Palette selection has also been integrated with the gallery feature so you can select a palette along with a gallery chart.

Using Palette Files

Harvard Graphics palettes consist of 16 different color elements. The program automatically assigns the color elements, by number, to specific elements within a chart. By default Harvard Graphic loads a palette file called HG23.PAL as the default color palette. The purpose of the color palette is to assign specific color values to each of the 16 different color elements used in Harvard Graphics charts. Table 9-3 shows the standard color assignments.

Table 9-3. Palette Color Assignments.

Chart Element	Color Number Assigned	Default palette color-HG23.PAL
Charts titles	1	White
Chart labels	5	Light cyan
Normal chart text	7	White
Dark Text	4	Light blue
Data series 1	2	Dark cyan
Data series 2	3	Blue
Data series 3	4	Light blue
Data series 4	5	Light cyan
Data series 5	6	Light yellow
Data series 6	7	White
Data series 7	2	Dark cyan
Data series 8	3	Blue
Chart Background	8	Black

continued...

...from previous page (Table 9-3)

Chart Element	Color Number Assigned	Default palette color-HG23.PAL
Symbols	9	White
	10	Light gray
	11	Black
	12	Red
	13	Green
	14	Blue
	15	Yellow

An important point is that there are two ways to change how colors are used in Harvard Graphics.

Color Number   You can change the color of a chart element, such as a specific data series, by changing the color number assigned to that element in the chart options screen. For example, data series 1 is automatically assigned color 2 (dark cyan) by default. If you changed the color number to 6 the data series would be displayed as color 6 — yellow.

Palette Color   You can also alter the color of a charge element by changing the palette so that a given color number now displays a different color. For example, if you change the palette definition of color 7, from the default of white to red, all the elements in the chart assigned color 7 (the main chart title and data series 6) will change from white to red.

Which method you use depends on how you want the change to affect your charts. Changing the color number of a chart element effects **only** that one chart. Changing the color used for a specific color number will effect **all** charts using that color palette. This means you should change the color used in the palette only when you want to make a change that effects a group of charts, not the colors for a single chart.

Palette operations in Harvard Graphics 2.3 fall into two categories.

Color palette   The **Color palette options**, located on the Setup menu, provide commands for creating, editing or selecting palettes. Palette editing allows you to control the exact colors used for the 16 color elements defined by a palette.

Gallery   Palette selection has been integrated into the gallery feature. You can use the [F5] and [F6] keys to change the color palette. The gallery is supplied with 11 palette files that you can cycle through using the [F5] and [F6] keys. When you change the palette, the gallery menu changes to reflect immediately the new color assignments.

Changing Palettes in the Gallery

The simplest way to work with color palettes is through the gallery. Display the gallery menu by entering

1 8

Change the palette by entering

[F6] *(3 times)*

The palette colors change each time [F6] is pressed. The current palette is palette 4. The gallery display makes it easy to select a palette because you see the palette color applied immediately to the current display. You can skip backwards through the palettes with [F5]. Enter

[F5]

The colors change to those of the new current palette (3). When you select a chart from the gallery, Harvard Graphics loads the current color palette along with the chart. Return to the main menu by entering

[Esc]

The Palette Menu

The Palette menu allows you to make more detailed changes to color palettes, should you find the Gallery palette options not sufficient. Display the Color Palette menu by entering

9 7

The menu lists three options.

Create palette   This option allows you to create a palette. When you select this option, the displayed palette editing screen is **not** blank. Rather, the screen is a copy of the current palette, which is assigned the new palette file name you select. This means you never begin the creation of a new palette from scratch. You start with an existing palette.

Edit palette   This option displays the settings of the current palette file and allows you to edit those values. Take care in using this option because any changes made to the palette are automatically saved to the palette file when you exit with either [F10] or [Esc]. Unlike most menus, pressing [Esc] does **not** ignore changes.

Select palette   This option allows you to load a palette from the disk.

Display the current palette by entering

> **2**

The palette screen displays a chart that contains data on all 16 colors available in a palette. Each color is defined by a combination of three primary colors: red, green and blue. Each primary color is given an intensity value from 0 to 1000. For example, white is created by setting all three primary colors to 1000. Conversely, black is created by setting all three primary colors to 0. Colors in between are created by different combinations of the primary colors. Note that because of the improved color gradations available on VGA screens, some colors will have subtle shade differences that will not appear on EGA screens. EGA screens will provide four basic levels of intensity (0=none, 250=low, 500-medium and 750-1000=high) for each color. Values that fall below the values are treated as the next intensity down. For example, a value of 650 would be the same intensity as 500 — medium.

The screen has two sets of primary colors for each color element. One is the combinations used to produce the screen color, while the second is the intensity levels used for output to photographic file recorders. Be aware that the dyes used in photographic film do not respond to exposure in a strict linear progression. The printed color may, therefore, be different than what was seen on the the screen.

Pressing [F2] displays a screen that shows the effects of the current color definition.

> **[F2]**

The program displays a screen that shows how the specified colors will look when implemented in Harvard Graphics charts.

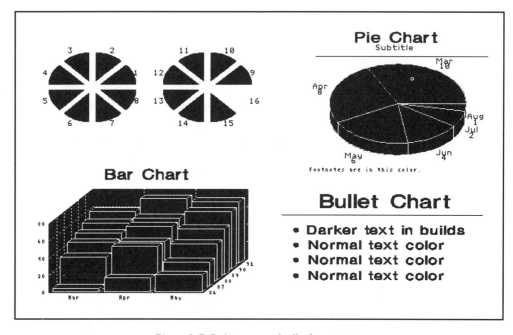

Figure 9-7. Palette example display screen.

Return to the palette display by entering

[Esc]

Return to the palette menu by entering

[F10]

To load a different color palette, enter

7 3

The program displays a list of all the palette files, PAL extensions, in the current directory. One useful palette is the BW.PAL. This is a palette that displays charts in black and white. This palette is useful when you are using printed output, since it will display charts in black and white and eliminate gray tones or colors. Enter

BW [return]

Display the palette screen by entering

7 2 [F2]

Note that the palette uses red as the background color, and colors for the drawing symbols. You may want to change all those options to black or white if you want to get a completely accurate display. Return to the palette editing display by entering

[Esc]

Adding a Palette to the Gallery

Harvard Graphics allows you to add four additional palettes to the gallery. The palettes are automatically added to the Gallery display if they are saved in the \HG\GALLERY directory and are given the numeric names 12, 13, 14 or 15.

For example, suppose you want to add the black and white palette currently loaded into Harvard Graphics, to the Gallery palettes. The first step is to create a new palette file. Enter

[F10] 7 1

The first step in creating the desired file is to change the directory to **\HG\GALLERY**. Enter

[Shift-Tab]
C:\HG\GALLERY [Tab]

Enter the name for this palette. To work with the gallery the files must be either 12, 13, 14 or 15. Harvard Graphics automatically adds the PAL file extension. Enter

12 [F10]

Note that the palette file is not immediately created. Instead, the program displays the palette editing screen. You can make modifications to the color at this point if you desire. When the palette is complete, save the new palette by entering

[F10]

When you exit the editing screen, the data is written to the specified disk file. the black and white palette is now part of the gallery. To test this out, display the chart gallery by entering

[Esc] 1 8
[F6] *(12 times)*

The 12th palette that appears is the black and white palette you have just added to the **\HG\GALLERY** directory. Exit the gallery by entering

[Esc]

Note that you can remove a palette from the gallery by using DOS to delete the palette file. For example, to delete the black and white palette from the gallery you would enter this command at the DOS prompt: **DEL\HG\GALLERY\12.PAL** [return]

APPLICATIONS MENU

The applications menu allows Harvard Graphics to function as a *shell* program. In DOS terms, a shell is a program that allows you to load and execute other programs usually from a menu. This shell feature was added so that the Draw Partner program could be smoothly integrated with the main program. The feature also allows you to setup the applications menu to run programs of your own choosing, as well as Draw Partner.

When you run an application from the application menu, the current Harvard Graphics session is suspended, but not terminated, while the selected application runs. When you exit the application, Harvard Graphics is restored. This means the chart, if any, that you were working with, is still loaded into Harvard Graphics. For example, if you use Lotus 1-2-3 to prepare data for charts, you can place 1-2-3 on the application menu so you can modify a spreadsheet without having to save or lose the chart you are working on.

When you run an application from the applications menu, Harvard Graphics removes itself from memory so you will have sufficient memory to run the selected application. Only a small part of the Harvard Graphics program, about 12K, remains in memory as a link to the current Harvard Graphics session. This is required to restore Harvard Graphics when you exit the other application.

You can add your own applications to the Harvard Graphics application menu by using the **Applications** option found on the **Setup** menu. Enter

9 8

The **Applications** screen has room for 8 separate applications. If you have installed the Draw Partner program, that application is automatically entered into the menu. If you chose to install the VDI driver, the AGX Slider Service application is also automatically installed into the menu. The remainder of the menu is open for your own choices.

As an example, one handy application to add to the menu is DOS access. Adding DOS access to the menu will allow you to suspend Harvard Graphics, enter the DOS prompt mode, execute DOS commands and then return to the chart you were working on. This makes it possible to copy or delete files without having to quit Harvard Graphics.

To create a DOS access option on the applications menu, place the cursor on the **Menu item** line of the first available menu item. In most cases this would be item 2. Enter a title that will appear in the application menu.

Access DOS [Tab]

The next entry is the maximum amount of memory you want used for the application. In most cases you can leave this blank, telling Harvard Graphics to give the program as much memory as possible. Enter

[Tab]

The last line of the menu setup is used to hold the exact name of the program you want to run. But what *program* is used to run DOS? The answer is that the DOS prompt user interface is the result of running the program stored in the COMMAND.COM file, which can be found in the root directory of the drive from which the computer was booted. When you are working with a program that has a shell feature, running the COMMAND.COM program file will start a DOS session from within the shell program. Assuming your computer booted from hard disk letter C, you would enter

C:\COMMAND.COM [return]

Save the modified applications menu setup by entering

[F10]

Return to the main menu by entering

[Esc]

From the main menu you can display the applications menu by entering [F3]. Enter

[F3]

Harvard Graphics displays the applications menu. If you have installed Draw Partner it will be the first item on the menu. You will also see the *Access DOS* option you have added to the menu. Select the number of the DOS access option. Enter

2

When you make the selection, Harvard Graphics will take a moment to save information about the current Harvard Graphics session. When this is done, the program will activate DOS. Note that the message *Type EXIT to return to Harvard Graphics* will appear at the top of the screen above the DOS prompt. EXIT refers to the DOS exit command. EXIT is used when you are running DOS from within a shell application. The command terminates the current DOS session and returns you to the application from which the DOS session was started. However, once you start to work with DOS, the message will disappear and you will have to remember that you must enter EXIT when you want to get back to Harvard Graphics. If you forget you are running DOS inside Harvard Graphics and you turn off the computer without returning to Harvard Graphics, any unsaved material in the current Harvard Graphics session will be lost.

Enter the DOS directory command.

DIR [return]

The command operates just it normally does. Return to harvard Graphics by entering

EXIT [return]

Harvard Graphics reloads the program and returns you to the current session at the same point at which you left.

Setting Paths for Applications

In general you can set up any application such as Lotus 1-2-3 or WordPerfect, to run from the Harvard Graphics application menu, in the same manner as you added DOS access. For example, suppose you want to run Lotus 1-2-3 from the applications menu. Instead of entering COMMAND.COM as the program, you would enter 123.EXE. Assuming that the Lotus 1-2-3 program is stored in a directory called \LOTUS on the C drive, you would enter the command as **C:\LOTUS\123.EXE**.

However, most large applications like Lotus 1-2-3 consist of several different program files. For example, in order for 1-2-3 to load the 123.EXE program you will need to access a file called 123.CMP, which is also stored in the \LOTUS directory. In order for 1-2-3 to be able to find and read all the files it needs to run, a DOS path must be opened to the directory that contains the 1-2-3 program, e.g., \LOTUS. A path is the name of a directory that DOS should search when a request is made for a specific file. You can store a list of search paths for DOS, using the PATH command. A PATH command is usually included in the AUTOEXEC.BAT file in the root directory of the boot disk. If you want to execute 1-2-3 from Harvard Graphics you must make sure a path is opened to the correct directory **before** running Harvard Graphics. For example, the following command opens search paths to \WP for WordPerfect, \DOS for the DOS utility programs and \LOTUS for Lotus 1-2-3.

PATH C:\WP;C:\DOS;C:\LOTUS;

A command similar to this should be included in the AUTOEXEC.BAT file.

HYPERSHOW BUTTONS

If you create slide show presentations with Harvard Graphics, and you have a mouse, you can add *hypershow* buttons to your slide show screen. A hypershow button allows you to execute slide show options with the mouse instead of The keyboard.

The following section will illustrate how you can use hypershow buttons with a Harvard Graphics slide show. Begin by creating three charts to use as part of the slide show. This can be done very quickly using the gallery feature. Enter

1 8 2 2 [F9]

Save this chart as SLIDE1 by entering

[F3] SLIDE1 [return] [return]

Create a chart called SLIDE2 from the Gallery's bar chart menu. Enter

[F10] 1 8 3 4 [F9]
[F3] SLIDE2 [return] [return]

Create a third chart by entering

[F10] 1 8 4 8 [F9]
[F3] SLIDE3 [return] [return]

Begin a fourth chart as a free form blank chart. This chart will be used to create three hypershow buttons that will display the charts from the files SLIDE1, SLIDE2 and SLIDE3 when the buttons are clicked. Enter

[F10] 1 1 6

Display the Draw/Annotate screen by entering

[F4]

The purpose of this chart is to create symbols, which when clicked with the mouse, will activate a given portion of the slide show. A button actually consists of two parts.

Graphic Object   You need to create an object, text or graphic, to be the visual symbol that will represent the option. The graphic symbol has no actual effect on the slide show but is used to establish an area on the screen that can be clicked in order to make a selection.

Button Area   The button area is a rectangular area drawn around the graphic object. The actual button area is invisible on the displayed chart. When the user points and clicks the mouse at the symbol enclosed by the button rectangle, the program will execute the command assigned to the button area.

The graphic object and the button area work together to create the illusion that the user is clicking on an object to execute an command. Keep in mind that a graphic object is not required for a button. The button rectangle will function the same way even if the drawing is blank. The purpose of the graphic object is to indicate to the user where on the drawing they are supposed to click.

In this example, you have three charts form which the user can choose: SLIDE1 which is a pie chart, SLIDE2 which is a bar chart and SLIDE3 which is a line chart. You need to create graphics that represent these options. Keep in mind that text can be used with or instead of graphics if you desire. For example, you might want to place the word PIE inside a circle as the symbol for SLIDE1.

Note that in this section instructions will be given as key strokes, since it it difficult to accurately express mouse actions. However, when you are working you will probably find it easier to use the mouse. Add a circle to the drawing by entering

1 5 [return]
[Home] *(5 times)*
[return]

A white circle appears in the center of the drawing. Add text to the circle by entering

[Esc] 1
PIE

Change the size and color of the text by entering

[F8] 10 [Del]
[Tab] 8
[F8] [return]

Position the text inside the white circle.

[down] *(6 times)*
[right] *(6 times)*
[return]

The word PIE appears inside the circle. In order to assign a hypershow button to this graphic, you need to draw a button rectangle around the object. The rectangle does not need to fit exactly around the button, but be close enough so that a person using the mouse would be able to click anywhere on the object and still activate the button command. Select the Button option from the add graphic menu.

[Esc] 7

The button operation begins with the button option box, which displays the button number. Each button is assigned a number from 1 to 10. It is the button number that is used to link the button with a specific GOTO action, such as GOTO slide 2 or GOTO slide 3. Each screen can have up to 20 buttons. This means you can define more than one button with the same number. In other words, you can GOTO an action from more than one place on the screen. You can have up to 20 buttons but only 10 different actions.

In addition to the user-defined buttons, you can use 7 special buttons numbered 211 through 217, as seen in Table 9-4. These buttons have predefined command functions that match the standard command keys used in slide shows.

Table 9-4. Special button numbers.

Button Number	Key Command	Function
211	[Left]	Display previous slide
212	[Right]	Display next slide
213	[Home]	Display first slide
214	[End]	Display last slide
215	[Space bar]	Pause slide show
216	[Ctrl-e]	Display chart data entry entry
217	[Esc]	Terminate slide show

In this case leave the button number at 1. Enter

[return]

The cross hair target appears in the drawing area. You need to draw the button rectangle around the object. Move the target to the point where the upper left corner of the button should be placed.

[up] (6 times)
[left] (5 times)
[return]
[down] (9 times)
[right] (9 times)
[return]

You have now created the graphic object and the button that will work together to form the hypershow button, as seen in Figure 9-8.

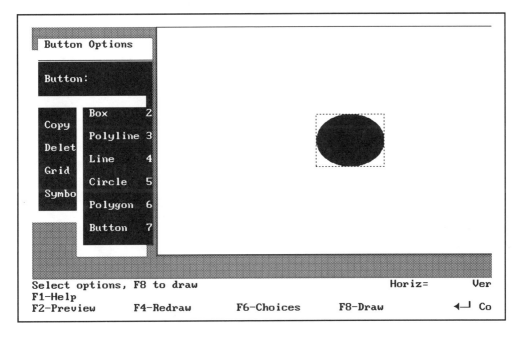

Figure 9-8. Graphic enclosed in button

The next symbol will be for the bar chart. In this case the symbol will be two rectangles of different sizes. Add a box to the drawing by entering

[Esc] 2 [Ctrl-left]
[right] *(5 times)*
[return]
[up] *(7 times)*
[right] *(3 times)*
[return]

Add a second box but change its color to black with a white border. Enter

[F8]
[Tab] *(5 times)*
n [F8]
[up] *(2 times)*
[return]
[right] *(3 times)*
[down] *(9 times)*
[return]

Draw a button rectangle designated as button 2, around the bars.

[Esc] 7 2 [return]
[return]
[up] *(9 times)*
[left] *(6 times)*
[return]

The last button will be for the line chart. In this case, create an irregular line with the polyline feature. Enter

[Esc] 3 [Ctrl-right]
[left] *(5 times)*
[return]
[End] *(3 times)*
[return]
[Home] *(2 times)*
[return]
[End] *(3 times)*
[return] [Esc]

Draw a button rectangle assigned to button 3, around the polyline.

[Esc] 7 3 [return]
[return]
[up] *(5 times)*
[right] *(9 times)*
[return]

You have now created the screen that you will use in the slide show to function as a hypershow menu for the three charts you want to present. Remember that the dotted lines created when you drew the buttons will **not** appear on the chart when it is displayed. Only the graphics will be visible and as far as the user is concerned, it will be those graphics, not the invisible button rectangle, that they will be selecting with the mouse.

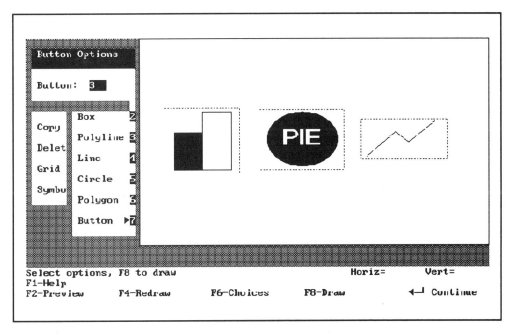

Figure 9- 9. Buttons created with draw/annotate

Save this display as a chart named BUTTONS by entering

[Esc] *(3 times)*
[F3] buttons
[F10] [Esc]

Slide Shows with Hypershow Buttons

You can now put the charts to work by combining them into a single slide show presentation. Create a new slide show that you will call HYPE. Enter

7 1
HYPE [F10]

The first chart in the slide show should be the BUTTONS.CHT chart. Move the highlight down to BUTTONS.CHT and enter

[return]

Repeat the process for the files SLIDE1.CHT, SLIDE2.CHT and SLIDE3.CHT.

When you have the four charts selected, move to the **Add ScreenShow effect** screen by entering

[F10] 3

In this example you are interested in connecting the slides with the buttons displays so that BUTTONS functions as a hypershow menu. The idea is that each button in the BUTTONS display is assigned to the chart file that matches the graphic used with the button, e.g., SLIDE1, the pie chart, is assigned to button 1, the circle graphic. Place the cursor on the line for the BUTTONS chart. by entering

[down]

To assign the buttons to slide, display the hypershow menu by entering

[F8]

The menu has three columns. The first lists the button numbers 1-10. The second column is used for assignment of number keys 0-9 to buttons. The third column is used to enter the number of the chart that should be displayed when the button is clicked or the key, if assigned, is entered. In this case you want to assign button 1 on the BUTTONS chart to go to chart 2, the pie chart. Enter

2 [return]

Button 2 should go to slide 3. Enter

3 [return]

Finally button 3 should activate slide 4.

4 [F10]

In order to create a slide show that will return to the menu after each chart is shown, you will have to set SLIDE1, SLIDE2 and SLIDE3 to return to the BUTTONS slide. Move down to SLIDE1 and set the hypershow to return to the first slide. Enter

[return] [F8]
[Tab] 1 [F10]

Repeat the process for the remaining two slides.

[return] [F8]
[Tab] 1 [F10]
[return] [F8]
[Tab] 1 [F10]

Run the slideshow by entering

[F10] 4

The program displays the BUTTONS chart. Select the line chart to be displayed.

Click on the line graphic

The line chart appears. Return to the BUTTONS display by entering

[return]

Access the bar chart.

Click on the bar symbol

This time the slide show displays the bar chart. Return to the BUTTONS display by entering

[return]

Exit the slide show by entering

[Esc] *(2 times)*

DRAW PARTNER

The Draw Partner program is a separate application that is integrated into Harvard Graphics through the applications menu. Draw Partner is a graphics drawing program that has a number of sophisticated features that provide you with drawing tools more powerful than those provided in the Draw/Annotate. You would use Draw Partner to create graphics from scratch, or modify a symbol from the clip art collection supplied with Harvard Graphics.

Note that the Draw Partner program will store graphics in files with a .DP extension. Draw Partner can also import Harvard Graphics symbol files, .CGM graphics and Lotus 1-2-3 .PIC chart files.

A full discussion of Draw Partner is beyond the scope of this book, but the following section contains a short example of how to use Draw Partner in conjunction with Harvard Graphics.

Drawing with Draw Partner

You can access the Draw Partner program by selecting it from the applications menu. The assumption is made that you chose to install Draw Partner when you installed Harvard Graphics. If you did not do so originally, you can run the install program again and select to install Draw Partner on your hard disk. As part of the installation process, Harvard Graphics places Draw Partner onto the applications menu. You can also activate Draw Partner with the [Ctrl-d] speed key.

Draw Partner can be used to annotate a chart, just as you would use the draw/annotate feature, as well as for creating graphics from scratch. While Draw Partner and Harvard Graphics are separate applications, the images created are transferred between programs. For example, if you currently have a chart defined, that chart is transferred to Draw Partner when it is activated. Conversely, if you start drawing from scratch in Draw Partner and return to Harvard Graphics, the Draw Partner image appears as a Harvard Graphics free-form chart.

For example, use Draw Partner to add a special text effect to a pie chart. Begin by creating a new pie chart in Harvard Graphics. Enter

1 2

Leave the titles empty and add the following data items.

[Tab] *(3 times)*
Slice A [return]
Slice B [return]
Slice C
[Tab]
[up] *(2 times)*
100 [return]
50 [return]
25

Instead of using a standard title for the chart, use Draw Partner to add one of its special features, circular text, to the chart. Activate Draw Partner by entering

[Ctrl-d]

In order to run Draw Partner, Harvard Graphics enters its shell mode in which most of the Harvard Graphics program is removed from memory, while the application, in this case Draw Partner, is executed. When Draw Partner is loaded, you see a screen display that looks very much like the draw/annotate screen in Harvard Graphics, except the menu is more elaborate. The pie chart is in the drawing area of the display.

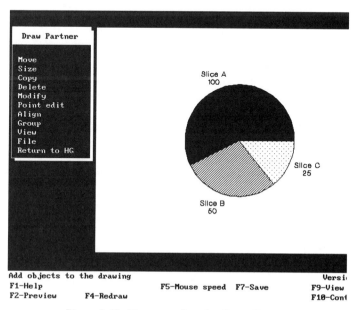

Figure 9-10. Chart transferred to Draw Partner

To add circular text, select the **Adoption**. Enter

[return]

Select the **Circular text** option by entering

C C [return]

The program places its target in the center of the pie. In order to place a circular title over the pie, you can select the center of the pie as the starting location. Enter

[return]

Expand the circle until it is is wider than the pie chart by entering

[up] *(11 times)*

In the case of drawing circular text, the circle that appears represents the guide line for the text to follow. When you complete the command, you will not see this line but will see the text placed along the path of the circle. Continue to the next step by entering

[return]

A short menu appears from which you can select text to be placed at the top or the bottom of the circular path. Select top by entering

[return]

Enter the text that will be placed on the circular path. As you enter the text, two vertical lines show the extent of the arc that will be filled with text.

Title of Pie Chart [return]

The text is placed along the top of the circular path. You can continue to add graphics items to the chart until you are satisfied with the results. When you return to Harvard Graphics the modified image is transferred to the program. This means you can switch back and forth between Harvard Graphics and Draw Partner as much as needed, in order to create the desired chart. Return to Harvard Graphics by entering

[Esc] *(2 times)*
[End] [return]

Display chart current chart by entering

[F2]

The chart, shown in Figure 9-11, combines the pie chart created with Harvard Graphics and the circular text added with Draw Partner.

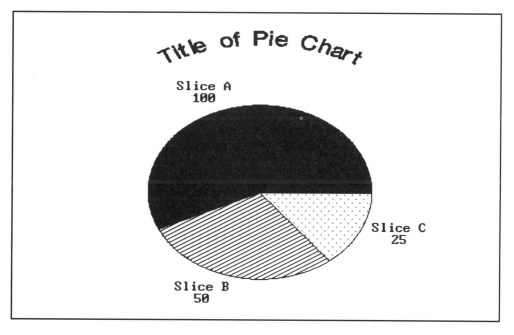

Figure 9-11. Circular text added to chart

Return to the main menu by entering

[Esc] [F10]

SUMMARY

This chapter discussed new features added to Harvard Graphics with the release of version 2.3.

Gallery Harvard Graphics allows you to create charts by selecting a predefined chart from the chart gallery. The gallery contains 76 different charts, covering all the chart types available in Harvard Graphics. You can select an entire chart (data and settings) or select only the settings, leaving the data area blank. You can also select a color palette for use with the selected chart.

Palette You can now easily load and modify any of 33 palettes supplied with the program. You can also create your own palette files based on existing palettes or from scratch. In addition, Palette selection is integrated with the gallery feature.

Applications   Harvard Graphics provides an applications menu that allows you to run other applications from within Harvard Graphics. If Draw Partner is installed it is automatically added to the applications menu. You can add 7 more programs of your own choosing to the menu, if desired.

Hypershow Buttons   You can now create mouse sensitive areas on charts used as part of slide show displays.

Draw Partner   *Draw Partner* is a separate program from Harvard Graphics that provides enhanced drawing features that can be used to annotate charts or create graphics. Changes made with Draw Partner will also appear on the current Harvard Graphics chart, if any.

Excel   Harvard Graphics can now import Excel spreadsheet data (.XLS files) and charts (.XLC files.)

CGM Support   You can directly export your Harvard Graphics charts to Compugraphics Metafile format files or import .CGM graphics into Harvard Graphics.

New Font   Harvard Graphics has added a new font called Traditional to its list of fonts displayed on the Setup menu.

Showcopy   The utility program called SHOWCOPY will read the contents of the slide show file and automatically copy all the required files to a different disk.

Speed Keys   Harvard Graphics Version 2.3 supports the use of special speed keys to execute commonly-used operations, such as getting or saving a chart.

Index